CULTURAL CRIMINOLOGY

CULTURAL CRIMINOLOGY

AN INVITATION

JEFF FERRELL | KEITH HAYWARD | JOCK YOUNG

SAGE

Los Angeles • London • New Delhi • Singapore • Washington DC

First published 2008

SAGE Publications Ltd
1 Oliver's Yard
55 City Road
London EC1Y 1SP

SAGE Publications Inc.
2455 Teller Road
Thousand Oaks, California 91320

SAGE Publications India Pvt Ltd
B 1/I 1 Mohan Cooperative Industrial Area
Mathura Road, New Delhi 110 044
India

SAGE Publications Asia-Pacific Pte Ltd
33 Pekin Street #02-01
Far East Square
Singapore 048763

British Library Cataloguing in Publication data

A catalogue record for this book is available
from the British Library

ISBN 978-0-4129-3126-7
ISBN 978-0-4129-3127-4

Library of Congress Control Number Available

Typeset by C&M Digitals (P) Ltd., Chennai, India
Printed in Great Britain by Cromwell Press Ltd, Trowbridge, Wiltshire
Printed on paper from sustainable resources

contents

list of plates

acknowledgements

The existence of a book like *Cultural Criminology: An Invitation* suggests something of the collective project that cultural criminology has now become. Over the past decade or so cultural criminology has grown to include more and more students, scholars, and academic programmes in the United States, the United Kingdom, and elsewhere, and has become manifest in increasing numbers of books, articles, and conferences. While any book's list of those to be thanked and acknowledged is surely incomplete, then, this one seems especially so – and we apologize to all those participants in cultural criminology's collective project whom we have inadvertently omitted.

The said, we'll at least make an effort, and so for their generous contributions of ideas, information, and perspective, we thank Kester Aspden, Frankie Bailey, Carla Barrett, Nachman Ben-Yehuda, David Bradbury, Dave Brotherton, Phil Carney, Grey Cavender, Isaac Enriquez, Ruben Flores-Sandoval, Michael Flynn, Chris Greer, Mark Hamm, Philip Jenkins, Paul Leighton, Marilyn McShane, Vince Miller, Jayne Mooney, Wayne Morrison, Stephen Muzzatti, Ben Penglase, Jean Pockrus, Greg Snyder, Ken Tunnell, Tim Turner, Robert Weide, Iain Wilkinson, Trey Williams, Catriona Woolner, and Cećile Van de Voorde. Our thanks also to both Joe Wilkes for his advice regarding the filmography and for his inspiring music (www.joewilkes.co.uk) and to 'writers' Colt 45 and Rasta 68 for their aesthetic assistance. A special thank you is also due to Majid Yar for his careful reading of, and helpfully critical comments on, the book manuscript. Any errors or infelicities are, of course, ours alone.

Our editor at SAGE, Caroline Porter, has been a source of ceaseless intellectual encouragement and good will, and we thank her and the production team at SAGE for their professionalism and their dedication to scholarly work.

Jeff Ferrell, Keith Hayward, and Jock Young
May 2008

cultural criminology: an invitation

Investigating a brutal beating in the spring of 2006, police in Arlington, Texas, turn up something odd: the beating has been videotaped. In fact, the whole assault has been staged for the camera by a group of local teenagers producing a series of amateur 'fight videos' and selling them from MySpace.com websites. 'These are not necessarily people who don't like each other', says James Hawthorne, a local deputy police chief. 'It's just for the video.' Police leaders and the local media describe the teenagers as 'a loosely organized ... gang known as PAC, or "Playas After Cash"' – but in its day-to-day activities, the gang seems to operate more like a video director and his first unit crew. During that savage beating, gang 'ringleader' Michael G Jackson can be heard directing the action, and as the beating ends, another participant takes time to turn to the camera and shout the title of the video. Jackson subsequently edits footage of DJs from a popular local radio station into his fight videos, sets the videos to a hip hop soundtrack, and links his webpage to other fight video sites. Even James Hawthorne has to admit that, as disturbed as he is by the fight video, it is 'a nicely produced piece of work' (Agee, 2006a: 1A, 17A; Ayala and Agee, 2006: 1A).

A few months later in an up-market central London street, eight people are arrested for attempting to deface a government building. The arrestees aren't young graffiti writers, though, but political protesters – and their medium isn't Krylon paint but projected light. The eight are part of an organized protest against violent repression, vote tampering, and the suppression of free speech in the Mexican state of Oaxaca; their crime is an attempt to project the final footage of American *Indymedia* reporter Brad Will on to the façade of the Mexican Embassy. In Mexico, municipal officials and police loyal to Oaxaca's corrupt governor have recently murdered Brad Will and two other participants in a demonstration organized by striking teachers and sympathetic activists. Demonstrators' demands include shoes, uniforms and breakfasts for school-children, and better pay and medical services for teachers.[1]

Each of these incidents embodies fundamental issues for cultural criminology. Whether the brutally hyper-masculine world of for-profit fight videos, or the contested representational dynamics of political exploitation and globalized protest, both illustrate one of cultural criminology's founding concepts: that *cultural dynamics carry within them the meaning of crime*. Given this, cultural criminology explores the many ways in which cultural forces interweave with the practice of crime and crime control in contemporary society. It emphasizes the centrality of meaning, representation, and power in the contested construction of crime – whether crime is constructed as videotaped entertainment or political protest, as ephemeral event or subcultural subversion, as social danger or state-sanctioned violence. From our view, the subject matter of any useful and critical criminology must necessarily move beyond narrow notions of crime and criminal justice to incorporate symbolic displays of transgression and control, feelings and emotions that emerge within criminal events, and public and political campaigns designed to define (and delimit) both crime and its consequences. This wider focus, we argue, allows for a new sort of criminology – a *cultural* criminology – more attuned to prevailing conditions, and so more capable of conceptualizing and confronting contemporary crime and crime control. This cultural criminology seeks both to understand crime as an expressive human activity, and to critique the perceived wisdom surrounding the contemporary politics of crime and criminal justice.

thinking about culture and crime

Cultural criminology understands 'culture' to be the stuff of collective meaning and collective identity; within it and by way of it, the government claims authority, the consumer considers brands of bread – and 'the criminal', as both person and perception, comes alive. Culture suggests the search for meaning, and the meaning of the search itself; it reveals the capacity of people, acting together over time, to animate even the lowliest of objects – the pauper's shopping cart, the police officer's truncheon, the gang member's bandana – with importance and implication.

For us, human culture – the symbolic environment occupied by individuals and groups – is not simply a product of social class, ethnicity, or occupation; it cannot be reduced to a residue of social structure. Yet culture doesn't take shape without these structures, either; both the cultural hegemony of the powerful and the subcultures of acquiescence and resistance of those marginalized are scarcely independent of social class and other forms of patterned inequality. Cultural forces, then, are those threads of collective meaning that wind in and around the everyday troubles of social actors, animating the situations and circumstances in which their troubles play out. For all the parties to crime and criminal justice – perpetrators, police officers, victims, parole violators, news reporters – *the negotiation of cultural meaning intertwines with the immediacy of criminal experience.*

As early work on 'the pains of imprisonment' demonstrated, for example, the social conditions and cultural dynamics of imprisonment form a dialectical relationship, with each shaping and reshaping the other. While all inmates experience certain pains of imprisonment, the precise extent and nature of these pains emerge from various cultures of class, gender, age, and ethnicity – the lived meanings of their social lives – that inmates bring with them to the prison. And yet these particular pains, given meaning in the context of pre-existing experiences and collective expectations, in turn shape the inmate cultures, the shared ways of life, that arise as inmates attempt to surmount the privations of prison life (Young, 1999). Facing common troubles, confronting shared circumstances, prison inmates and prison guards – and equally so street muggers and corporate embezzlers – draw on shared understandings and invent new ones, and so invest their troubles and their solutions with human agency.[2]

This shifting relationship between cultural negotiation and individual experience affirms another of cultural criminology's principal assumptions: that crime and deviance constitute more than the simple enactment of a static group culture. Here we take issue with the tradition of cultural conflict theory, as originated with the work of Thorsten Sellin (1938) and highlighted in the well-known subcultural formulation of Walter Miller (1958), where crime largely constitutes the enactment of lower working-class values. Such a reductionist position – Sellin's original formulation suggested that vengeance and vendetta among Sicilian immigrants led to inevitable conflict with wider American values – has clear echoes today in the supposition, for example, that multiculturalism generates ineluctable cultural collisions, most particularly those between Muslim and Western values. Yet as we will argue, and as cultural criminologists like Frank Bovenkerk, Dina Siegel and Damian Zaitch (2003; Bovenkerk and Yesilgoz, 2004) have well demonstrated, cultures – ethnic and otherwise – exist as neither static entities nor collective essences. Rather, cultural dynamics remain in motion; collective cultures offer a heterogeneous mélange of symbolic meanings that blend and blur, cross boundaries real and imagined, conflict and coalesce, and hybridize with changing circumstances. To imagine, then, that an ethnic culture maintains some ahistorical and context-free proclivity to crime (or conformity) is no cultural criminology; it's a dangerous essentialism, stereotypical in its notion of cultural stasis and detrimental to understanding the fluid dynamics connecting culture and crime.

In *Culture as Praxis*, Zygmunt Bauman (1999: xvi–xvii) catches something of this cultural complexity. There he distinguishes two discourses about culture, longstanding and seemingly diametrically opposed. The first conceptualizes 'culture as the activity of the free roaming spirit, the site of creativity, invention, self-critique and self-transcendence', suggesting 'the courage to break well-drawn horizons, to step beyond closely-guarded boundaries'. The second sees culture as 'a tool of routinization and continuity – a handmaiden of social order', a culture that stands for 'regularity and pattern – with freedom cast under the rubric of "norm-breaking" and "deviation"'.

Culture of the first sort fits most easily into the tradition of subcultural theory as developed by Albert Cohen (1955) and others. Here culture suggests the collective vitality of subversive social praxis, the creative construction of transgression and resistance, an outsider group's ability to symbolically stand the social order on its head. Culture of the second sort is more the province of orthodox social anthropology, of Parsonian functionalism and of post-Parsonian cultural sociology. Here, culture is the stuff of collective cohesion, the Durkheimian glue of social order and preservative of predictability, the *soi-distant* support of social structure. And if for this first cultural discourse transgression signals meaningful creativity, for the second transgression signifies the very opposite: an absence of culture, an anomic failure of socialization into collective meaning. Yet the two discourses are not irreconcilable; both suggest an ongoing and contested negotiation of meaning and identity. Of course, the notion of culture as existing somehow outside human agency, as a functional and organic prop of social structure, is preposterous. But the collective *belief* in tradition, the emotional embracing of stasis and conformity, the ideological mobilization of rigid stereotype and fundamental value – and against this, the *disbelief* among others in the social order itself, and so a willingness to risk inventing collective alternatives – now *that* is indeed a significant subject matter, and one embraced by cultural criminology.

A cultural criminology that foregrounds human agency and human creativity, then, does not ignore those cultural dynamics that sometimes involve their renunciation. People, as David Matza (1969) famously pointed out, have always the capacity to transcend even the most dire of circumstances – but they also have the capacity for acting 'as if' they were cultural puppets unable to transcend the social order at all. If, in Dwight Conquergood's (1991) wonderful phrase, we are to view culture as a verb rather than as a noun, as an unsettled process rather than a *fait accompli*, then we must remember that this verb can take both the passive and the active tense. Culture suggests a sort of shared public performance, a process of public negotiation – but that performance can be one of acquiescence or rebellion, that negotiation one of violent conflict or considered capitulation.

In this sense cultural criminology, by the very nature of its subject matter, occupies a privileged vantage point on the everyday workings of social life. Its twin focus on culture and crime – put differently, on meaning and transgression – positions it at precisely those points where norms are imposed and threatened, laws enacted and broken, rules negotiated and renegotiated. Such a subject matter inevitably exposes the ongoing tension between cultural maintenance, cultural disorder, and cultural regeneration – and so from the view of cultural criminology, the everyday actions of criminals, police officers, and judges offer not just insights into criminal justice, but important glimpses into the very process by which social life is constructed and reconstructed. As we will see, this subject matter in turn reveals the complex, contested dynamic between cultures of control (control agencies' downwards symbolic constructions) and cultures of deviance (rule breakers' upwards counter-constructions).

cultural criminology old and new

Talk of culture, subculture and power evokes the rich tradition of subcultural theorization within criminology – and certainly cultural criminology draws deeply on subcultural research, from the early work of the Chicago School to the classic delinquency studies of the British Birmingham School. Likewise, cultural criminology is greatly influenced by the interactionist tradition in criminology and the sociology of deviance, as embodied most dramatically in labelling theory, and as taken up in the 1960s at the London School of Economics. Labelling theories, and the broader symbolic interactionist framework, highlight the conflicts of meaning that consistently animate crime and deviance; they demonstrate that the reality of crime and transgression exists as a project under construction, a project emerging from ongoing negotiations of authority and reputation. In fact, these and other intellectual traditions are essential to the development of cultural criminology – and the following chapter will explore how cultural criminology represents perhaps their culmination and reinvention.

Yet, in addressing the question of 'whether cultural criminology really does represent a new intellectual endeavour rather than a logical elaboration of previous work on deviant subcultures' (O'Brien, 2005: 600), we would firmly answer for the former. Cultural criminology actively seeks to dissolve conventional understandings and accepted boundaries, whether they confine specific criminological theories or the institutionalized discipline of criminology itself. From our view, for instance, existing subcultural and interactionist perspectives only gather real explanatory traction when integrated with historical and contemporary criminologies of power and inequality. Likewise, cultural criminology is especially indebted to theories of crime founded in the phenomenology of transgression (e.g. Katz, 1988; Lyng, 1990; Van Hoorebeeck, 1997) – yet here as well, our goal is to develop these approaches by situating them within a critical sociology of contemporary society (Ferrell, 1992; O'Malley and Mugford, 1994; Hayward, 2004: 152–7).

And cultural criminology consciously moves beyond these orientations in sociology and criminology; as later chapters will show, it incorporates perspectives from urban studies, media studies, existential philosophy, cultural and human geography, postmodern critical theory, anthropology, social movements theory – even from the historical praxis of earlier political agitators like the Wobblies and the Situationists. As much as cultural criminology seeks to ground itself in the best of existing criminology and sociology, it seeks also to reinvigorate the study of crime by integrating a host of alternative perspectives. Our intention is to continue turning the intellectual kaleidoscope, looking for new ways to see crime and the social response to it.

This strategy of reinvigoration is as much historical as theoretical; if we are to engage critically with the present crisis in crime and crime control, intellectual revivification is essential. Many of the perspectives just noted were forged from existing orientations during the political fires of the 1960s and 1970s, or in other cases out of the early twentieth-century blast furnace of industrial capitalism and the emerging nation state. Developing what was to become labelling theory, for example, Becker (1963: 181) disavowed his work being anything more than the existing 'interactionist theory of deviance' – and yet his revitalized interactionist theory resonated with the uncertainties and inequalities of the 1960s, rattled the foundations of 'scientific' criminology, and softened up criminology for still other radical remakings. So it is with cultural criminology today. We're not at the moment organizing the 1912 Lawrence cotton mills with the Wobblies, or plastering Paris 1968 with Situationist slogans; we're working to make sense of contemporary conditions, to trace the emergence of these conditions out of those old fires and furnaces, and to confront a new world of crime and control defined by the manufactured image, the constant movement of meaning, and the systematic exclusion of marginal populations and progressive possibilities. To do so, we're pleased to incorporate existing models of criminological critique – but we're just as willing to reassemble these and other intellectual orientations into a new mélange of critique that can penetrate the well-guarded façades of administrative criminology, the shadowy crimes of global capitalism, and the everyday realities of criminality today.

Crucial to cultural criminology, then, is a critical understanding of current times, which, for want of a better term, we'll call *late modernity*. Chapter 3 will provide a fuller sense of late modernity, and of cultural criminology's response to it. For now, we'll simply note that cultural criminology seeks to develop notions of culture and crime that can confront what is perhaps late modernity's defining trait: a world always in flux, awash in marginality and exclusion, but also in the ambiguous potential for creativity, transcendence, transgression, and recuperation. As suggested earlier, human culture has long remained in motion – yet this motion today seems all the more apparent, and all the more meaningful. In late modernity the insistent emphasis on expressivity and personal development, and the emergence of forces undermining the old constants of work, family and community, together place a premium on cultural change and personal reinvention. Couple this with a pluralism of values spawned by mass immigration and global conflict, and with the plethora of cultural referents carried by the globalized media, and uncertainty is heightened. Likewise, as regards criminality, the reference points which give rise to relative deprivation and discontent, the vocabularies of motive and techniques of neutralization deployed in the justification of crime, the very *modus operandi* of the criminal act itself, all emerge today as manifold, plural, and increasingly global.

And precisely the same is true of crime as public spectacle: experiences of victimization, justifications for punitiveness, and modes of policing all circulate widely and ambiguously, available for mediated consumption or political contestation.

Under such conditions, culture operates less as an entity or environment than as an uncertain dynamic by which groups large and small construct, question, and contest the collective experience of everyday life. Certainly, the meaningful moorings of social action still circulate within the political economy of daily life, and in the context of material setting and need – and yet, loosened in time and space, they circulate in such a way as to confound, increasingly, the economic and the symbolic, the event and the image, the heroic and the despicable. If the labelling theorists of a half-century ago glimpsed something of the slippery process by which deviant identity is negotiated, how much more slippery is that process now, in a world that cuts and mixes racial profiling for poor suspects, pre-paid image consultants for wealthy defendants, and televised crime personas for general consumption? If the subcultural theorists of the 1950s and 1960s understood something of group marginalization and its cultural consequences, what are we to understand of such consequences today, when globalized marginalization intermingles with crime and creativity, when national authorities unknowingly export gang cultures as they deport alleged gang members, when criminal subcultures are packaged as mainstream entertainment?

All of which returns us to those American fighters, those Mexican strikers and British street protesters, their violent images and their political conflicts circling the globe by way of do-it-yourself videos, video projections, websites, news coverage, and alternative media. In the next section we look further at fights and fight videos, and at the larger late modern meaning of symbolic violence. In the chapter's final section we return to politics and political conflict. There we'll make clear that we seek to revitalize political critique in criminology, to create a contemporary criminology – a cultural criminology – that can confront systems of control and relations of power as they operate today. There we'll hope to make clear another of cultural criminology's foundational understandings: that to explore cultural dynamics is to explore the dynamics of power – and to build the basis for a cultural *critique* of power as well.

meaning in motion: bloody knuckles

Amidst the cultural motion of late modernity, here's one movement you might not think of as cultural at all: the quick, snapping trajectory of arm, elbow and fist as a punch is thrown. That movement seems more a matter of bone and muscle than culture and meaning – and if that punch strikes somebody in the mouth, there are the bloody knuckles that are pulled back in the next motion. And if that somebody calls the cops? Perhaps the punch-thrower ends up in jail, staring down at those bloody knuckles to avoid staring at the other people in the holding cell. And eventually, they all get bailed out or they don't, they go to trial or they don't, they get convicted or they don't, they move back to their home or on to prison. Nothing much cultural about it, not much meaning to interrogate – just the everyday rhythms of skin and blood and criminal justice.

Well, yeah, except who was that somebody who got hit in the mouth, anyway? A boyfriend? A girlfriend? A police officer? An opponent standing toe-to-toe with another in the ring? Each incident will provoke a different reaction – and this must be because it *means* something different to strike your partner than it does to strike an officer of the state or a boxing opponent.

Oh yeah, and when did it happen? Was it the 1940s, for example, or now? See, we want to argue that this is part of the meaning, too, because sad as it is to say, in the 1940s a man could all too often hit a woman in the mouth and it meant … well, not much. 'Domestic violence' hadn't yet been invented as a legal and cultural (there's that word again) category – that is, it hadn't been widely defined, acknowledged, and condemned as a specific type of criminal behaviour. It took the radical women's movement and decades of political activism to get that accomplished (see Dobash and Dobash, 1992; Mooney, 2000; Radford et al., 2000). Today the process continues, with mandatory arrest laws for domestic violence, restraining orders, and other legal innovations. So before that, back in the day, as long as a women could hide the swollen lip and the man could hide the bloody knuckles, sometimes the violence didn't mean much at all – at least not publicly, at least not in the way it might and should.

And here's something else to think about: sometimes people in 1940 claimed – hell, sometimes men today still claim – that a swollen lip and bloody knuckles mean 'I love you'. A sadly warped rationalization, it goes something like this: 'Hey, I know I shouldn't hit you, but you know how it is, I just get so jealous, I just love you so much I don't ever want to lose you.' Notice here the power of the social and cultural context – of patriarchy and gender objectification and possessiveness – to operate as a sort of depraved magic, a magic so twisted that it can transform interpersonal violence into symbolic affection. And clearly, as long as this pernicious logic continues to circulate, so will women's victimization. So again: maybe it's not so much the bloody knuckles and the swollen lips as whose lips and knuckles they are, and who gets to decide what they mean.

If that's the case, then it seems that physical violence may start and stop, but that its meaning continues to circulate. It also seems that most violence, maybe all interpersonal violence, involves drama, presentation, and performance – especially gendered performance (Butler, 1999; Miller, J., 2001) – as much as it does blood and knuckles. So, if we hope to confront the *politics* of violence – that is, to understand how violence works as a form of power and domination, to empathize with the victimization that violence produces, and to reduce its physical and emotional harm – we must engage with the *cultures* of violence. Even this most direct of crimes – flesh on flesh, bloody knuckles and busted lips – is not direct at all. It's a symbolic exchange as much as a physical one, an exchange encased in immediate situations and in larger circumstances, an exchange whose meaning is negotiated before and after the blood is spilt.

Sometimes such violence is even performed for public consumption, and so comes to circulate as entertainment. A televised pay-per-view title fight, for example, can be thought of as a *series* of performances and entertainments: before the fight, with the press conferences, television commercials, and staged hostilities of the weigh-in; during the fight itself, with the ring rituals of fighter introductions, ringside celebrities, and technical knockouts; and after the fight, with the press coverage, the slow-motion replays of punches and pain, the interviews with the winner and the loser. If a boxing commission inquiry happens to follow, or if a 'moral entrepreneur' (Becker, 1963) decides later to launch a crusade against pugilistic brutality, another series of performances may unfold – and another series of meanings. Now the fight's entertainment will be reconsidered as a fraud, or a fix, or as evidence of what used to be called 'man's inhumanity to man'. Now other press conferences will be staged, other moments from the fight rebroadcast in slow motion, and all of it designed to go another round in staging the fight and its implications.

Even without a television contract or a boxing commission inquiry, the same sort of performative spiral often comes into play. Remember our opening story about the Texas fight video? Well, after the fight video had been discovered, after Deputy Chief Hawthorne had admitted that the video was nicely produced, he added something else. The participants in the video seemed to be fighting 'for 15 minutes of fame', Hawthorne said, offering a police assessment that echoed, of all people, 1960s underground artist Andy Warhol, and Warhol's dark vision of mediated spirals spinning so quickly that eventually 'everyone will be famous for fifteen minutes'. Yet the spirals of fame, infamy, and misfortune in this case hardly ended after fifteen minutes. In response to the fight videos and publicity surrounding them, local politicians set up a commission on youth violence, and investigated the involvement of the radio station in the videos. Legal authorities indicted four of the participants on serious felony charges: aggravated assault and engaging in organized crime. While the grandmother of the beating victim urged Jackson to spend some of his video profits on her grandson's hospital bills, Jackson's MySpace.com page filled up with 'Free Mike Jack' posts from supporters. And at his website, fight videos were still for sale, still making a profit. Only now the price had gone up, and now local police had notified the IRS of possible tax law violations in relation to the sales.[3]

When police officials paraphrase Andy Warhol, when in the midst of administering a vicious beating a participant addresses the camera, when footage of that and other fights is edited into entertainment, the meaning of violence is indeed being made in motion, and physical violence has become inextricably intertwined with mediated representation. The immediate, vicious physicality of violence – the beating victim suffered a brain hemorrhage and a fractured vertebra – now elongates and echoes through video footage, legal charges, and public perception. As it does, the linear sequencing of cause and effect circles back on itself, such that Jackson's fight video comes to be seen as crime, as evidence of crime, as a catalyst for later crime, even as the imitative product of existing mediated crime. And when, still later, the national media picked up the story, the fight videos and their meanings, their causes and effects, were once again set in motion.

In August 2006, national newspaper *USA Today* featured a story on the Texas fight videos – but now with more spirals of mediated meaning. Beginning with bloody knuckles – an alliterative description of 'bare knuckle brawlers brutally punching each other' – the *USA Today* article moved to an image of Brad Pitt from the 1999 film *Fight Club* (Dir. David Fincher) and the claim that fighters in Texas and elsewhere 'follow [the] advice' offered in the film, then alluded to the film *A Clockwork Orange* (Dir. Stanley Kubrick, 1971). It noted the use of instant messaging and cellphone cameras in staging the videotaped fights, adding that one Texas fight video depicted teens watching an earlier fight video. The article even resurrected Warhol with a quote from a university professor: 'This does seem a phenomenon of the *Mortal Kombat*, violent video game generation. [It] offers a chance to bring those fantasies of violence and danger to life – and maybe have your 15 minutes of fame in an underground video.' Most significantly, *USA Today* recast the fight videos themselves as products of 'teen fight clubs' and a 'disturbing extreme sport', and claimed that these extreme sport/fight clubs have now 'popped up across the nation' (McCarthy, 2006: 1, 2). Already confounded with mediated representation and entertainment, the violence as presented in the *USA Today* article now became another sort of entertainment – an 'extreme sport' – and emerged as evidence of organized youth subcultures. As a writer from the *Columbia Journalism Review* noted in response to the *USA Today* feature, this mediated violence had now been 'repackaged' as a 'national trend' (Gillette, 2006) – or as criminologist Stan Cohen (2002) might say, re-presented as a purported reason for 'moral panic'.

Interestingly, the *USA Today* article also took pains to claim that these fights and fight videos – or maybe fight clubs, or extreme sports – were not the products of power and inequality, citing one legal authority who claimed that 'it's not a race issue, it's not a class issue', and another who emphasized that the problem 'crosses all socioeconomic bounds' (McCarthy, 2006: 2). Maybe so – but we suspect that, in one form or another, power and inequality do in fact underwrite the fight videos. The videos certainly portray the sort of pervasive leisure-time violence that Simon Winlow and Steve Hall (2006) have documented among young people increasingly excluded from meaningful work or education. They offer direct evidence of media technology's seepage into the practice of everyday life, such that kids can now stage, for good or bad, elaborate images of their own lives. Most troubling, they suggest the in-the-streets interplay between a mean-spirited contemporary culture of marketed aggression and an ongoing sense of manliness defined by machismo, violence, and domination. Hunter S Thompson (1971: 46) once said of a tawdry Las Vegas casino that it was 'what the whole ... world would be doing on Saturday night if the Nazis had won the war'. Yeah, that and brutalizing each other on video-tape, selling it for a profit, and watching it for entertainment.

violence, power, and war

Other sorts of violence show us something about power and inequality as well. As already seen, domestic violence explodes not only out of angry situations, but from longstanding patterns of interpersonal abuse and gendered expectation. As we'll discuss in later chapters, various contemporary forms of violence as entertainment – 'bum fights', extreme fighting, war footage – each invoke particular social class preferences and political economies of profit, offering different sorts of flesh for different sorts of fantasies. As we'll also see, knuckles bruised and bloodied in pitched battles between striking factory workers and strike-breaking deputy sheriffs suggest something of the structural violence inherent in class inequality; so do the knuckles of young women bloodied amidst the frantic work, the global assembly-line madness, of a maquiladora or Malaysian toy factory. As Mark Hamm (1995) has documented, young neo-Nazi skinheads, jacked up on beer and white power music and mob courage, write their own twisted account of racism as they beat down an immigrant on a city street, or bloody their knuckles while attacking a gay man outside a suburban club.

Significantly for a cultural criminology of violence, episodes like these don't simply represent existing inequalities, or exemplify arrangements of power; they *reproduce* power and inequality, encoding it in the circuitry of everyday life. Such acts are *performances* of power and domination, offered up to various audiences as symbolic accomplishments. A half-century ago, Harold Garfinkel (1956: 420) suggested that there existed a particular sort of 'communicative work ... whereby the public identity of an actor is transformed into something looked on as lower in the local scheme of social types', and he referred to this type of activity as a 'degradation ceremony'. Violence often carries this sort of communicative power; the pain that it inflicts is both physical and symbolic, a pain of public degradation and denunciation as much as physical domination. And in this sense, once again, it is often the *meaning* of the violence that matters most to perpetrator and victim alike. A wide and disturbing range of violent events – neo-Nazi attacks, fraternity hazing traditions, gang beat-downs, terrorist bombings and abduction videos, public hangings, sexual assaults, war crimes – can be understood in this way, as forms of ritualized violence designed to degrade the identities of their victims, to impose on them a set of unwanted meanings that linger long after the physical pain fades. To understand violence as 'communicative work', then, is not to minimize its physical harm or to downgrade its seriousness, but to recognize that its harms are both physical and symbolic, and to confront its terrible consequences in all their cultural complexity.

So violence can operate as image or ceremony, can carry with it identity and inequality, can impose meaning or have meaning imposed upon it – and in the contemporary world of global communication, violence can ebb and flow along long fault lines of war, terror, and ideology. Among the more memorable images from the US war in Iraq, for example, are those photographs of prisoner abuse that emerged from Abu Ghraib prison. You know the ones: the hooded figure standing on a box with wires running from his hands, the pile of men with Lyndie England leering and pointing down at them, the prisoner on the leash held by England. You know, and we know, because those photographs have been so widely circulated as to become part of our shared cultural stockpile of image and understanding. But before we go any further, a question: Did a US soldier at Abu Ghraib ever sodomize a prisoner, murder a prisoner, hit a prisoner and pull back bloody knuckles? These things may or may not have happened, but if we've seen no photographic evidence of them, then they won't seem – can't seem – as real or as meaningful to us as those acts that were photographed. And so the suspicion arises: Was the 'problem' at Abu Ghraib the abuse, or the photographs of the abuse? And if those photographs of abuse had not been taken, would Abu Ghraib exist as a contested international symbol, a public issue, a crime scene – or would a crime not converted into an image be, for many, no crime at all (Hamm, 2007)?

Those photos that *were* taken have certainly remained in motion since they were first staged, spinning off all manner of effects and implications along the way. To begin with, the photos didn't just capture acts of aggressive violence; they operated, as Garfinkel would argue, as a system of ritualized degradation in the prison and beyond, exposing and exacerbating the embarrassment of the prisoners, recording it for the amusement of the soldiers, and eventually disseminating it to the world. For the prisoners and the soldiers alike, the abuse was as much photographic as experiential, more a staged performance for the camera than a moment of random violence. The responses of those outraged by the photos in turn mixed event, emotion, and image: on the walls of Sadr City, Iraq, a painting of the hooded figure, but now wired to the Statue of Liberty for all to see; and in the backrooms of Iraqi insurgent safe houses, staged abuses and beheadings, meant mostly for later broadcast on television and the internet (Ferrell et al., 2005: 9).

And yet for the soldiers back on the opposite side, for those US soldiers who took the Abu Ghraib photographs, a not-so-different sensibility about the image: a sense that cell phone cameras, digital photographs emailed instantaneously home, self-made movies mixing video footage and music downloads, all seem normal enough, whether shot in Boston or Baghdad, whether focused on college graduation, street fights, or prisoner degradation. Here we see even the sort of 'genocidal tourism' that cultural criminologist Wayne Morrison (2004a) has documented – where World War II German Police Reservists took postcard-like photographs of their atrocities – reinvented in an age of instant messaging and endless image reproduction. And like Michael G Jackson and other fight video makers, we now see soldiers and insurgents who produce their own images of violence, find their own audiences for those images, and interweave image with physical conflict itself.

Violence, it seems, is never only violence. It emerges from inequities both polit-ical and perceptual, and accomplishes the symbolic domination of identity and interpretation as much as the physical domination of individuals and groups. Put in rapid motion, circulating in a contemporary world of fight videos and newscasts, images of violence double back on themselves, emerging as crime or evidence of crime, confirming or questioning existing arrangements. From the view of cultural criminology, there is a *politics* to every bloody knuckle – to knuckles bloodied amidst domestic violence or ethnic hatred, to knuckles bloodied for war or profit or entertainment, to knuckles bloodied in newspaper photos and internet clips. As the meaning of violence continues to coagulate around issues of identity and inequality, the need for a *cultural* criminology of violence, and in response a cultural criminology of social justice, continues too.

the politics of cultural criminology

If ever we could afford the fiction of an 'objective' criminology – a criminology devoid of moral passion and political meaning – we certainly cannot now, not when every bloody knuckle leaves marks of mediated meaning and political consequence. The day-to-day inequalities of criminal justice, the sour drift towards institutionalized meanness and legal retribution, the ongoing abrogation of human rights in the name of 'counter-terrorism' and 'free trade' – all carry criminology with them, willingly or not. Building upon existing inequalities of ethnicity, gender, age, and social class, such injustices reinforce these inequalities and harden the hopelessness they produce. Increasingly crafted as media specta-cles, consistently masked as information or entertainment, the inequitable dynamics of law and social control remain essential to the maintenance of polit-ical power, and so operate to prop up the system that produces them.

In such a world there's no neat choice between political involvement and criminological analysis – only implications to be traced and questions to be asked. Does our scholarship help maintain a fraudulently 'objective' criminol-ogy that distances itself from institutionalized abuses of power, and so allows them to continue? Does criminological research, often dependent on the good will and grant money of governmental agencies, follow the agendas set by these agencies, and so grant them in return the sheen of intellectual legiti-macy? By writing and talking mostly to each other, do criminologists absent themselves from public debate, and so cede that debate to politicians and pun-dits? Or can engaged, oppositional criminological scholarship perhaps help move us towards a more just world? To put it bluntly: What is to be done about domestic violence and hate crime, about fight videos and prison torture – and about the distorted images and understandings that perpetuate these practices as they circulate through the capillaries of popular culture?

Part of the answer we've already suggested: critical engagement with the flow of meaning that constructs late modern crime, in the hope of turning this fluidity towards social justice. In a world where, as Stephanie Kane (2003: 293) says, 'ideological formations of crime are packaged, stamped with corporate logos, and sent forth into the planetary message stream like advertising', our job must be to divert the stream, to substitute hard insights for advertised images. Later chapters will discuss this strategy of cultural engagement in greater depth, but here we turn to an issue that underlies it: the relationship of crime, culture, and contemporary political economy.

capitalism and culture

For us, that issue is clear: unchecked global capitalism must be confronted as the deep dynamic from which spring many of the ugliest examples of contemporary criminality. Tracing a particularly expansionist trajectory these days, late modern capitalism continues to contaminate one community after another, shaping social life into a series of predatory encounters and saturating everyday existence with criminogenic expectations of material convenience. All along this global trajectory, collectivities are converted into markets, people into consumers, and experiences and emotions into products. So steady is this seepage of consumer capitalism into social life, so pervasive are its crimes – both corporate and interpersonal – that they now seem to pervade most every situation.

That said, it's certainly not our contention that capitalism forms the essential bedrock of all social life, or of all crime. Other wellsprings of crime and inequality run deep as well; late capitalism is but a shifting part of the sour quagmire of patriarchy, racism, militarism, and institutionalized inhumanity in which we're currently caught. To reify 'capitalism', to assign it a sort of foundational timelessness, is to grant it a status it doesn't deserve. Whatever its contemporary power, capitalism constitutes a trajectory, not an accomplishment, and there are other trajectories at play today as well, some moving with consumer capitalism, others moving against and beyond it. Still, as the currently ascendant form of economic exploitation, capitalism certainly merits the critical attention of cultural criminology.

And yet, even as we focus on this particular form of contemporary domination and inequality, we are drawn away from a simple materialist framework, and towards a cultural analysis of capitalism and its crimes. For capitalism is essentially a *cultural* enterprise these days; its economics are decisively cultural in nature. Perhaps more to the point for criminology, contemporary capitalism is a system of domination whose economic and political viability, its crimes and its controls, rest precisely on its cultural accomplishments. Late capitalism markets lifestyles, employing an advertising machinery that sells need, affect and affiliation as much as the material products themselves. It runs on service economies, economies that package privilege and manufacture experiences of imagined indulgence. Even the material fodder for all this – the cheap appliances and seasonal fashions – emerges from a global gulag of factories kept well hidden behind ideologies of free trade and economic opportunity. This is a capitalism founded not on Fordism, but on the manipulation of meaning and the seduction of the image; it is a cultural capitalism. Saturating destabilized working-class neighbourhoods, swirling along with mobile populations cut loose from career or community, it is particularly contagious; it offers the seductions of the market where not much else remains.

As much as the Malaysian factory floor, then, *this* is the stuff of late capitalism, and so the contested turf of late modernity. If we're to do our jobs as criminologists – if we're to understand crime, crime control, and political conflict in this context – it seems we must conceptualize late capitalism in these terms. To describe the fluid, expansive, and culturally charged dynamics of contemporary capitalism is not to deny its power but to define it; it is to consider current conditions in such a way that they can be critically confronted. From the Frankfurt School to Fredric Jameson (1991) and beyond, the notion of 'late capitalism' references many meanings, including for some a fondly anticipated demise – but among these meanings is surely this sense of a capitalism quite thoroughly transformed into a cultural operation, a capitalism unexplainable outside its own representational dynamics (Harvey, 1990; Hayward, 2004).

The social classes of capitalism have likewise long meant more than mere economic or productive position – and under the conditions of late capitalism this is ever more the case. Within late capitalism, social class is experienced, indeed constituted, as much by affective affiliation, leisure aesthetics, and collective consumption as by income or employment. The cultural theorists and 'new criminologists' of the 1970s first began to theorize this class culture, and likewise began to trace its connection to patterns of crime and criminalization. As they revealed, and as we have continued to document (Hayward, 2001, 2004; Young, 2003), predatory crime within and between classes so constituted often emerges out of *perceptions* of relative deprivation, other times from a twisted allegiance to consumer goods considered essential for class identity or class mobility (Featherstone, 1991; Lury, 1996; Miles, 1998). And yet, even when so acquired, a class identity of this sort remains a fragile one, its inherent instability spawning still other crimes of outrage, transgression, or predation. If crime is connected to social class, as it surely is, the connective tissue today is largely the cultural filaments of leisure, consumption, and shared perception.

crime, culture, and resistance

In the same way that cultural criminology attempts to conceptualize the dynamics of class, crime, and social control within the cultural fluidity of contemporary capitalism, it also attempts to understand the connections between crime, activism, and political resistance under these circumstances. Some critics argue that cultural criminology in fact remains *too* ready to understand these insurgent possibilities, confounding crime and resistance while celebrating little moments of illicit transgression. For such critics, cultural criminology's focus on everyday resistance to late capitalism presents a double danger, minimizing the real harm done by everyday crime while missing the importance of large-scale, organized political change. Martin O'Brien, for example, suggests that 'cultural criminology might be best advised to downgrade the study of deviant species and focus more attention on the generically political character of criminalization' (2005: 610; see Howe, 2003; Ruggiero, 2005). Steve Hall and Simon Winlow (2007: 83–4) likewise critique cultural criminology's alleged tendency to find 'authentic resistance' in every transgressive event or criminal subculture, and dismiss out of hand forms of cultural resistance like 'subversive symbol inversion' and 'creative recoding' that cultural criminologists supposedly enjoy finding among outlaws and outsiders.

In response, we would note that cultural criminology doesn't simply focus on efflorescences of resistance and transgression; it also explores boredom, repetition, everyday acquiescence, and other mundane dimensions of society and criminality (e.g. Ferrell, 2004a; Yar, 2005). Cultural criminology's attention to meaning and micro-detail ensures that it is equally at home explaining the monotonous routines of DVD piracy, or the dulling trade in counterfeit 'grey' automotive components, as it is the *sub rosa* worlds of gang members or graffiti artists. As cultural criminologists, we seek to understand all components of crime: the criminal actor, formal and informal control agencies, victims, and others. In this book's later chapters, for example, we develop cultural criminology's existing focus on the state (e.g. Wender, 2001; Hamm, 2004). For cultural criminology, attention to human agency means paying attention to crime and crime control, to emotion and rationality, to resistance and submission.

Then again, it's probably the case that we and other cultural criminologists do take special pleasure in moments of subversive resistance; as Jean Genet once admitted to an interviewer, 'obviously, I am drawn to peoples in revolt ... because I myself have the need to call the whole of society into question' (in Soueif, 2003: 25). But maybe it's also the case that illicit cultural practices like 'subversive symbol inversion' and 'creative recoding' *do* now constitute significant opposition to capitalism's suffocations – and have in the past as well. Long before capitalism's late modern liquidity, back in the period of nuts-and-bolts industrial capitalism, one group most clearly and courageously engaged in organized, in-your-face confrontation with capitalism's predatory economics: those Wobblies we mentioned earlier, more formally known as the Industrial Workers of the World (IWW). Indeed, the Wobblies were known for their ability to organize itinerant and marginal workers, for their dedication to direct economic action – and for their facility at subversive symbol inversion and creative recoding. In fact, it was just this sort of symbolic sleight of hand that allowed this ragtag group of low-wage peripatetic outsiders to organize, fight – and often win – against the robber barons and deputy sheriffs of industrial capitalism.

Looking to create a culture of union solidarity, the Wobblies converted well-known church hymns into rousing union anthems. Facing legal injunctions against advocating sabotage or organizing, they posted 'silent agitators' (union organizing stickers), published notices that spelled out 'sabotage' in code, and issued communiqués that surely seemed to support the legal authorities – since these communiqués provided such detailed instructions to IWW members regarding what forms of sabotage they should (not) employ. Like other progressive groups of the time, the Wobblies were animated by – in many ways *organized by* – shared symbols, subversive recodings, and semiotic inversions of the existing order.

So if we can find illicit symbolic subversion and cultural recoding sparking 'authentic resistance' even in an early capitalist period characterized by material production and circumscribed communication, what might we find under the current conditions of late capitalism, with its environments of swirling symbolism and pervasive communication? To start, we might find the women's movements or gay/lesbian movements or anti-war movements of the past few decades, staging illegal public spectacles, confronting mediated representations of women and men and war, and recruiting members through channels of alternative communication. We might spot activists on New York City's Lower East Side, recalling the Wobblies as they organize opposition to the Giuliani administration's criminalization of informal public notices by distributing informal public notices saying, 'Warning! Do Not Read This Poster' (Patterson, 2006). With the historian John Bushnell (1990), we might even find a parallel dynamic outside the bounds of Western capitalism, noting how the emergence of street graffiti in the Soviet Union exposed the totalizing lies of the Soviet authorities, and ultimately helped organize successful resistance to them.

And if you're a cultural criminologist, you might pay particular attention to the ways in which new terms of legal and political engagement emerge from the fluid cultural dynamics of late capitalism. To summarize some of our recent studies in crime and resistance: when gentrification and 'urban redevelopment' drive late capitalist urban economies, when urban public spaces are increasingly converted to privatized consumption zones, graffiti comes under particular attack by legal and economic authorities as an aesthetic threat to cities' economic vitality. In such a context legal authorities aggressively criminalize graffiti, corporate media campaigns construct graffiti writers as violent vandals – and graffiti writers themselves become more organized and politicized in response. When consumer culture and privatized transportation conspire to shape cities into little more than car parks connected by motorways, bicycle and pedestrian activists create collective alternatives and stage illegal public interruptions. When late capitalist consumer culture spawns profligate waste, trash scroungers together learn to glean survival and dignity from the discards of the privileged, and activists organize programmes to convert consumer 'trash' into food for homeless folks, clothes for illegal immigrants, and housing for the impoverished. When the same concentrated corporate media that stigmatizes graffiti writers and trash pickers closes down other possibilities of local culture and street activism, a micro-radio movement emerges – and is aggressively policed by local and national authorities for its failure to abide by regulatory standards designed to privilege concentrated corporate media (Ferrell, 1996, 2001/2, 2006).

In all of these cases easy dichotomies don't hold. These aren't matters of culture or economy, of crime or politics; they're cases in which activists of all sorts employ subversive politics strategies – that is, various forms of organized cultural resistance – to counter a capitalist economy itself defined by cultural dynamics of mediated representation, marketing strategy, and lifestyle consumption. Likewise, these cases don't embody simple dynamics of law and economy, or law and culture; they exemplify a confounding of economy, culture, and law that spawns new forms of illegality and new campaigns of enforcement. Similarly, these cases neither prove nor disprove themselves as 'authentic' resistance or successful political change – but they do reveal culturally organized opposition to a capitalist culture busily inventing new forms of containment and control.

Most significantly, the cultural criminological analysis of these and other cases neither accounts for them as purely subjective moments of cultural innovation, nor reduces them to objective byproducts of structural inequality. Among the more curious claims offered by cultural criminology's critics is the contention that cultural criminology has abandoned structural analysis and 'criminological macro-theories of causality' in favour of 'subjectivist-culturalism' (Hall and Winlow, 2007: 83, 86). In reality, since its earliest days, cultural criminology has sought to overcome this very dichotomization of structure and agency, of the objective and the subjective, by locating structural dynamics within lived experience. This is precisely the point of Stephen Lyng's (1990) 'edgework' concept, embodying both Marx and Mead in an attempt to account for the interplay between structural context and illicit sensuality. Likewise, Jack Katz's (1988) 'seductions of crime' are meant as provocative engagements with, and correctives to, 'criminological macro-theories of causality'. As Katz argues, a criminology lost within the abstractions of conventional structural analysis tends to forget the interpersonal drama of its subject matter – or paraphrasing Howard Becker (1963: 190), tends to turn crime into an abstraction and then study the abstraction – and so must be reminded of crime's fearsome foreground. Clearly, cultural criminology hasn't chosen 'subjectivist-culturalism' over structural analysis; it has chosen instead a style of analysis that can focus structure and subject in the same frame (Ferrell, 1992; Hayward, 2004; Young, 2003). Perhaps some of our colleagues only recognize structural analysis when encased in multi-syllabic syntax or statistical tabulation. But structural analysis can be rooted in moments of transgression as well; it can show that 'structure' remains a metaphor for patterns of power and regularities of meaning produced in back alleys as surely as corporate boardrooms.

commodifying resistance? romanticizing resistance?

Engaging in this way with the politics of crime, resistance, and late capitalism requires yet another turn as well, this one towards a central irony of contemporary life: the vast potential of capitalism to co-opt illicit resistance into the very system it is meant to oppose, and so to transform experiential opposition into commodified acquiescence. This homogenizing tendency constitutes an essential late capitalistic dynamic, and the most insidious of consumer capitalism's control mechanisms. The ability to reconstitute resistance as commodity, and so to sell the illusion of freedom and diversity, is powerful magic indeed. Because of this, a number of cultural criminological studies have explored this dynamic in some detail. Meticulously tracing the history of outlaw biker style, Stephen Lyng and Mitchell Bracey (1995) have demonstrated that early criminal justice attempts to criminalize biker style only amplified its illicit meanings, while later corporate schemes to incorporate biker style into mass production and marketing effectively evacuated its subversive potential. More recently, we have outlined the ways in which consumption overtakes experiences of resistance – indeed, most all experiences – within the consumerist swirl of the late capitalist city (Hayward, 2004). Likewise, Heitor Alvelos (2004, 2005) has carefully documented the appropriation of street graffiti by multinational corporations and their advertisers. And he's right, of course; as the illicit visual marker of urban hipness, graffiti is now incorporated into everything from corporate theme parks and Broadway musicals to clothing lines, automobile adverts, and video games. When it comes to the politics of illicit resistance, death by diffusion – dare we say, impotence by incorporation – remains always a real possibility.

And yet again, a dichotomized distinction between authentically illicit political resistance and commodified market posturing does little to explain these cases, or the fluidity of this larger capitalist dynamic. From one view, of course, this dynamic would suggest that there can be no authentic resistance in any case, since everything – revolutionary tract, subversive moment, labour history – is now automatically and inescapably remade as commodity, re-presented as image, and so destroyed. A more useful view, we think, is to see this dynamic as one of complexity and contradiction. As seductive as it is, the late capitalistic process of incorporation is not totalizing; it is instead an ongoing battleground of meaning, more a matter of policing the crisis than of definitively overcoming it. Sometimes the safest of corporate products becomes, in the hands of activists or artists or criminals, a dangerous subversion; stolen away, remade, it is all the more dangerous for its ready familiarity, a Trojan horse sent back into the midst of the everyday. Other times the most dangerously illegal of subversions becomes, in the hands of corporate marketers, the safest of selling schemes, a sure bet precisely because of its illicit appeal. Mostly, though, these processes intertwine, sprouting further ironies and contradictions, winding their way in and out of little cracks in the system, often bearing the fruits of both 'crime' and 'commodity'.

A new generation of progressive activists born to these circumstances seems well aware of them, by the way – and because of this, well aware that the point is ultimately not the thing itself, not the act or the image or the style, but the activism that surrounds and survives it. So, anti-globalization activists, militant hackers, urban environmentalists and others project images on to an embassy, throw adulterated representations back at the system that disseminates them, organize ironic critiques, recode official proclamations, and remain ready to destroy whatever of their subversions might become commodities. Even within late capitalism's formidable machinery of incorporation, the exhaustion of meaning is never complete, the illicit subversion never quite conquered. The husk appropriated, the seed sprouts again.

Our hope for cultural criminology – that it can contribute to this sort of activism, operating as a counter-discourse on crime and criminal justice, shorting out the circuitry of official meaning – is founded in just this sensibility. We don't imagine that cultural criminology can easily overturn the accumulated ideologies of law and crime, but we do imagine that these accumulations are never fully accomplished, and so remain available for ongoing subversion. In fact, the logic of resistance suggests that it is the very viability of crime control as a contemporary political strategy, the very visibility of crime dramas and crime news in the media, that makes such subversion possible, and possibly significant. In a world where political campaigns run loud and long on claims of controlling crime, where crime circulates endlessly as image and entertainment, we're offered a symbolic climate ready-made for a culturally attuned criminology – and so we must find ways to confound those campaigns, to turn that circulation to better ends. And as those in power work to manage this slippery world, to recuperate that meaning for themselves, we must remain ready to keep the meaning moving in the direction of progressive transformation.

This hope for social and cultural change, this sense that even the sprawling recuperations of late capitalism can be resisted, rests on a politics that runs deeper still. Certainly, the 'cultural' in cultural criminology denotes in one sense a particular analytic focus: an approach that addresses class and crime as lived experience, a model that highlights meaning and representation in the construction of transgression, and a strategy designed to untangle the symbolic entrapments laid by late capitalism and law. But the 'cultural' in cultural criminology denotes something else, too: the conviction that it is shared human agency and symbolic action that shape the world. Looking up at corporate misconduct or corporate crime, looking down to those victimized or in revolt, looking sideways at ourselves, cultural criminologists see that people certainly don't make history just as they please, but that together, they do indeed make it.

For this reason cultural criminologists employ *inter alia* the tools of interactionist and cultural analysis. From our view, notions of 'interaction' or 'intersubjectivity' don't exclude the sweep of social structure or the real exercise of power; rather, they help explain how structures of social life are maintained and made meaningful, and how power is exercised, portrayed, and resisted. To inhabit the 'social constructionist ghetto', as Hall and Winlow (2007: 89) have accused us of doing, is in this way to offer a radical critique of authorities' truth claims about crime and justice, and to unravel the reifications through which progressive alternatives are made unimaginable. That ghetto, we might add, also keeps the neighbouring enclave of macro-structural analysis honest and open; without it, such enclaves tend to close their gates to the ambiguous possibilities of process, agency, and self-reflection. And so an irony that appeals especially to 'ghetto' residents like ourselves: the categories by which serious scholars deny 'culture' and 'interaction' as essential components in the construction of human misconduct are themselves cultural constructions, shaped from collective interaction and encoded with collective meaning.

And further into the politics of cultural criminology, and into some controversial territory indeed. Cultural criminology is sometimes accused of 'romanticism', of a tendency to embrace marginalized groups and to find among them an indefatigable dignity in the face of domination. As regards that critique, we would begin by saying ... yes. A sense of human possibility, not to mention a rudimentary grasp of recent world history, would indeed suggest that human agency is never completely contained or defined by dominant social forces, legal, capitalist, or otherwise. The Warsaw ghetto, the Soviet gulag, the American slave plantation – not even the horrors of their systematic brutality was enough to fully exhaust the human dignity and cultural innovation of those trapped within their walls. If, as someone once suggested, law is the mailed fist of the ruling class, then those hammered down by that fist, those criminalized and marginalized and made out-laws, carry with them at least the seeds of progressive opposition, offering at a minimum a broken mirror in which to reflect and critique power and its consequences. Marginalization and criminalization certainly produce internecine predation, but they also produce, sometimes in the same tangled circumstances, moments in which outsiders collectively twist and shout against their own sorry situations. From the Delta blues to Russian prison poetry, from the Paris Commune to anti-globalization street theatre, there is often a certain romance to illicit cultural resistance.

Or is there? In common usage, 'romanticization' suggests a sort of sympathetic divergence from reality; for some of our critics, it suggests that we create overly sympathetic portraits of criminals and other outsiders, glorifying their bad behaviour, imagining their resistance, and minimizing their harm to others. Yet embedded in this criticism is a bedrock question for cultural criminologists: What *is* the 'reality' of crime, and who determines it? After all, a charge of romanticizing a criminalized or marginalized group implies a solid baseline, a true reality, against which this romanticization can be measured. But what might that be, and how would we know it? As we'll see in later chapters, police reports and official crime statistics certainly won't do, what with their propensity for forcing complex actions into simplistic bureaucratic categories. Mediated representations, fraught with inflation and scandal, hardly help. And so another irony: given the ongoing demonization of criminals and dramatization of crime in the interest of prison construction, political containment, and media production values, it seems likely that what accumulates as 'true' about crime is mostly fiction, and that 'romanticism' may mostly mark cultural criminologists' diversion from this fiction as they go about investigating the complexities of transgression.

When critics chide cultural criminologists for romanticizing crime and resistance, then, they risk reproducing by default the manufactured misunderstandings that should in fact be the object of criminology's critical gaze. The same danger arises when they critique cultural criminology's alleged focus on 'little delinquents' and 'petty misdemeanors' (Hall and Winlow, 2007: 83, 89), on 'graffiti writing or riding a motorcycle' (O'Brien, 2005: 610), rather than on larger crimes of greater political import. As we'll show in Chapter 4, criminal acts are never quite so obviously little or large, never inherently inconsequential or important; they're made to be what they are, invested with meaning and consequence, by perpetrators, victims, lawyers, news reporters, and judges, all operating amidst existing arrangements of power. Delinquents and death-row inmates, petty misdemeanours and high crimes all emerge from a process so fraught with injustice that it regularly confounds life and death, guilt and innocence – and so, again, this process must be the *subject matter* of criminology, not an a priori foundation for it. When urban gentrification is underway, little criminals like homeless folks and graffiti writers get larger, at least in the eyes of the authorities. When the Patriot Act passes, petty misdemeanours are reconstructed by some as terrorism and treason. With enough political influence, the high crimes of corporations can be made inconsequential, if not invisible. The key isn't to accept criminal acts for what they are, but to interrogate them for what they become.

Moreover, this sort of cultural criminological interrogation hardly necessitates that we look only at crimes made little, or only affirmatively at crime in general. Mark Hamm's (1997, 2002) extensive research on the culture of right-wing terrorism, Phillip Jenkins' (1999) analysis of anti-abortion violence and its 'unconstruction' as terrorism, Chris Cunneen and Julie Stubbs' (2004) research into the domestic murder of immigrant women moved about the world as commodities, our own work on pervasive automotive death and the ideologies that mask it (Ferrell, 2004b) – the lens used to investigate such crimes is critical and cultural, sometimes even condemnatory, but certainly not affirmative. In fact, it would seem that these and similar studies within cultural criminology address quite clearly any charge of ignoring 'serious' crimes of political harm and predation.

Still, we'll admit to a lingering fondness for those 'little delinquents' and 'petty misdemeanors' – since, we've found, they sometimes become powerful forces for political change. History, if nothing else, should tell us that.

notes

1 It is important to acknowledge the cultural complexity surrounding the Oaxaca teachers' strike. While there were and are legitimate demands in the realm of education, and sections of the movement were genuinely popular, the movement subsequently was co-opted by other regional groups in their power struggle against the Governor's hegemonic PRI party.
2 It is important here to briefly note our perspective on the social or criminological subject. Our central axiom is the creative nature of human action. Men and

women create culture, give meaning to their own particular cultural perspective, ableit in a moral and material world not of their own making. None of this rules out the mechanistic mores of habit and here we follow Matza (1969) – the ability to act 'as if' determined and the leap of bad faith that this entails. Human behaviour is shaped by the actors themselves. It is not merely the unfolding of preordained essences which have been encoded in some DNA sequence, or in the psychoanalytical drama of phallus and breast set in some conjectured encounter early in the family or the steady casual dominance of broken home or childhood poverty stretching through the actor's life. Rather, moral careers are contingent on the present, and the past appears to hold sway only when there has been a continuity of experience or a process of self-fulfillment where powerul actors reinforce notions of a fixed self and powerless subjects come to belive these narratives. Motives are cultural products not essences revealed. In a hyper plural society there is a multitude of vocabularies of motives available; and these are picked not willy nilly but in relationship to the perceived problems of the individual, whilst the self has a unitary quality as a centre of the human construction of meaning, albeit in a world riven by a plurality of meanings. To postulate that human beings are narrative creators who constantly rewrite and reshape their personal narratives does not imply a lack of unity of the self but the very opposite. A common human predicament is that of ontological insecurity where groups or whole sectors of the population feel that their social status is threatened and their identity disembedded. Such a situation, as we will see in Chapter 3 is particularly prevalent in late modernity. One solution to this is the process of 'othering' where actors actively embrace narratives about themselves and others which deny human creativity and prioritize the preordained and the fated. Othering is the projection of essentialist attributes on another and, by means of this, oneself in order to justify privileges and deference and to stem feelings of ontological insecurity. It promises fixed lines of orientation in a late modern world of hyper pluralism and disembeddedness; it guarantees structures of superiority and inferiority. It is a guard against the vertigo of late modernity (Young, 2007). It utilizes binaries of supposed essential differences whether based on gender, or nation or race or religion or class, etc. A particularly potent source of such differences centres on crime and deviance: thus the 'normal' is contrasted with the 'deviant' and the law-abiding with the criminal (very frequently linked to class and race etc). Virtue is contrasted with vice, their vice corroborates our virtue. Such an act of othering allows vice to be seen as a lack of culture and very frequently forms the basis of a determinism which is presumed to propel the deviant actor. This, as we will see later, is often the basis of much orthodox positivist criminology. Layered onto this are psychodynamic processes which add intensity and passion to this process of othering. Chief of these are the sense of moral indignation where those cast as Others are castigated for cheating at the rules of reward and evading the sacrifices which the virtuous citizens perceive as the nature of responsibility and duty (e.g., living on the dole, having housing freely provided, being single dependent mothers etc). This is particularly exacerbated where such deviants are seen as directly causing problems for the virtuous (e.g., immigrants, the underclass). Such psychodynamics does not involve the enactment of determinants set up in a psychoanalytical past (e.g., Gadd and Jefferson, 2008) but are the result of current problems and pressures occuring in particular parts of the social structure (e.g., the impact of downsizing, chronic job insecurity, deskilling etc), of mistaken beliefs about their causes and processes of bad faith and self-mystification. It is a psychosocial criminology which is existentially based and grounded in the present structural problems of late modernity.

3   Agee, 2006a: 1A; Agee, 2006b: 8B; Ayala and Agee, 2006: 1A, 23A; Jones, 2006a: 5B; Jones, 2006b: 10B; Mitchell, 2006: 23A.

A selection of films and documentaries illustrative of some of the themes and ideas in this chapter

THE WIRE (series, 5 parts), Creator: David Simon
Perhaps the greatest TV crime series ever, *The Wire* unfolds over five series like a filmic textbook on cultural criminology: the micro-street practices of drug sellers, post-industrial urban decay, the strengths and weaknesses of contemporary police work, transnational people smuggling, corruption in the prison and criminal justice system, the manipulation of crime statistics, money laundering, and the failing US education system – the list of criminologically-related themes is endless. The first series takes a few episodes to warmup, but stick with it and you will be rewarded as *The Wire's* expansive narrative gathers pace and focus.

THE CORPORATION, 2003, Dirs Jenifer Abbott and Mark Achbar
An insightful and entertaining documentary, *The Corporation* charts the rise to prominence of the primary institution of capitalism – the public limited company. Taking its status as a legal 'person' to the logical conclusion, the film puts the corporation on the psychiatrist's couch to ask 'What kind of person is it?' The answers are disturbing and highlight the problems associated with unchecked capitalism. The film also includes over 40 interviews with critics and corporate insiders, including Noam Chomsky, Naomi Klein, Milton Friedman, Howard Zinn, and Michael Moore. See the film's excellent website www.thecorporation.com for some great links, information on how to study and teach the themes raised by the movie, and a number of case studies and strategies for change.

THE POLITICS OF NIGHTMARES (2004) (3 parts), Dir. Adam Curtis
A controversial but compelling three-part BBC series that draws some unlikely parallels between the US neo-conservative political elite and the architects of radical Jihadist Islam. Curtis's ultimate thesis is that, in a post-Cold War world, fear and paranoia about terrorism and extremism are major tools of Western governments.

KAMP KATRINA, 2007, Dirs David Redmon and Ashley Sabin
An achingly poignant documentary about the trials and tribulations of a group of New Orleans residents who, left homeless by Hurricane Katrina, attempt to rebuild their lives in a small tent village set up by a well-intentioned neighbour. This is no alternative utopia, though, and very soon the frailties of humanity become all too apparent. See also Spike Lee's hard-hitting 2006 documentary *When the Levees Broke*, which focuses not just on the human suffering wrought by Katrina, but importantly the ineptitude of the US Federal government before and after the disaster. Lee's film poses serious questions about whose lives count in Bush's America.

DOGVILLE, 2003, Dir. Lars von Trier
A minimalist parable about a young woman on the run from gangsters, *Dogville* is a treatise on small-town values and perceptions of criminality. It is a story that also has much to say about both 'community justice' and ultimately revenge, as each of the fifteen villagers of Dogville are faced with a moral test after they agree to give shelter to the young woman.

the gathering storm

Sometimes you know things have to change, are going to change, but you can only feel it. ... Little things fore-shadow what's coming, but you may not recognize them. But then something immediate happens and you're in another world. ... It's a reflective thing. Somebody holds the mirror up, unlocks the door – something jerks it open and you're shoved in and your head has to go into a different place....

Bob Dylan (2004: 61–2), on arriving
in New York City, 1961

Ideas do not emerge from nothingness; they occur and recur at particular times and places, in specific cultural and economic contexts. They are not concocted in the seclusion of quiet seminars, however much the scholar might think, but in the cafés and bars, in the city streets, amidst the background babble of everyday life.

In this chapter we go backwards to go forwards. We look at the extraordinary developments in sociology and criminology in the 1960s and 1970s – developments that laid the foundation for cultural criminology, and continue to animate it today. Specifically, we review some (but not all) of the theoretical perspectives and ideas that have influenced and inspired cultural criminology – and note some of their limitations as well.

the cultural turn: the emergence of new deviancy theory

In a period of just over ten years, roughly 1955–1966, a spate of books and articles published in the USA dramatically transformed our thinking about crime and deviance – and for a time placed the sociology of deviance at the centre of sociological thinking and debate. This body of work, the new deviancy theory, was constituted by two strands: subcultural theory and labelling theory, which developed sometimes at loggerheads and frequently in debate, but which shared in common a distinctly *cultural* approach to the explanation of crime and deviance.

It was a time of awakening. The United States had gone through an uninterrupted phase of economic growth from the late 1930s onwards. Unlike Europe, it hadn't experienced the desolation of war and the rationing and reconstruction in its aftermath. US prosperity soared to heights unknown; its cars, kitchens, supermarkets, and cinema were the envy of the world. Yet just at this point the American Dream seemed to falter. Crime rose despite prosperity, the Dream excluded many, affluence itself revealed great rifts within the country, and the Dream itself began to seem somehow insubstantial. The blatant racial segregation of the South and the stark inequalities in the North became all the more apparent in the arc light of prosperity, and in a society where meritocracy was so proudly proclaimed as the American way.

The 'naturalness' of both exclusion and inclusion came into question, whether based on notions of inferior biology, inferior intelligence, or cultural inadequacy. And such querying of the taken-for-granted world extended from race to the other constituencies of exclusion: women, youth, class, and sexuality. The paradox of liberal democracy was pronounced: the claim to treat the diverse equally, to include all citizens on the basis of liberty, equality, and fraternity – yet, in fact throughout history the formal and informal exclusion of whole categories of people on the basis of biology and culture. The working class, women, youth – all, historically, fell outside the boundaries of citizenship: indeed slavery, the most despotic of all exclusions, was at its height precisely at the time that the Enlightenment proclaimed the universal nature of human rights. Demarcation disputes about the right to be included and, paradoxically, the rules of exclusion were long-standing (Macpherson, 1977) – and the intense social conflicts which so deeply divided the United States in the 1950s and 1960s echoed this.

Timeline: Storm Clouds Gather

1955	*Rebel Without a Cause* (Dir. Nicholas Ray)	*Delinquent Boys: The Culture of the Gang*, Albert Cohen
	Howl, Allen Ginsberg	*The Sane Society*, Erich Fromm
	Rosa Parks refuses to give up her bus seat to a white man in Montgomery, Alabama	

1956	Elvis Presley enters the charts and the American consciousness with his first hit 'Heartbreak Hotel' and a subsequent appearance on the *Ed Sullivan Show*	*The Power Elite,* C Wright Mills
1957	*On the Road*, Jack Kerouac	
1958	Bertrand Russell founds the Campaign for Nuclear Disarmament and the 'peace sign' is commissioned	*The Memoirs of a Dutiful Daughter*, Simone de Beauvoir *Society of Captives*, Gresham Sykes
1959	Fidel Castro and Che Guevara seize power in Cuba *Naked Lunch*, William Burroughs	*The Presentation of Self in Everyday Life,* Erving Goffman *The Sociological Imagination*, C Wright Mills
1960	In the United States the FDA (Federal Drug Administration) approve the oral contraceptive pill Andy Warhol starts painting Campbell's soup cans and other mass-produced items	*Delinquency and Opportunity*, Richard Cloward and Lloyd Ohlin *The Organisation Man,* William F Whyte *Resistance, Rebellion and Death*, Albert Camus
1961	*Catch-22,* Joseph Heller	*Asylums*, Erving Goffman *The Death and Life of Great American Cities*, Jane Jacobs
1962	The Rolling Stones make their debut and The Beatles are signed by Parlophone *A Kind of Loving* (Dir. John Schlesinger)	*The Other America*, Michael Harrington *Phenomenology of Perception*, Maurice Merleau Ponty
1963	March on Washington: Martin Luther King 'I Have a Dream' speech Assassination of J F Kennedy Bob Dylan releases 'Blowin' in the Wind'	*Outsiders*, Howard Becker *The Feminine Mystique*, Betty Friedan
1964	Malcolm X announces the formation of a Black nationalist party Berkeley Free Speech Movement commences *Last Exit to Brooklyn* Hubert Selby Jnr	*One Dimensional Man*, Herbert Marcuse *Understanding Media*, Marshall McLuhan *Delinquency and Drift*, David Matza
1965	Watts Riot, Los Angeles John Coltrane releases 'A Love Supreme' and The Velvet Underground form	*For Marx*, Louis Althusser
1966	*The Crying of Lot 49*, Thomas Pynchon	*The Delinquent Solution*, David Downes

	The Battle of Algiers (Dir. Gillo Pontecorvo)	*Complexity and Contradiction in Architecture*, Robert Venturi *The Social Construction of Reality*, Peter Berger and Thomas Luckmann
1967	Race Riots in Newark and Detroit	*The Phenomenology of the Social World,* Alfred Schutz *The Politics of Experience*, R D Laing *Human Deviance, Social Problems and Social Control*, Ed Lemert
1968	May–June: student revolts in Paris The Tet Offensive and the My Lai Massacre take place in Vietnam. *Do Androids Dream of Electric Sheep?* Philip K Dick	First National Deviancy Conference, University of York, UK
1969	Woodstock *Easy Rider* (Dir. Dennis Hopper) *I Know Why the Caged Bird Sings*, Maya Angelou	*Becoming Deviant*, David Matza *Symbolic Interactionism*, Herbert Blumer
1970	Kent State Massacre Jim Morrison of The Doors is found guilty of profanity and indecent exposure	*La société de consommation,* Jean Baudrillard *The Coming Crisis in Western Sociology*, Alvin Gouldner
1971	Attica Prison Revolt *A Clockwork Orange* (Dir. Stanley Kubrick)	*The Drugtakers*, Jock Young
1972	Watergate Scandal breaks The feminist publication *Spare Rib* is first published in London The porn movie *Deep Throat* (Dir. Gerard Damiano) becomes a major box office hit	*Subcultural Conflict and Working Class Community*, Phil Cohen *Folk Devils and Moral Panics*, Stan Cohen
1973	Oil crisis	*The New Criminology*, Ian Taylor, Paul Walton, Jock Young
1974	US President Richard Nixon resigns after lying to the American people over Watergate	*Soft City,* Jonathan Raban *Housewife*, Ann Oakley
1975	*One Flew Over the Cuckoo's Nest* (Dir. Milos Forman) Sex Pistols play their first show	*Discipline and Punish: The Birth of the Prison,* Michel Foucault
1976	Soweto Riots, South Africa Bob Marley leaves Jamaica for England and records 'Exodus'	*Resistance through Ritual*, Stuart Hall and Tony Jefferson *Women, Crime and Criminology*, Carol Smart
1977	Hanifa Muslim extremists take over three buildings in Washington, DC, taking 130 hostages	*Learning to Labour*, Paul Willis *Outline of a Theory of Practice*, Pierre Bourdieu

	The Clash release their debut album	*Sexual Politics*, Kate Millett
1978	*The Deer Hunter* (Dir. Michael Cimeno)	*Policing the Crisis*, Stuart Hall et al. *Orientalism*, Edward Said
1979	Margaret Thatcher elected UK Prime Minister Tens of thousands of gay rights supporters march on Washington, DC	*Subculture: The Meaning of Style*, Dick Hebdige *The Culture of Narcissism*, Christopher Lasch *The Postmodern Condition*, Jean-François Lyotard
1980	Ronald Reagan defeats Jimmy Carter in US Presidential elections	*Sociology of Youth Culture*, Mike Brake *Culture, Media, Language*, Stuart Hall, Dorothy Hobson, Andrew Lowe, Paul Willis
1981	Brixton Riot, precipitating a summer of race riots in the UK	*Culture*, Raymond Williams *Pornography: Men Possessing Women*, Andrea Dworkin

It was out of such struggles, and out of fundamental debates on the nature of diversity and inclusion in liberal democracy, that the revolt in criminology emerged. The binaries of inequality in terms of race, gender, age, and sexuality were generalised to those designated 'normal' and those labelled 'deviant', the 'law-abiding' and the 'criminal'. This started within the sociology of deviance and then rolled out into criminology proper. The sociology of deviance deals with the *demi-monde*, those on the margins of society, those caricatured as lacking biologically and culturally: homosexuals, illicit drug users, the mentally ill, alcoholics. The sociology of crime and delinquency focuses even more closely on those socially and politically excluded in liberal democracies: the black, the young, the undeserving poor, the recalcitrant male. Indeed, the criminal justice system focuses precisely on those excluded from civil society. The very categories of orthodox criminology resonate with intimations of biological, social and cultural inferiority, from the atavism of Lombroso (2006 [1876]) and the low self-control instilled into children by 'weak' families (Gottfredson and Hirschi, 1990), to the destructive attributes of lower-class culture as defined by Walter Miller (1958).

If, then, the politics of liberal democracy focus on the inclusive society yet concern themselves with criteria for exclusion, orthodox criminology has mirrored this political philosophy, focusing on the excluded and making a science of the criteria for inclusion. So it was no accident that the new deviancy theory emerged in this period, on the back of the civil rights struggles, followed by the women's and gay rights movements – the ever-widening politics of inclusion. For this new deviancy theory was, above all, concerned with the unfairness of social exclusion (whether political, legal, or economic), and the falsity of attempting to explain such imposed deviance as the result of individual organic or cultural deficits. The new deviancy theory targeted three exclusionary issues: first, the notion that deviance was due to a lacking of culture, over and against a presumed cultural consensus; second, the claim that the cause of such a deficit was individual defect, as sustained by genetics, family, or social inadequacy; and third, the idea that the criminal justice system and other agencies of social control rightfully imposed such interpretations on the recalcitrant – that is, rightfully labelled the deviant as an individual lacking in culture.

But the gathering storm didn't just sweep up the excluded; it caught those who were most definitely *included*, those who were the supposed success stories of the American Dream. Affluence itself, the corporate culture, the ever-bigger car and kitchen, the ideal home and family and job – all of these began to look somehow shabby, repressive, tedious. Some, then, were excluded from the Dream, some began to realize that they had been relegated to bit parts in a male drama, and others began to rail at the monotony of success and to question the very premises of the Dream, its prizes and its promises. As Betty Friedan (1963) asked in her pathbreaking feminist book, *The Feminine Mystique:* 'Is this all there is?'

The emergence of feminism, the explosive development of youth cultures, the left-leaning new bohemianism – all these spread changing attitudes through society, shaking the mostly complacent world of the early 1960s. They stressed active transformation of life and lifestyle; sensitivity to the cultural creativity of women, ethnic minorities, and the poor; and critique of those presuming to represent social consensus and mainstream values. Add to such powerful cultural forces the plurality of values circulated by immigration, tourism, and the mass media, and we have a 'market of worlds' (Schelsky, 1957), which profoundly influenced the new deviancy theory.

the new deviancy explosion

In addition to ... being more understandable than much sociological writing, half of *Outsiders* consisted of empirical studies ... of topics that were 'interesting' to the generation of students then entering American universities ... These topics, intersecting more or less with their own lives, made the book one that teachers, many of whom shared the student interest in drugs and music, liked to assign to students to read. And so the book became a sort of standard text in classes of younger students.

Howard Becker (2005: 1), on his 1963
book *Outsiders*

The new deviancy theory took shape in response to the problems of inclusion and of diversity. The shock of the plural is the jarring of lifestyles, of subcultures whose existence points to alternative possibilities and tantalizing choices, all of which present troubling potentials and possibilities. The existence of pluralism, the possibility of diversity immediately poses fundamental questions of inclusion: Into what social world are we being included? Does it fit our needs, satisfy our dreams? Both are questions of normality. If orthodox criminology attempted to demarcate the normal and the deviant, and posit a 'normal' consensual culture, the new deviancy theory agitated for eroding the distinction between normality and deviance, and so argued for the inherent diversity of culture. The twin problems of distinction and diversity began to confront criminological thinking.

Ultimately, a widespread crisis of legitimacy unfolded: a younger generation learnt of not only the limits of the system, the barriers to inclusion, but the prejudices and repression against new ideas and cultures. They witnessed the repression of ethnic minorities and the poor as these groups fought for civil rights, and they directly experienced the backlash of police and other legal authorities against the anti-Vietnam War movement. The tear gas that hung over college campuses, the massacre of students at Kent State University by the National Guard, confirmed the worse fears of a generation. And by the early 1970s, as Robert Lilly and his co-authors note, 'The state's moral bankruptcy seemed complete with the disclosure of the Watergate scandal, which showed that corruption not simply penetrated but rather pervaded the government's highest echelons' (Lilly et al., 1989: 130).

In this historical context, the intellectual impact of the new deviancy theorists was enormous, their influence for a time seemingly irreversible. Their contribution was *to bring culture into the study of crime and deviant behaviour* – not simply by acknowledging the obvious presence of culture in social life, but by stressing the creative characteristic of culture, and hence the human creation of deviance *and* the human creation of the systems attempting to control it.

For orthodox criminology, 'normal' law-abiding behaviour had been seen as conformity to the mainstream culture, crime and deviance as a *lacking* of culture, and social control as the rather automatic and mechanistic enforcement of cultural norms. In this view crime is caused by institutions unable to transmit cultural norms, or individuals unable to receive them; by social disorganization on a societal level, or lack of cultural socialization on a personal level; or by some combination of the two. Such a positivist criminology seeks to explain, through factors like broken families or genetic predisposition, why such a socialization into an unquestioned consensus of cultural values has not come about. Crime is, in short, the failure of society to inculcate culture and, as such, criminological analysis can be seen as an act of othering and exclusion. It is the presumed 'well-socialized' analyzing the 'under-socialized', the social viewing the asocial, the culturally evolved examining the atavistic, the meaningful world explaining 'meaningless' forms of violence and misbehaviour.

The role of the new deviancy theory, in stark contrast, was to grant criminal and deviant behaviour *cultural meaning* – and, as we will see, the power of the new labelling theory was to explain the cultural process by which othering and exclusion occurred, the process by which criminological theory, the mass media and the wider public defined deviancy, distorted and took away its meaning, and so created the very stereotype they imagined. You'll recall that in Chapter 1 we noted two notions of 'culture', the first conceptualizing culture as the consensual cement of society, the second seeing culture as a font of creativity, a source of creative challenges to reification, social order, and acceptability. The new deviancy theorists wholeheartedly embraced the latter – culture as innovation and resistance. Yet they also took care to expose the cultural work of the powerful, who attempt to maintain the myth of normative culture as natural, an inevitability beyond human action. From this view, a thoroughgoing analysis of crime and deviance examines how human action invokes the creative generation of meaning, but also how powerful agencies attempt to steal creativity and meaning away from the deviant and the criminal – indeed, away from all those whom they subordinate. The first of these realms became the focus of subcultural theory – the second the focus of labelling theory; the first was concerned primarily with the cultural origins of deviant behaviour, the second was concerned with the social *reaction* to deviance, with social control and cultural intervention.

These new approaches didn't disavow all previous theorizing, though; like cultural criminology today, they reached back to rediscover and reinvent earlier understandings of deviance, crime, and culture. Among the major influences on subcultural theory was Émile Durkheim. Durkheim's view of the relationship between human nature and society was crucial – yet it is almost invariably misconstrued. Only too frequently criminologists take Durkheim to be saying that human nature is essentially insatiable, with the role of culture to serve as a civilizing block which can somehow hold back the potential flood of deviance (e.g. Lilly et al., 1989; Vold et al., 1998; Downes and Rock, 2007). Culture here becomes the opposite of deviance, and the lack of cultural socialization its cause.

Yet this is in reality almost the opposite of his viewpoint. For Durkheim, organic needs and animal desires are satiable and limited; it is *culturally induced aspirations* which are potentially without limit, which create incessant and interminable want, which cause human beings to suffer, as he puts it, 'the sickness of infinity'. Durkheim was writing in the midst of France's rapid industrialization, and he witnessed a massive transformation in social structure and social ethos – in particular the rise of a culture of individualism and a decline in more solidaristic, traditional values. He adamantly argued that a society whose core cultural values exalted individual competition and offered incessant and ever-retreating goals was one which would inevitably be unstable and conflict-ridden. For him, such a condition was not 'natural' but rather the cultural creation of a capitalist society – and so a society with less crime and conflict could occur if a unifying culture were developed out of trust, meritorious reward, and finite achievement.

Durkheim, then, based his explanation of crime and deviance in the cultural realm, and he further insisted that deviance is a cultural product, and hence a product of cultural definition. In *The Rules of Sociological Method*, he famously noted that even in a 'society of saints' some would come to be defined as criminal (Durkheim, 1964: 68–9), and he frequently pointed out that deviance arises not from the act itself, but from the cultural rules that forbid (e.g. Durkheim, 1965: 43).

When in 1938 Robert Merton published the most influential piece yet written on the causes of crime and deviance, 'Social Structure and Anomie', he drew on Durkheim to explicitly critique both individual and social positivism. Like Durkheim, he demonstrated that crime and deviance, rather than being a matter of individual pathology, are in fact 'normal' responses to particular cultural and structural circumstances. But his critique of social positivism is also of interest. Simple equations like 'poverty causes crime', Merton showed, do not hold. Rather, the stress on the American Dream, the notion that success and social mobility is open to all, grinds against the actual structural limitations on success. Ironically, it is precisely the most legitimate of American values – the 'American Dream' – that causes deviance and disorder, or, as Merton puts it, 'anti-social behavior is in a sense "called forth" by certain conventional values *and* by a class structure involving differential access to the approved opportunities…' (1938: 24, emphasis in original).

And Merton emphasized another criminogenic aspect of American culture: the overemphasis on success goals, rather than the means of achieving them. In combination, Merton suggested, these two elements – cultural emphasis on success at any cost, and limited opportunities – created a terrible strain indeed. In his well-known typology of adaptations to this strain, Merton imagined several options, one being crime – that is, the innovative creation of new means to achieve cultural goals of success. And it is out of this insight that subcultural theory emerges, where crime and deviance are seen as cultural and material *solutions* to contradictions in the wider society.

subcultural theory

Subcultural approaches to crime and deviance have a long history, dating to the vivid descriptions of criminal underworlds in the Victorian era. For all their fine detail, though, early subcultural accounts tended to mix moralism with description – but to omit theory. They described subcultural values, showed how these values were *transmitted* in a normal process of socialization, but did not explain their *origins*. It is the ability to explain both the transmission of deviant cultural values and their origins which is the hallmark of what one might term 'mature subcultural theory'. Such an approach commenced in the late 1950s and early 1960s with the pioneering work of Albert Cohen and Richard Cloward in the field of delinquency, and Gresham Sykes and Erving Goffman in their studies of total institutions.

The concept of 'subculture' in mature subcultural theory is clearly linked to the notion of culture developed within social and cultural anthropology – that subcultural responses can be thought of as jointly elaborated solutions to collectively experienced problems. Deviant behaviour is viewed as a meaningful attempt to solve the problems faced by an isolated or marginalized group; it is necessary, therefore, to explore and understand the subjective experiences of subcultural members. Culture in this anthropological sense constitutes the innovations people have evolved in collectively confronting the problems of everyday life. These include language, ways of dress, moral standards, myths, political ideologies, art forms, work norms, modes of sexuality – in sum, all creative and collective human behaviour. Finding themselves in certain shared structural positions demarcated by age, class, gender, or race, for instance, people evolve shared and meaningful solutions to whatever problems such positions pose.

But of course these positions come alive in particular contexts – city or country, 1908 or 2008, prison or school or workplace – and so shared problems and their subcultural solutions vary tremendously, overlapping at times, diverging at others, and always evolving. As human creations, subcultures can vary as widely as the collective experience and imagination of those involved. In this sense all people create subcultural formations; police officers, plumbers, and politicians all evolve collective rituals, styles, and codes in their daily round. But for deviance theorists and criminologists, there is a more precise focus: the subcultures of those defined as deviant or criminal, those that the law marginalizes and excludes.

With this focus, subculture theorists developed an insight as simple as it was important: subcultural responses are not empty, not absurd, but *meaningful*. Just think about it: In our public discourse, sometimes in orthodox criminology as well, a whole series of common terms serves to dismiss the possibility of deviant behaviour being meaningful, of it having subcultural meaning. Terms like 'mob', 'hyperactive', 'primitive', 'savage', 'mindless', and 'mad' all serve the purpose of defining deviant behaviour as simply aberrant and so lacking in any meaning or value. In contrast, subcultural theory argues that human behaviour is fundamentally meaningful – fundamentally cultural, that is – and that differences in social behaviour represent specific problems and specific solutions.

Indeed, subcultural theory from the 1950s onwards set itself the task of explaining deviant behaviours commonly assumed to be simply irrational and unproductive. Again, echoes of anthropology could be heard, echoes of anthropologists' efforts to explain the meaning and purpose of seemingly bizarre cultural customs: unspeakable kinship rituals, taboos and fetishes, cargo cults. Notice, though, that in this way subcultural theory quickly moved from the Mertonian claim that crime constitutes a utilitarian alternative for reaching consensual goals, and onwards to a focus on behaviour which on its face appeared self-defeating, if not entirely implausible.

In the classic subcultural text *Delinquent Boys: The Culture of the Gang*, Albert Cohen (1955) begins with the recognition that most delinquency is not a means to desired material goods, but rather is 'non-utilitarian, malicious and negativistic'. Stealing and then discarding goods, breaking glass, terrifying 'good' children, flouting the teacher's rules – this is 'anti-social' behaviour, at its core *transgressive*. Yet Cohen doesn't relegate this behaviour to mindless mischievousness; he points to the locus of such delinquency low in the social structure. And what is it, he asks, about 'growing up in a class system'? Cohen's answer is well known, and continues to be influential. At school, children are judged by middle-class values which lower-class children are hard-pressed to meet. The resulting experiences of status deprivation and humiliation are for these children the problem – and they can collectively, if provisionally, solve the problem by reacting strongly against these middle-class values, by negating and inverting them. So evolves a 'reaction forma-tion', a process of collective energy, intensity, and *cultural work*, whereby middle-class values are inverted and subcultural status is attained by this very rebellion.

Two decades later, subcultural theorist Paul Willis discovered, in his book *Learning to Labour* (1977), a similarly shared problem for lower-class kids: being asked to measure up to middle-class standards for which their back-ground ill-prepared them, in order to achieve academic qualifications irrele-vant to their future jobs. As Willis found, such kids culturally 'solve' the problem by playing up in the classroom and rejecting the teacher's discipline, while at the same time developing a subculture that rewards manliness and physical toughness with high status. Similarly, Ken Pryce's (1979) study of young blacks in the UK found that some evolve a leisure culture which helps them survive unemployment and racism, and enables them to meaningfully reject the few, menial jobs available.

Models which reduce the deviant activities of youth to the mental or physical failings of individuals are in this way rejected – since, from the view of sub-culture theory, such models cannot account for the meaningful, subcultural dynamics behind such behaviour. Subcultural theorists dare to see the world and its problems through the eyes of the subculture's members; they grant subjectivity and collective agency to the subcultures they study. For them, human subjectivity and interpretation – human *culture* – is the *sine qua non* for understanding human behaviour.

Proto-subcultural Theory: Writing from Below

Subcultural theory in each of its manifestations is an act of excavation, a delving into the depths of society to find what is bubbling underneath. Like the work of social historians, it is *writing from below*, giving voice to those that are 'hidden from history'.

The first manifestations were in Victorian London, at that time the largest city in the world, or in Manchester, the fastest-growing city of its era. Booth, Engels, Mayhew, Morrison, Dickens and others explored these 'Africas' of the city, these 'unknown continents' of the new metropolis.

The second was Chicago, the new Manchester, the city which expanded in a century from a trading post of 300 people to become, by 1910, one of the world's greatest cities with a population exceeding four million. With immigration of African-Americans from the South and Europeans from the Old World, it became a city of unparalleled diversity – and home of the Chicago School of sociology, where Robert Park famously exhorted his students to 'go get the seat of their pants dirty' in real research.

The third was the new deviancy theory of the 1950s and 1960s, poised between crime, delinquency and the exotic, with ethnographies of back streets and jazz clubs, of peers and 'queers', of marijuana smokers and poolroom hustlers.

The fourth was represented by the trans-Atlantic shift to Britain, a transposition of subcultural theories of delinquency to spectacular youth cultures: skinheads, teddy boys, rockers, mods and punks.

The fifth, today, moves from subculture to club culture, virtual culture, and the 'post-subcultural' world of late modernity – the arena of cultural criminology. It is a world of global gangs and techno-tribes, of hyperpluralism and global street culture, where old certainties lose their moorings amidst the mediated swirl of daily life.

labelling theory: the constructionist revolution

Deviance ... is a creation of the public imagination ... The act's deviant character lies in the way it is defined in the public mind ... [which] has, of course, drastic consequences for the person who commits it.

Howard Becker (1965 [1971]: 341)

This is a large turn from the older sociology which tended to rest heavily upon the idea that deviance leads to social control. I have come to believe that the reverse idea, i.e., social control leads to deviance, is equally tenable and the potentially richer premise for studying deviance in modern society.

Edwin Lemert (1967: v)

Labelling theory had a revolutionary impact on the sociology of deviance, turning the orthodox understanding of crime and deviance on its head. The lens of orthodox positivism promised to accurately reflect objective reality;

labelling theory showed that there was no objective reality to reflect, only a process of ongoing action and reaction, of contested meaning changing with audience and situation. 'Deviance', labelling theorists argued, is not an objective fact, waiting to be catalogued and analyzed, but rather a collective process of human creation and human subjectivity. Yet labelling theorists cautioned that not all creations, not all meanings, are of equal consequence in the construction of deviance. Some definitions and interpretations carry the imprimatur of authority, and the potency of legal sanction and enforced stigma; the labelling process is one of power and marginalization. And so, as with Edwin Lemert's insight above, labelling theory stood orthodox understanding on its head once again. If dominant definitions shape what comes to be 'deviant', then it may be that mainstream social institutions don't serve to control deviance – it may well be that they *create* it. From this view what we take to be 'deviance' results not from the failure of social control systems, but from their success.

Consider an example perhaps all too familiar to college students: alcohol and drinking. As one moves from student to student, from campus to campus, from the universities of one country to those of another, the variety of labels assigned to drinking, the variety of cultural and subcultural meanings it is given, are extraordinary. Some abhor drunkenness, some insist on it as a deserved pleasure. Some see drinking as a badge of masculinity, some a crutch for the weak. Some campuses ban alcohol entirely; others sponsor a variety of student pubs and drinking clubs. Some student groups embrace drinking games and ritualized consumption; some see these as signs of social immaturity or impediments to academic success. To be 'deviant' in one subculture or on one campus is to be 'normal' in another; drinking is *simultaneously* normal, deviant, legal, and illegal, depending on circumstance and perception. Certainly it is an objective fact that some people do drink – but whatever *deviancy* drinking may or may not carry cannot be inherent in their acts of drinking; it is instead a cultural construction, a shifting assignment of meaning and label.

But what of *serious* drinking? Surely there is some unanimity about its real dangers? Well, no – and not only because 'serious' drinking, drinking that badly damages body and soul, is commonly labelled as fraternity tradition, successful Super Bowl party, or writer's prerogative. More to the point, it's the issue of power, the cultural imposition of meaning from above. Even were we all to agree that 'serious' drinking constituted a social problem, there would still be the matter of contested definition. Various experts and organizations compete for the ownership of a problem; there are subcultures of control just as there are subcultures of deviance, and each develops its own legitimacy, language, and labels. Alcohol is a prime example. If indeed serious drinking is a problem, is it a moral failure and a sin? Is it a matter of 'binge drinking', in need of legal regulation? Or is it an illness called 'alcoholism'? And so, does the social control of serious drinking involve campus authorities, the police, Alcoholics Anonymous officials, or psychotherapists?

Significantly, each of these labels creates its own deviants and deviant trajectories. Labelling a serious drinker an alcoholic invokes a particular regime of treatment, a particular set of assumptions about illness, responsibility and relapse, and so a particular set of ongoing consequences for family and career; labelling a serious drinker a criminal invokes a very different set of meanings for self and society, and so sets that person on a different course regarding career and criminal justice. And it is in precisely this sense that labelling constructs deviance – that Alcoholics Anonymous decides the meaning of alcoholism, that police and the courts construct the reality of drunk driving, that campus authorities work to impose meaning on the phenomenon of student drinking.

Moreover, as this process of meaning imposition continues, the assigned label often comes to publicly signify a person's master status, and so becomes the lens through which the individual's past and future behaviour are now viewed. Whether fairly or not assigned the label of 'sex offender', for example, a person's past actions will now be unfavourably reconsidered, and future actions cast already under suspicion. In this way labelling not only imposes meaning but *removes* it, precluding other options for status or identity. As discussed in the previous chapter, this dynamic is exemplified in Garfinkel's (1956) notion of 'degradation ceremonies', designed to 'deculture' a person as part of imposing a new status. Witness the shaving of heads, removal of everyday clothes, verbal abuse, humiliation, and rigid regulations imposed as prisons, drug rehabilitation units like Synanon, and Marine training programmes work to construct new identities (see Goffman, 1961).

values and the lust for kicks

With the new deviancy theory, with subcultural theory and labelling theory, some of the essential foundations for cultural criminology were built: the understanding that deviance and criminality inevitably embody contested meanings and identities. The sense that all parties to crime and deviance – courts, cops, criminals, everyday citizens, media institutions – engage in cultural work as they negotiate these meanings and identities; that is, they work to assign labels, negotiate symbolic status, and find collective solutions. The sensitivity to the subcultural roots of crime and deviance, and to the meaningful process by which subcultural members confront their shared problems. And an awareness that, overarching all this, a web of larger societal values, carrying with them the tensions of failure and success, and the politics of inclusion and exclusion.

These foundations were laid by American theorists, but before we cross the Atlantic to find their counterparts in the United Kingdom, there is one final and important American contribution, one that both complements and contests ideas we've already seen. This is the contribution of David Matza, and his collaborator Gresham Sykes. When in Chapter 6 we consider the distinctive methods of cultural criminology, Matza's influence will be evident. We will argue there, as did Matza, for *naturalism* in the study of deviance and crime, for a methodology faithful to the phenomenon under scrutiny. And he emphasized, as we will there, that faithfully studying human behaviour means taking notice of subjectivity, meaning, and emotion.

Here, though, we focus on Matza and Sykes' explorations of culture, subculture, and crime. In the late 1950s and early 1960s Matza and Sykes published two groundbreaking articles on juvenile delinquency and crime. They argued against the orthodox notion that delinquency was a result of abnormal personality – but they also questioned the newer notion that delinquency was necessarily the product of distinctive deviant subcultures. Rather, they maintained that delinquents were frequently of normal personality, and that they by and large adhered to the same values as the rest of the population. They maintained, in short, that there was no great gulf between the cultural universes of the law-abiding and the delinquent, between the 'normal' and the 'deviant'.

The first article, 'Techniques of Neutralization' (Sykes and Matza, 1957), is certainly the best known. In it they argued that delinquents 'neutralize' the thrall of conventional values though a series of normative 'techniques' such as denying their own responsibility, or disavowing that their acts cause injury or victimization. Such 'vocabularies of motive' (Mills, 1940) enable potential delinquents to set aside for a moment their conventional values, to temporarily loosen their bond to the moral order, and so to engage in delinquency. These techniques of neutralization, then, constitute the *cultural work* necessary to commit crimes, the creation of a narrative which particularizes and justifies a specific delinquent act while leaving larger moral prohibitions in place. A delinquent's motivation for theft, for example, likely wouldn't involve a sense that robbery should be universally accepted, but more a sense that in particular situations certain groups deserve to be targeted, or can afford the loss of stolen goods. Crime and delinquency, then, are not random occurrences, but negotiated relationships, meaningful relationships, between offender and victim.

This principle has been extended fruitfully to explanations of white-collar crime and police crime, and more recently war crimes (Cohen, 2002b). Likewise, Jayne Mooney (2007), in her study of domestic violence, has examined how domestic violence could flourish in a 'civilized' society where physical violence is held as an anathema. In answer, she found particular situations – spousal 'cheating', 'self-defence' – where male violence against women was recognized by both men and women as a likely response; it was not condoned, particularly by women, but is was normatively expected. Similarly, even the terrible question of how 'normal' people can come to commit collective genocidal atrocities has been answered in part through an understanding of these neutralizing techniques (Morrison, 2004b).

But the explanation offered by 'techniques of neutralization' has also become popular in orthodox criminology, in that it appears to confirm the existence of a single, consensual, law-abiding culture to which all belong, until such time as putative delinquents or other potential law-breakers negotiate temporary exception. In short, the thinking goes, there is no deviant culture, no criminal subculture, no alternative value system – only behaviour which on occasion deviates from the accepted norm. In this fashion, Matza and Sykes's work is seen as a useful adjunct, for example, to Travis Hirschi's (1969) control theory, for it seems to explain temporary detachments from the dominant culture.

Yet what those who would co-opt Matza and Sykes into orthodox criminology fail to acknowledge is the second of their two articles, 'Juvenile Delinquency and Subterranean Values' (1961). Here Matza and Sykes admit that their own analysis of techniques of neutralization 'leaves unanswered a serious question: What makes delinquency attractive in the first place?' In answer, they argue that it is … fun. Delinquents, they write, 'are deeply immersed in a restless search for excitement, "thrills", or "kicks". The approved style of life, for many delinquents, is an adventurous one. Activities pervaded by displays of daring and charged with danger are highly valued. … The fact that an activity involves breaking the law is precisely the fact that often infuses it with an air of excitement' (Matza and Sykes, 1961: 713). Note that deviant subcultures and alternative value systems, seemingly dismissed, now return with a vengeance, with thrills and kicks and the adrenalin rush of breaking the law! All of this of course recalls Cohen's *Delinquent Boys* (1955), and their enjoyment of transgression – and like Cohen, Willis, Pryce, and other subcultural theorists already seen, Matza and Sykes add to their list of delinquent values aggression and a disdain for work.

So in fact, according to Matza and Sykes, a viable delinquent culture does exist – but it is here that Matza and Sykes drop their bombshell: *this is the case not because this culture stands apart from dominant values, but because it is in many ways so similar to them.* Daring, adventure, and the rejection of the work, they argue, permeate our culture; even values of violence and aggression are rampant. Mainstream society, they write:

> exhibits a widespread taste for violence, since fantasies of violence in books, magazines, movies, and television are everywhere at hand. … Furthermore, disclaimers of violence are suspect not simply because fantasies of violence are widely consumed, but also because of the actual use of aggression and violence in war, race riots, industrial conflicts, and the treatment of delinquents themselves by police. There are numerous examples of the acceptance of aggression and violence on the part of the dominant social order. Perhaps it is more important, however, to recognize that the crucial idea of aggression as a proof of toughness and masculinity is widely accepted at many points in the social system. The ability to take it and hand it out, to defend one's rights and one's reputation with force, to prove one's manhood by hardness

and physical courage – all are widespread in American culture. (Matza and Sykes, 1961: 717)

Almost a half-century ago, Matza and Sykes were developing an analysis that would become central to cultural criminology: the understanding that criminal violence may at times be condemned – but it is also widely commodified, consumed, and celebrated. And as we will show throughout the book, and especially in Chapter 5, this is immeasurably more the case now than it was then.

Matza and Sykes were further suggesting that a fundamental cultural contradiction courses through all social strata – a set of *subterranean values* co-existing with, but also contradicting, overt or official social values. A critical example is the search for excitement, the lust for 'kicks'. Even within mainstream society, certain institutionalized situations allow such subterranean values to flourish: organized celebrations, holidays, carnivals, festivals and sports, where such values temporarily trump those of workaday existence (Presdee, 2000). In this sense, Matza and Sykes argue, this lust for kicks 'is not a deviant value, in any full sense, but must be held in abeyance until the proper moment and circumstances for its expression arrive' (1961: 716). Normally, then, such values are maintained in balance with the formal values, contained in this way, and allowed expression in leisure time. For many, such values only occasionally intrude on the quiet hum of everyday life, offering little moments of respite from the drone. Other individuals and groups, though, over-accentuate these values, disdain the workaday norms of official society, and so 'deviate' by breaking the balance that contains the contradiction.

Yet today, fifty years since Matza and Sykes, the balance is changing – or perhaps the contradiction is becoming more manifest and less containable. Late modernity, with its trajectories towards uncertain work, immediacy, short-term hedonism, night-time economies, and mediated aggression, pushes the subterranean lust for kicks ever more to the surface. Consider, as we will more carefully in later chapters, the close symbiosis between the frustrations of those low in the social structure and the aggressive narratives of the mainstream media. In his brilliant ethnography of the Philadelphian ghetto, for example, Carl Nightingale argues that:

> Whether the amount of violence in films and TV shows have contributed to the recent rise in homicides … is uncertain, but some of the ethical codes of aggression in [the] neighbourhood clearly have depended on the mainstream culture of violence for legitimacy … boys' efforts to compensate for humiliation and frustration owe some of their aggressive qualities to their identification with the heroes and values of the mainstream American culture of violence. (1993: 168)

And as we will see in subsequent chapters, it's not just Nightingale's ghetto kids that today over-script their lives in terms of kicks and violence – it's soldiers and students, cops and reporters, too.

the transition to late modernity: British subcultural theory

Originating in Victorian England, subcultural perspectives flourished with the emergence of the new deviancy theory in the United States of the 1950s and 1960s. Over the following decades subcultural theory's development continued in Britain, and specifically in the work of two British groups: the National Deviancy Conference (NDC), an organization of radical criminologists inaugurated at the University of York in 1968, and the Centre for Contemporary Cultural Studies (CCCS) of the University of Birmingham, widely known for its work on youth subcultures and its role in the development of cultural studies more generally. The timing of this shift to Britain resulted both from the later development in Europe of an affluent consumer society, and from the more general transition of all Western industrial societies to late modernity.

As we suggested in introducing this chapter, a 'Golden Age' (Hobsbawm, 1994) of general economic growth, prosperity, and social stability had emerged in Western industrial societies following World War II. The years that followed, though, saw a widespread restructuring of work and rise in unemployment, growing uncertainty and insecurity, increased marital breakdown, decline in community, and a wholesale contest of values. While the advent of the Golden Age had varied – with America finding prosperity earlier than did the war-torn societies of the UK and Europe – the timing of its demise was more precisely shared. From the late 1960s onwards, in the USA, Britain, France and elsewhere, both a cultural revolution and a fundamental economic restructuring were underway. These transformed the social order of the developed world; the tectonic shift into late modernity had begun (see Young, 1999). And it was at this cusp of change that an extraordinary burst of creativity occurred, this time on the British side of the Atlantic.

Over its roughly ten-year existence, the NDC became not only a major site of this intellectual tumult, but the source of an intellectual explosion that would reshape sociology and criminology – and further set the stage for what was later to become cultural criminology (see Cohen, 1981; Young, 1998). In its first five years, for example, the NDC heard from sixty-three British scholars, who went on to produce just under a hundred books on crime, deviance, and social control. And more than crime and deviance was at issue; others developed early work in gender studies (Mary McIntosh and Ken Plummer) and the first flourishes of what would later be known as 'cultural studies' (Dick Hebdige, Mike Featherstone, Stuart Hall, and Paul Willis). Interestingly, the basis of this work, and of the widespread interest it generated, was the early development of 'postmodern' themes. As Stan Cohen said, some thirty years later: 'After the middle of the Nineteen Sixties – well before Foucault made these subjects intellectually respectable and a long way from the Left Bank – our little corner of the human sciences was seized by a deconstructionist impulse' (1988: 101). Indeed, the arrival of Foucault's *Discipline and Punish* in English translation in 1977 was scarcely a revelation; its themes and concepts had already been well rehearsed within the NDC.

In fact, the NDC was thoroughly deconstructionist and anti-essentialist, evoking myriad voices and viewpoints, and bent on unravelling the social construction of gender, sexual proclivity, crime, suicide, drugs, and mental state. It inverted hierarchies, and saw mainstream culture from the perspective of outsiders like mods, rockers, teddy boys, hippies, and skinheads. Tracing the cultural bricolage by which these new 'spectacular' youth cultures constituted themselves, it focused on their media representations and the fashion in which media stereotypes of them and others shaped social reality. And beneath it all was a critique of state intervention, of positivism and classicism; the twin meta-narratives of modernist progress, social engineering and the rule of law were subject to ongoing criticism. Positivism was perhaps the main enemy. It drained creativity and meaning from deviant action, the NDC argued, erecting an imaginary normative consensus against which to judge and condemn outsiders. Its methodology elevated alleged experts to the role of 'scientists' discovering the 'laws' of social action, and its policy – whether in the mental hospitals, social work agencies or drug clinics – mystified human action while remaking human beings in its own narrow image.

The rule of law came under sharp scrutiny as well. The NDC saw the criminal justice system as selective and ineffective – saw that while crime occurred endemically, the justice system focused on the working class and the young, ignoring the crimes of the powerful and tolerating the deviancy of the middle class. And at the end of this justice process, the prison: brutalizing, blaming, and ultimately counter-productive; in fact two of the most blistering indictments of the prison system, *Psychological Survival* (Cohen and Taylor, 1976) and *Prisoners in Revolt* (Fitzgerald, 1977), spring from this view. Further, the NDC realized that irrational and counter-productive social reactions to crime were not limited to the institutions of the state. They also circulated in civil society, with the mass media targeting deviant groups, creating folk devils, and engendering moral panics (see Young, 1971; Cohen, 1972).

As we have seen, this critical, deconstructionist impulse had commenced in the United States, around the work of the labelling theorists. It was theoretically revolutionary in its discourse (social control generates deviance rather than deviance necessitating social control), relativistic in its analysis (deviance is not inherent but interactional), and anarchic in its inversion of orthodoxies, as it rejected the received wisdom of positivism and celebrated human diversity. In short, it was tremendously *attractive* to the young and the radical during this time of fundamental social change, in Britain and elsewhere.

At the same time that this radically deconstructionist literature was being imported to Britain, a second and more muted strand of the American new deviancy theory arrived: subcultural theory, in particular work on gangs and delinquency (Cohen, 1955; Cloward and Ohlin, 1960) and studies of prison subcultures (Clemner, 1940; Sykes, 1958). Sociologists at the London School of Economics became a major intellectual conduit for this theory, beginning with Herman Mannheim's *Juvenile Delinquency in an English Middletown* (1948), moving through Terence Morris's *The Criminal Area* (1957) and Terence and Pauline Morris's *Pentonville* (1963), and culminating in David Downes's influential *The Delinquent Solution* (1966). Out of this tradition there also emerged Stan Cohen's PhD thesis (1972) on mods and rockers, and related studies: Jock Young's work on drugtakers (1971), for example, and Mike Brake's (1980) research on youth culture (see Hobbs, 2007).

the British synthesis

In the debates and presentations that animated the NDC, American labelling and subcultural theories were transformed, primarily through a synthesis of the two. This synthesis was facilitated by the logic of their two foci: labelling theory focused on constructions downwards (the *reaction* against deviance) and subcultural theory on constructions upwards (deviant *actions* and responses). Moreover, the sometimes wooden tone of American subcultural theory was given a zest, an energy, a feeling of cultural creativity; top-down reactions to deviance were also invested with this sensibility. Transgressive and deviant acts were in turn given a more positive valuation. Rightly or wrongly, deviance was a sign of resistance, an effort at overcoming, a creative flourish; it was not predominantly a site of failure or grudging adaptation. The American sociology of deviance became a British sociology of transgression.

This synthesis, and these strands of energy and resistance, were transposed and interwoven in the emerging British deviancy theory. In a British society more attuned than American society to class relationships, and during this period quite thoroughly transfixed on the emergence of ebullient and dynamic youth cultures, class and youth emerged as the major areas of research and writing (with, unfortunately, gender and ethnicity to come only later). Bringing a synthesis of labelling theory and subcultural theory to bear on these issues, British scholars could complement labelling theory's groundbreaking analysis of social reaction/interaction with subcultural theory's attentiveness to the dynamics of deviant behaviour. Attuned to cultural energy and excitement, they could in turn add a sense of transgressive creativity to subcultural theory's somewhat formulaic understandings of deviant behaviour.

The task of British theorization, then, was threefold: to deal with the nuances of both action and reaction, to conceptualize human actors who were neither capriciously free-willed nor stolidly over-determined, and to locate meaningful action in the context of small-scale situations as well as wider social frameworks. As regards the analysis of these larger social frameworks, the NDC sensed that both labelling theory and subcultural theory could be usefully supplemented. Labelling theory in particular was concerned very fruitfully with the immediate interaction between the actor and the labelling process, but it offered little in the way of a theory of the total society, other than a keen sense of moral entrepreneurs and their enterprise (Becker, 1963). Subcultural theory well understood the contradiction between structure and culture on a societal level, but like labelling theory did not overtly theorize the dynamics of society as a whole (see Taylor, 1971: 148).

The attempt to achieve these syntheses and supplements shaped a key text to emerge from this period: Ian Taylor, Paul Walton, and Jock Young's *The New Criminology* (1973). This text proposed an explanatory framework which would serve to create 'a fully social theory of deviance'. Building from C Wright Mills famous exhortation in *The Sociological Imagination* (1959) – that we must situate human biography in history and in structure, and so bridge the gap between the inner life of actors and the outer dynamics of the historical and social setting – the book inquired into the wider origins of the deviant act within the structure of the total society. Yet it also attempted to understand deviancy's immediate origins in the psychodynamics of subcultures as members confront perceived problems. Further, the book attempted to develop this analysis symmetrically, to explain equally the social reaction against deviance and the subculture of deviance itself. This effort at holistic theory was evident also in *The Drugtakers* (Young, 1971), *Policing the Crisis* (Hall et al., 1978), and *The Sociology of Youth Culture* (Brake, 1980).

A final influence on the British development of cultural and subcultural theory was the work of socialist historians; this was especially the case with the Centre for Contemporary Cultural Studies under the directorship of Stuart Hall. With the influence of socialist historians like Edward Thompson, Eric

Hobsbawm, Sheila Rowbotham, Christopher Hill, and Stuart Cosgrove, subcultures came to be conceptualized as places of imagination and creativity rather than flatness and determinism, sites of resistance rather than retreatism. The world of leisure emerged alongside the world of school and work as a domain worth studying, and in all these worlds, human meaning trumped mechanistic malfunction (see Cohen, 1980; Downes and Rock, [1988] 2007). Critical here is the notion of *'writing from below'*, of history written from 'the material experiences of the common people rather than from above in the committee chambers of high office' (Pearson, 1978: 119); the goal, to quote the title of Sheila Rowbotham's (1973) book, is to reveal that which is 'hidden from history'. As Chapter 6 will show, this ethos of writing from below, of writing from the streets and alleys, remains very much alive in cultural criminology.

The Centre for Contemporary Cultural Studies

The Centre for Contemporary Cultural Studies (CCCS) was a powerhouse in contemporary sociology. The CCCS was interdisciplinary *par excellence*, iconoclastic, and immensely innovative. The list of scholars who worked at the Centre is itself impressive: Stuart Hall, Dick Hebdige, Paul Willis, Angie McRobbie, Tony Jefferson, Chas Critchner, John Clarke, Paul Gilroy, and Dave Morley, among others. These scholars reconstituted cultural studies, reshaped sociologies of education, identity, ethnicity, youth culture, and the mass media – and, of course, reinvented the sociology of deviance. In doing so they crossed disciplinary boundaries separating sociology, literary studies and social history; embraced the new American work in the sociology of deviance and subcultural theory; and evoked an array of authors from Raymond Williams to Edward Thompson, from Althusser to Gramsci, from Barthes to Lévi-Strauss. From Raymond Williams they learned to take seriously the creativity of popular culture, and to understand culture as the sum total of people's identities. From Edward Thompson they embraced the notion of writing history from below. From both they saw subculture as a text to be read, learning to treat lived practices and symbolic materials as the very stuff of human creativity, and to see art in the everyday (see Willis, 2000). Their gaze was wide focus; it disdained the narrow optic of orthodox criminology. In this sense, to the extent that they influenced criminology, it was because crime and deviance crossed their span of attention, not because of any disciplinary affiliation.

This writing from below offered another critical advantage: by paying appreciative attention to the activities and aspirations of lowly people, social and feminist historians could discover the dynamics of the total society as well. And so for British subcultural theorists, a similar insight: subcultures could be 'read' as texts, texts that revealed the nature of power and inequality – and popular culture could be more relevant and revealing than high culture. Thus Phil Cohen's (1972) account of 'skinheads' exposes the dynamics of urban dislocation, working-class deskilling, and destruction of community. The analysis of changing youth culture forms by John Clarke and his colleagues (1976) clues us in to wider processes of embourgeoisement, mass culture, and affluence. As seen earlier, Paul Willis's (1977) attentive study of working-class lads, their intransigence and bloody-mindedness, becomes also a study of Pyrrhic resistance to wage labour and subordination.

But it was not only deviant action which was given larger meaning within this more holistic analysis; so was the reaction against deviance. In precisely parallel fashion, labelling theory was reworked and recast as moral panic theory. For if subcultural theory makes sense of the seeming irrationality of delinquency, moral panic theory offers the possibility of *making sense of* the seemingly ill-conceived and irrational reactions to deviance by authorities and the wider public. Just as delinquent vandalism appears on a superficial level negativistic and unproductive, yet becomes meaningful and understandable in its wider social context, so moral panics about crime – though disproportionate, wrong-headed, and counter-productive – become understandable and 'reasonable' when considered in the context of existing societal conflicts. Of course none of this is to say that subcultural responses are always tenable, or that moral panics are ultimately justified. Rather it is to stress, once again, that both deviant action and the reaction against it constitute *meaningful* human behaviour – beset like all human behaviour by mistake and misinterpretation, but hardly mindless or without implication.

moral panic theory

It's 1964, a cold, wet Easter on an English beach at the small seaside town of Clacton. Two groups of kids get into a spat: the mods, with their motorscooters and sharp suits, and the rockers, astride motorcycles more in the style of the American biker. Some bikes and scooters roar up and down the front, some windows are broken, some beach huts are wrecked. It's no great disturbance on the beach – the TV footage shows that – but there's an extraordinary disturbance in the mass media, with heavy coverage and angry commentary, and among members of the public. 'There was Dad asleep in the deckchair and Mum making sandcastles on the beach', says The Daily Express newspaper – one pictures them relaxed, pink in the sun – and suddenly a 'Day of Terror', and the 'Wild Ones' who 'Beat Up the Town'. Over a two-year period similar reports emanated from other seaside towns: roaming gangs of mods and rockers 'from London', periodically 'invading', causing mayhem, displayed their arrogance and new-found affluence, insulting decent people – in a memorable phrase, 'sawdust Caesars' puffed up with their own cowardice and aggression.

It was this world – this world of mods and rockers, mums and dads, and media – that Stan Cohen memorably investigated in *Folk Devils and Moral Panics*

(1972; 3rd edition, 2002a); and it was from this world, and from Cohen's brilliant analysis of it, that moral panic theory developed. Certainly one of the most influential models of crime, deviance, and the media – an essential model today for cultural criminologists and others – moral panic theory is nonetheless often mischaracterized and misunderstood.

Commonly, 'moral panic' is understood as a collective mistake in understanding. From this view, an event of little consequence occurs (for reasons that are unimportant), but it is mistakenly reported and exaggerated by the mass media, such that those involved in the event become 'folk devils' over which the general public feels unjustified 'moral panic'. Yet this simple, linear model of the media imparting unnecessary panic to the public scarcely captures the complexity – and importance – of 'moral panic'. Missing is the sense of creative energy and collective intensity that animate the events; missing also is a sense of the representational loops and spirals by which moral panic emerges as a *collective endeavour*, an endeavour in which the youth, the media, the moral entrepreneurs, the control agents, and the public are all accomplices in the action.

In reality, three dimensions of moral panic must be addressed if the theory is to succeed in untangling the relationship between crime, deviance, the media, and public perception:

1 **Symmetry.**   Both the subculture and the moral panic – that is, both the action and the reaction – must be explored, and explored symmetrically. Both the subculture and the moral panic must be read as narratives in which actors attempt to solve problems facing them. In this sense, both those made into folk devils and those who panic morally over them can be understood as exhibiting cultural creativity. Moral panics tell us something significant about those who panic; moral panics are not mere misperceptions implanted by the mass media or agencies of control. Adding further complexity is the fact that there is not a single unitary panic, not a single simple text to be read by the researcher; different audiences create different texts, and in so doing reveal much about themselves and their particular cultural circumstance.

2 **Energy.**   A pulse of energy intrudes at each stage. The kids on the beaches are driven by the creativity and exuberance of their own subculture. They thrill to their own transgression, to the reaction it creates and the attention it receives; in Dick Hebdige's (1988: 8) evocative description, 'spectacular youth cultures convert the fact of being under surveillance into the pleasure of being watched'. The mums and dads, the public watching the skirmishes, aren't passive spectators, either; they're morally indignant, cheering the police as they arrest the thugs (Cohen, 2002a: 134), glad that police and the magistrates reaffirm the boundaries of decency and propriety. They, and those who later encounter mediated versions of these happenings are not merely manipulated recipients of media messages – they *want* those messages, they

read the morning paper and turn on the television with anticipatory gusto. The media, meanwhile, have learnt that there is a ready market in agitating audiences; they themselves have institutionalized moral indignation with self-righteous enthusiasm (see Cohen and Young, 1973).

In this way, as we will see in subsequent chapters, moral panic theory anticipates the phenomenology of transgression and vindictiveness in Jack Katz's *Seductions of Crime* (1988), and cultural criminology generally. Here moral panic theory also exposes the exquisite, energetic tension between the fanciful and the visceral. Youth cultures like mods and rockers of the past, Goths or gutter punks now, certainly harbour the fanciful; they identify with those of other times and places, subvert conventional lines of race or gender, conjure up music from across borders, and bricolage styles of dress, demeanour and patois. They even magically remake banal commodity into subversive meaning. Again, Dick Hebdige:

> the mods could be said to be functioning as *bricoleurs* when they appropriated ... commodities by placing them in a symbolic ensemble which served to erase or sub-vert their original straight meanings. Thus pills medically prescribed for the treat-ment of neuroses were used as ends-in-themselves, and the motor scooter, originally an ultra-respectable means of transport, was turned into a menacing sym-bol of group solidarity. ... More subtly, the conventional insignia of the business world – the suit, collar and tie, short hair, etc. – were stripped of their original connotations – efficiency, ambition, compliance with authority – and transformed into 'empty' fetishes, objects to be desired, fondled and valued in their own right. (1979: 104–5)

With these transformations, though, the fanciful begins to edge up to the transgressive – and more subversive still is the attempt by certain subcultures to unbalance the *moral equation*, the normative balance between work and leisure. The mods, as Stan Cohen put it, 'made a calculated attempt to live in leisure time' (2002a: 158), to live a life of excitement and elegance that escaped the world of work. Thus the bell-hop hero of the film *Quadrophenia* (1979, dir. Franc Roddam), a fictional retelling of the mod experience, creates a glamorous role at night, bridged by the 'alchemy of speed', despite a servile role during the day. The expressive existence of the subculture constitutes a *collective accomplishment*, albeit a precarious one, always in danger of exhaustion by the demands of criminal law or material economy.

But back to those who panic – here too energy is being expended. Listening to their comments, as Stan Cohen did, we hear a litany of vindictiveness: calls for corporeal punishment or forced labour, demands for state controls and detention centres. Such visceral reactions, heavy with emotional energy, are a key feature of moral panics; Young (1971) found a very similar response to hippies and drug users, where there was a general revulsion from police officers and members of the public over imagined filth and degradation. The text of panic is, therefore, a transposition of fear; the very disproportional excess of the language, the venom of the stereotype, signifies that something more than simple reporting is afoot, as in this much-quoted *News of the World* (1969) account of a London hippie squat:

> Drug-taking, couples making love while others look on, a heavy mob armed with iron-bars, filth and stench, foul language, that is the scene inside the hippies' fortress in London's Piccadilly. These are not rumours but facts, sordid facts which will shock ordinary decent living people. Drugtaking and squalor, sex ....

Savour if you will the mixture of fascination and repulsion, attraction and condemnation, as the text mixes fragments of truth with doses of sensationalized outrage (see Young, 1971; Brake, 1985; Cohen, 1997). And consider this: today, around what sorts of group might similarly overblown reporting, and similarly panicked perceptions, develop? Immigrants? Terrorists? Graffiti writers? Gangs?

3 The real problem and the real significance.   Cohen stresses a key dimension of moral panic analysis, and one that we would stress as well: moral panic is not simply illusion or misperception; it signifies that, somewhere beyond the hype, a significant issue does exist. In Cohen's case study, the hedonistic spontaneity of the new youth cultures *did* threaten the normative standards of the older generation:

> The mods and rockers symbolised something far more important than what they actually did. They reached the delicate and ambivalent nerves through which post-war social change in Britain was experienced. ... Resentment and jealousy were easily directed against the young, if only because of their increased spending power and sexual freedom. When this was combined with a too-open flouting of the work and leisure ethic, with violence and vandalism and drugtaking, something more than the image of a peaceful [holiday] at the sea was being shattered. (2002a: 161–2)

When moral panic occurs, then, it often involves a displacement of another fear, or a mystification of a deeper threat – but it is collective panic nonetheless, and if 'read' carefully, can teach us much about the cultural dynamics of fear and the structural crises that underlie it. Further, it can reveal the degree to which such deep crises operate on the level of meaning, symbol, and emotion. After all, the violence and vandalism of the mods and rockers would have mattered little, save that it came to symbolize an attack on mainstream values; as Cohen tellingly puts it, 'Whatever the "devil" was in the seaside towns it was not in the vandalism' (2002a: 114).

Indeed, if one revisits the three original studies of moral panics – Cohen's study of mods and rockers, Young's study of cannabis and hippies in *The Drugtakers* (1971), and the collective study of mugging in *Policing the Crisis* (Hall et al., 1978) – they can all be seen to reveal major structural and cultural changes in advanced industrial societies, as refracted through the prism of youth. Drifting towards late modernity, seismic realignments were underway, primary among them the shift from a society of work discipline and deferred gratification to one which stressed both work and leisure; commitment to work but also an emphasis an immediacy, enjoyment and consumption. As usual, youth cultures prefigured these changes, and so moral panics over mods and rockers, hippies, anti-war protestors, and minority kids echoed them. As later chapters will show, panics over immigrants or terrorists or graffiti writers resound with similar echoes today.

towards a cultural criminology

Cultural criminology is today known for, among other things, its transnational character; its theories and its theorists regularly criss-cross the Atlantic in the process of research, analysis, and intellectual collaboration. As must be obvious by now, this is no accident. The combined work of American and British scholars over the second half of the twentieth century in many ways established what cultural criminology was to become. Their work showed that subcultural dynamics, mediated representation, and collective perception are integral to the construction of crime and deviance. It found the roots of particular crimes and subcultures in larger cultural contradictions and patterns of social change, and in turn demonstrated the role of the media in masking and remaking these relationships. Ultimately, their work affirmed that the most important of issues – exclusion and inclusion, crime and control, human identity itself – cannot be understood apart from issues of emotion, meaning and power.

As the world has moved deeper into late modernity, though – and as cultural criminology has emerged as a distinct criminology of the late modern condition – this intellectual process hasn't halted. Honing the analysis already developed, theorists and researchers have further refined it by exploring ongoing tensions and contradictions.

Take, for example, the tension between affirming the cultural creativity of deviants and criminals, and on the other hand acknowledging the claustrophobic and self-destructive character of some deviant and criminal behaviour. This was of course a tension that Albert Cohen confronted with his delinquent boys – and it is one that contemporary cultural criminology continues to confront. One way of exploring this tension has been already suggested by labelling theory, and its notion of self-fulfilling social dynamics. Convicting a person of drug use may well close off legitimate avenues of work or school, negatively shape the person's self-image, and so predispose that person to ongoing drug use. Likewise, a lifetime of brutalization in prison may well produce prisoners who seem little more than … brutes. Research shows, for example, that the heavy use of solitary confinement and disciplinary cells tends to launch an insidious ratcheting up of discipline, with prisoners who are disabled by long-term isolation acting out in such a manner as to invoke further punishment and isolation (Grassian and Friedman, 1986).

This sense of progressive alienation from society, this downward drift of increasing social reaction and increasing deviance, has also been encoded in the concept of the 'deviancy amplification theory' – a concept particularly associated with the work of the NDC (e.g. Young, 1971; Cohen, 1972; Ditton, 1979). Here, spirals of social rejection are not only interpersonal but mediated, as media images, expert opinion, and the workings of the criminal justice system conspire to create the very 'folk devils' that are imagined. As subsequent chapters will show, this amplifying spiral operates even more powerfully today – and so cultural criminologists continue to explore it, and to trace the ways in which image intertwines with action.

Another significant aspect of this tension between cultural creativity and dehumanization involves, ironically, the ability of individuals and groups to create cultural practices that deny their own creativity and human agency, operating *as if* human action were merely the unfolding of destiny. Earlier in this chapter we considered Paul Willis's *Learning to Labour* (1977), and his discovery that working-class boys rebel against middle-class school standards by creating rituals of toughness and disobedience. But that's not the end of their story, as the book's subtitle – *how working-class kids get working-class jobs* – suggests. As Willis shows, working-class boys soon enough begin to realize that school offers only limited possibilities of mobility, and that their attempt to 'succeed' in the educational rubric of the school is largely a charade. Yet the subculture that they create in response – with its stress on the physical and the masculine, its rejection of intellectual achievement, and its elevation of solidarity over social mobility – only further *prepares* the boys for a life of manual labour and hard graft. Their insight into the charade of an open class structure is a Pyrrhic victory, helping to insure the very social immobility that they sense. This subtle, poignant analysis of the tension between subcultural creativity and social entrapment continues to be immensely influential. It forms the theoretical undercurrent, for example, in Philippe Bourgois' *In Search of Respect* (1995), and is a major motif of Jay McLeod's *Ain't No Making It* (1995).

A second tension is equally important – and as we continue to explore it, we move ever closer to the contemporary realms of late modernity and cultural criminology. For British theorists, you'll recall, a subculture constituted a 'text' to be 'read' for its meanings; it was a text, a story, in which a subculture attempted to find a meaningful solution to some shared problem. The East London skinheads of the 1970s and 1980s, for example, were read as a response to the steep decline of traditional work, the beginning of gentrification, and the death of small craft industries. Since all of these trends operated to remove the social and economic props of working-class masculinity, as grounded in traditional skills and physical prowess, a 'solution' was invented: the revanchist machismo of the skinheads, the shaved heads, Doc Marten boots, and reactionary songs and rituals (Hamm, 1995). This shared subcultural narrative, this text, was seen as clear-cut, unified, and readable for its particular meanings and implications. Distinctive subcultures were defined by precise styles and types of member; they offered signs of resistance, indicators of symbolic subversion against the hegemony of the dominant culture.

Hidden in this sense of subculture as readable text, though, is a tension – and one that has only increased under late modernity. This is the tension between the subculture and the larger culture; put differently, the tension between inclusion and exclusion, between integration and diversity. As we suggested earlier in this chapter, alternative and 'subterranean' values now percolate throughout late modern culture, carried along by the media and by global migration, by mainstream advertisers as much as by subcultural adversaries. As we'll show in subsequent chapters, this shifting, uncertain cultural landscape eventually blurs even the distinction between violence and entertainment, or crime and crime control. In such a swirling environment, then, the tendency can be to overstate the integrity of the subcultural 'text', and to assume too clear-cut a delineation of the subculture itself.

Perhaps in such a world subcultural identity is not so distinct, subcultural messages not always so dramatic. Increasingly, we realize that at least some subcultures must be understood, in Peter Martin's words, as 'fluid, porous, amorphous and transitory' (2004: 31), with young people capriciously adopting one subcultural role or another, playing with subcultural identities and discarding them (McRobbie, 1994), or occupying multiple subcultural worlds at once. If there remains a subculture text to be read in such cases, that text will be hybrid, plural, and adulterated, borrowing from other subcultures and the mediated subterranean values of the wider society, along the way 'scrambling fixed signs of identity' (Cohen, 1997: 261) and perhaps even embracing its own demonization (McRobbie and Thornton, 1995). As Ferrell has found (1998), in such circumstances even a relatively *distinct* subculture can nonetheless define itself by dislocation, anonymity, and movement. None of this discards the notion of subculture, of course; rather it suggests that, as social, cultural, and subcultural conditions change, so must our analysis of them.

And as we'll argue in the next chapter, it is under these late modern conditions that a cultural criminology becomes essential. In late modernity the tectonic plates of gross inequality and widespread social stigmatization continue to grind below the social surface, erupting endemically in crime and disorder, more dramatically in riots, terrorism, and the 'reconnaissance battles' (Bauman, 2005) associated with contemporary warfare. In this world of dizzying instability and insecurity, exclusionary processes continue and accelerate, pushed along by mediated representation and global fluidity. Meanwhile, subcultures of resistance, reaction, and desperation flourish and fade, reminding us that something remains amiss, that the social world grows only more unstable and fissiparous. Here, crime and deviance mirror the disorder of the everyday.

Under these conditions orthodox criminology won't suffice. The late-modern world requires a criminology that is something more than the white noise of the criminal justice system, a criminology that accounts for meaning rather than dismissing it. It demands a criminology designed to explore mass representation and collective emotion, not a criminology bent on reducing cultural complexity to atomized rational choice. If it is to be made better, this world needs not a criminological culture of control (Garland, 2001) founded in practicality and conservatism, but a criminology animated by cultural innovation and dedicated to progressive possibility.

Long gathering, the storm has now broken. There's no turning back from it.

A selection of films and documentaries illustrative of some of the themes and ideas in this chapter

GOODFELLAS, 1990, Dir. Martin Scorsese
Goodfellas is Scorsese's masterpiece about the true story of mobster Henry Hill and his association with the New York Mafia. The film is illustrative of a number of classic criminological theories, including the Chicago School concepts of 'differential association' and 'cultural transmission'. However, in terms of the specific relationship to this chapter, *Goodfellas* is interesting in that the film unknowingly evokes two of David Matza's theories – the notion of 'delinquency and drift' (the idea that individuals drift into deviance – see the opening scenes of the film which chart Hill's tentative entry into the Mafia); and his famous 'Techniques of neutralization' (or the processes by which individuals and groups rationalize and explain their criminality).

THIS IS ENGLAND, 2006, Dir. Shane Meadows
Set in 1983 in a small English coastal town, *This is England* is the personal story of an 11-year-old boy's brief association with a group of skinheads. Set against the backdrop of Margaret Thatcher's Britain, *This is England* is interesting in that it deals with the allure of subcultures, but also the personal psychological differences of the group's members – differences that ultimately tear the group apart and force the film's central character to question his values.

THE BATTLE OF ALGIERS, 1966, Dir. Gillo Pontecorvo
The winner of multiple awards, *The Battle of Algiers* uses intense realism to depict the Algerian Liberation Front's struggle against French colonial power. With scenes of violence, police torture, political assassinations, and terrorist bombings, the film blends dramatic scenes and recreations of historically accurate events to show the unfolding of colonial and postcolonial violence and its role in the creation of the contemporary world order. Interestingly, it is alleged that the film was screened in the White House prior to the invasion of Iraq.

BERKELEY IN THE SIXTIES, 1990, Dir. Mark Kitchell
Historical documentary chronicling the 1960s counter-culture movement from its origins at the University of California, Berkeley. Using a mix of documentary footage and interviews with key players, such as Allen Ginsberg and Huey Newton, the film charts the blossoming of the anti-war movement, women's liberation, the rise and fall of the Black Panthers, and other products of this period of political protest.

A *TASTE OF HONEY*, 1961, Dir. Tony Richardson
Based on Shelagh Delaney's play, *A Taste of Honey* is a bitter sweet comedy-drama that sets out to question class and gender matters in 1960s Britain. Like a number of other classic films produced during this period (e.g. *Look Back in Anger*, 1959, Dir. Tony Richardson, *A Kind of Loving*, 1962, Dir. John Schlesinger, and *The Loneliness of The Long Distance Runner*, 1962, Dir. Tony Richardson), *A Taste of Honey* was highly influential in the way it challenged notions of the 'nuclear family' and the class rigidities of mid-twentieth-century Britain.

the storm breaks: cultural criminology now

Concluding the previous chapter, we suggested that a new world is emerging – a world of 'late modernity' – and that cultural criminology is designed to resonate with this world, and so to penetrate its obfuscations and critique its injustices. This chapter develops both claims. First offering a fuller sense of the late modern world, it next turns to cultural criminology's engagement with it.

late modernity

In the world of late modernity, space and time compress under the forces of economic and cultural globalization, culture comes loose from locality, and material and virtual realities intermingle, with many people consequently experiencing a profound sense of disembeddedness and dislocation. Here mass media, new media, and alternative media proliferate, forming a tangled spider's web of constant, if virtual, interconnection. Here hyperpluralism prospers – a contested diversity of values encountered on the screen and in the street, an unprecedented plurality of cultural perspectives circulating amidst state and corporate attempts at the monopolization of meaning.

In the world of late modernity, certainties of just reward and confident identity fade away, or re-present themselves chaotically. Ontological insecurity runs rampant, stereotypes scuttle around the mediated social structure in an ongoing festival of othering – and so identity politics take centre-stage while class conflicts morph into 'culture wars' against the poor and disenfranchised.

All of this anomic insecurity is cut through with gross inequality. While bankers drink custom cocktails at £330 a glass in trendy London bars, and undocumented workers remodel $3 million Brownstones in Brooklyn for the wealthy, others wander the streets, collecting bottles and cans in purloined supermarket carts. In the USA, the top 1% of the population owns 40% of the financial wealth, the bottom 80% owns a mere 9% – and the UK and its inequalities aren't far behind.

As these inequalities increase within the First World, they increase *between* the First World and the Third World as well. One half of the world now lives on less than $2 a day; the three richest men in the world possess wealth equal to that of the poorest 48 nations combined. With a globalized media and economy, such inequalities become all the more unbearable, all the more culturally discordant, and so in the war zones of the Middle East, the projects of East New York and the sink estates of South London, the *banlieues* of France and the poppy fields of Afghanistan, they play out. Between the global extremes of wealth and deprivation, a panicked 'middle class' remains all too ready to project its fears upon the underclass (Young, 2007) – and the disadvantaged react to their structural humiliation, sometimes righteously, sometimes terribly, and most always in ways that authorities label crime, terrorism, or immorality.

The puzzle of Riker's Island

Eight miles from Manhattan is the largest penal colony in the world, a place most New Yorkers could not find on the map if they knew it existed at all. Home to 15,000 inmates, Riker's Island is just over the waterway from La Guardia International Airport. It is a place of invisibility where, paradoxically, the inmates live next to a global transportation hub, and view the skyline of one of the great global cities – both no doubt tantalizing exacerbations of their misery.

This world of secret punishment poses certain puzzles for the criminologist. Why, first of all, is punishment hidden when in the past, as the French philosopher Michel Foucault (1977) pointed out, it was out front and ostentatious, with the public gallows, the whipping post, the village stocks? And why do so many people *need* to be punished in a rich, developed country that, supposedly, is the homeland of Western civilization and liberal democracy? In the United States there are over two million people behind bars at any one time, and prison building, management, and maintenance has itself become a giant industry, vigorously sought by state and local authorities for its promise of employment and pollution-free 'industry'.

Riker's Island itself is the size of a small town, with its own schools, bakers, tailor shop, medical centre, nursery, and religious facilities. Yet it is scarcely economically sufficient: Riker's costs the US taxpayer over $800 million a year to run. Indeed, the average cost of keeping an inmate is $60,000 a year compared to the average US wage of $37,000. As for efficiency: about 75% of inmates will return to Riker's within a year of release. So a further problem occurs for the criminologist: how is such an irrational process possible and why does it persist, not only in the USA but across the 'developed' world?

Then there are the inmates themselves: what strikes the criminologist immediately is the demographic profile of Riker's, one scarcely representative of the wider society. Over 90% of the inmates are black and Latino, they are nearly all men, one-quarter have been treated for mental illness, and 80% have a history of substance abuse. Most definitively, they are poor: 30% previously homeless, 90% lacking a high school diploma (see Wynn, 2001). Why is the US criminal justice system, like others, skewed in such a direction? What does this hidden prison, and its population, tell us about the problems of late modernity?

Amidst all this, in the cities and towns, the criminal justice system and the prison–industrial complex continue. Were all those imprisoned or supervised by the US system put together, they would constitute the second largest city in the United States, only a million short of New York City. Meanwhile, in the streets of London one is rarely beyond the scope of the CCTV (Closed Circuit Television) cameras – the average Londoner comes into view of the estimated 500,000 cameras 300 times a day. And even with crime in decline over the past decade, many in London or New York or Paris continue to clamour for more cameras, more police officers, more 'security'.

We suspect that this desire for 'security' reflects far more than simple fear of crime. Where social commentators of the 1950s and 1960s berated a complacent, comfortable, 'never had it so good' generation, today commentators talk of a risk society where social uncertainty has emerged as the constant dynamo of existence. This uncertainty pervades both production and consumption. The world of productive work has, for many, unravelled; as the primary labour market of secure employment and 'safe' careers has withered, the secondary labour market of short-term contracts, flexibility, and expendability has grown, and with it an 'underclass' of the unemployed and underemployed. The world of leisure and consumption has likewise been transformed into a kaleidoscope of choice and presumed preference, turned relentlessly by the stress on immediacy, hedonism, and self-actualization (see Campbell, 1989; Featherstone, 1991; Young, 1999). And these anomic circumstances become even more precarious in light of two late modern contradictions: the heightened demand for self-identity at a time when pervasive social disruption undermines any such self-assurance, and the heightened demand for the sorts of immediacy and excitement that a commodified culture industry is hard-pressed to deliver.

Little of this is inherently new. Mass migration, labour flexibility, mass media influence, and social instability all presented themselves dramatically in the past; indeed, as we've seen, the subcultural tradition emerged to make sense of precisely such disruptive developments and their consequences. What *is* new is the combined force of such developments today, their greater orbit, and their dangerous juxtaposition. Dramatic declines in First World industry and manufacturing dissolve not only stable workplaces and reliable incomes, but stabilities of identity and community. Increased geographic mobility and hyper-individualism further disintegrate traditional human communities; growing numbers of divorced couples and single parents reflect and exacerbate this trajectory. Ultimately, these factors conspire to replace the American Dream of material comfort with a new First World Dream where meaning and expression are paramount, where finding yourself becomes an ongoing task of uncertain reinvention.

In late modernity, this new dream is primarily scripted and marketed by way of mediated communications. Television and radio now occupy roughly half the waking hours of citizens in the UK and the USA – and of course to this must be added video games, popular films, internet entertainment, and other mediated diversions. In late modernity communications media morph and proliferate, creating and servicing a diversity of audiences, replacing weakened traditional communities with communities of virtual meaning and emotion. In this process two social identities are created and contrasted: positively the celebrity, and negatively various deviants, criminals, and outcasts – though, as we will see, these two identities are often made to intersect. Powerful but ambiguous orientations to crime and crime control, to morality and immorality, are in this way circulated through a world hungry for just such direction. As personal identity disintegrates, virtual identity becomes more desirable, more dangerous – even more 'real'.

All the while the labour demands of global capital and the commodified seductions of global media breach borders real and imagined, mobilizing desires and populations alike. In Europe, relatively homogeneous populations have now, for good or bad, become manifestly multicultural; in Europe and elsewhere, the sheer variety of cultures now interspersed with one another – crossing borders, contesting cultural identities, sharing mediated dreams – marks the pluralism of late modernity.

late modern pluralism, late modern predicaments

Late modernity's pluralism can be understood as a kind of *hyperpluralism*, a swirling proximity of discordant values that confounds the global and the local. The shock of the plural, the uncertainty of the hyperplural, derive from everyday exposure to an inordinate variety of cultural meanings, subcultural styles, and definitions of propriety or deviance. Here meanings overlap, values hybridize, and identities collapse into each other – to the point that 'normal' is no longer a certainty, and the taken-for-granted world begins to blur. Texting a friend in Chicago, catching an email from an acquaintance in Greece, chatting with your Nigerian immigrant classmate before your class on modern French literature, watching a foreign film on your car's headrest monitor or reading the ads for Spanish language classes on the city bus, wearing cowboy boots with your retro-1970s disco outfit, going home to your neighbourhood's mix of ethnic histories and contemporary subcultures, the everyday world of late modernity swarms with a plurality of meaning and value.

This shock, this *defamiliarization*, is a regular occurrence also for the immigrant, the traveller, the seasonal labourer on the move – ever-larger parts of the late-modern population. On the move and caught between many worlds, day-to-day routines unravel and the most 'natural' of tasks becomes problematic – even 'home' loses its certainty once left behind. With mass migration and global tourism, with the ever-arriving influx of other people and other ideas, indigenous populations begin to lose their citadels of symbolic security as well. On the move, the world turns inside out.

For good or bad, a sort of cultural chaos ensues. Certainties as to equality or fairness are replaced by a sense of arbitrariness; clear measures of personal worth or professional achievement recede. People come and go, jobs come and go – the rice terraces of an earlier class structure are breached, ploughed under, replaced with a slash-and-burn economic ecology. Not surprisingly, the luck industries – casinos, online gambling, televised poker tournaments, state-sponsored lotteries – flourish. For most, insecurity, uncertainty and debt make a mockery of meritorious progress towards accumulated wealth or secure retirement. The sham dream of instant fame and fortune, of winning a tele-vised talent contest or the lottery, remains.

On one level, hyperpluralism and other late modern dislocations create great human potential – the potential for people to cast off the heavy weight of transmitted culture, with its deference and unthinking acceptance, and its mythologizing of tradition. At another level, these late modern uncertainties spawn great human misery, forcing into the foreground feelings of profound insecurity, social vertigo, even existential emptiness. From within this predica-ment, the choices are twofold: to change, reinvent and resist, or to choose to deny choice itself, and instead retreat to essentialist and fundamentalist notions of oneself and others.

As regards the first choice, we will simply mention here the multitude of late modern resistance movements, from radical post-industrial environmentalists to anti-globalization protesters, from South American political artists to African women's rights activists. We will also note, and in later chapters return to, the widening horizons of resistance within late modernity. A new generation of activists is not so much interested in older models of mass social movements as they are in mining the hyperplurality of everyday life, and launching there moments of self-determination, autonomy, and cultural hybridity (Maffesoli, 1996, 2004; Ferrell, 2001/2). These activists also understand the particular dynamics of late modernity – understand that moments of leisure and pleasure can hold radical possibilities, that the street can talk politics with the internet, that mediated representations can be subverted and reversed.

But of course there's that second choice as well, the choice for essentializing and othering. A common salve for feelings of insubstantiality and worthlessness is to maintain that there is something essential about oneself or one's beliefs that in fact guarantees superiority. Gender, class, race, nation, religion – all can be invoked

Plate 3.1 Signs of uncertainty in Lexington, Kentucky and London, England
Credit: Photographs Terry Cox, Keith Hayward, and Jeff Ferrell (2006)

in the search for self-assessed superiority, and in the creation of an outsider group that is 'naturally' inferior. All provide narratives of difference, moral castigation of the other, a neat division of an increasingly complex and confounded world into a hierarchy of innate merit. Importantly, this is not only a process of cultural dehumanization; it is a facilitator of violence. It acts as a collective technique of neutralization, promoting both the vindictive punitiveness of the master and the transgressive violence of the offender. The cruel and unusual punishments of the American prison system, the terrorist bombing of the London underground, the many everyday acts of domestic violence or racist attack – all mix essentialism and 'othering' with dehumanization and violence.

precarious inclusion, tantalizing exclusion, and social bulimia

Social exclusion is often thought of as a binary; the securely included majority on the one side, the socially and morally excluded minority on the other. Under the conditions of late modernity, we would argue, a very different dynamic applies: many of the included are discontented, insecure, and disaffected, and many of those thought of as excluded are in fact only too well assimilated. In late modernity, precarious inclusion confronts tantalizing exclusion.

To remain 'included' in a late modern world of tenuous careers and economic disarray – that is, to maintain a 'decent' standard of living, to support a 'success-ful' lifestyle, to allay the constant fear of falling – requires unreasonable effort, self-control, and restraint. The job is insecure and the salary doesn't keep up with inflation, the work hours are long and getting longer, the weekend is short, and brief moments of enjoyment arrive only with the liberal aid of alcohol. Both parents work – or the single parent works two jobs – and then there are the kids' schedules of school and recreation and performance. And that's not to mention the traffic jams during the long commute to and from work, the crippling cost of housing, the rising cost of petrol and heating oil – and the sense that maybe none of this is sufficient for identity or security, that none of this measures up to the last generation or the last aspirational television programme watched.

The profoundly precarious position of most of those 'included' in late modern society in turn spawns anger, vindictiveness, and a taste for exclusion. From this precarious social perch, it can all too easily seem that the underclass unfairly live on *our* taxes and commit predatory crime against *us*. It can seem that *we* are afflicted by our own hard work and decency, while *they* are free to hang about and pursue pleasure. It can seem that they are all we are not, are not restrained by the same late modern inequities as are we. Such a process is, of course, not one of simple envy; the precariously included are seldom eager to swap places with the disgraced and impoverished excluded. But the very existence of the excluded, their imagined moral intransigence and unearned indulgence, makes the uncer-tain circumstances of the included somehow all the more unbearable.

Of course late modernity creates other sorts of contradictions for the excluded and the underclass. Elsewhere, we've investigated the American black underclass as a sort of test case – a test, that is, of exclusion and inclusion in late modern society (Young, 1999) – focusing particularly on Carl Nightingale's (1993) brilliant ethnography of the Philadelphia ghetto, *On the Edge*. What Nightingale discovered confounded any simple binary of exclusion and inclusion – for the ghetto, he found, is the apotheosis of America. Here is full immersion in mainstream American culture: a world worshipping money and success, hooked on Gucci, BMW, and Nike; a population watching television eleven hours a day, sharing mainstream culture's obsession with violence, lining up outside the cinemas, even embracing in some ways the racism of the wider society. The problem of the ghetto is not simple exclusion; rather, it is deep cultural inclusion confronting systematic exclusion from cultural and economic realization. It is a situation where inclusion and exclusion occur concurrently – *a bulimic world* where massive cultural inclusion is accompanied by systematic structural exclusion.

In the late modern world, then, the fundamental subject matter of criminology – crime and its causes, crime control, fear of crime, policing, punishment – is recast. Now, fear of crime may well emerge from mediated representation, punitive attitudes from social and personal precariousness. Crimes of acquisition may now mirror the ironies of late modern cultural inclusion, perhaps embodying also visceral reactions to particular modes of late modern disintegration. Forms of criminality once traceable to stable locales may now trace to individualized emotions, searches for lost identity, or collisions of migratory cultures. The criminal justice system will surely respond, will certainly play its own role in exclusion and inclusion, and in the policing of the image. A new sort of criminology will be needed.

a cultural criminology for late modernity

The late modern transformations and fluctuations just outlined have been the stuff of much debate in the social sciences; in particular the debate has been framed around epochs and eras. On one side is the view that such changes signal the demise of modernism and a transition into conditions of 'postmodernity' (e.g. Baudrillard, 1981; Lyotard, 1984; Jameson, 1991). The opposing perspective, generally associated with theorists such as Giddens (1984, 1990), Beck (1992), and Berman (1982), is more circumspect, suggesting instead that these changes don't involve anything as significant as a paradigm shift, and that current social and economic transformations remain situated in the realm of modernity. The debate turns around the knotty question of whether contemporary conditions represent a qualitative break with, or merely a quantitative intensification of, what has gone before. Whatever the case, though, we need a criminology that is not just aware of these debates (orthodox criminology generally is not), but capable of understanding, documenting, and reacting to the particulars of contemporary circumstances.

Whether or not our social order is currently undergoing a period of epochal structural transformation, it is clearly beset by significant, even extraordinary, modifications to many of the taken-for-granted assumptions and modes of organization associated with classic modernity. To understand contemporary patterns of crime and crime control, these transformations must be investigated – and an 'agnostic' position as regards postmodernity/modernity enables us to do so. From this stance, we can talk of our inhabiting (or perhaps travelling through) a continuous yet discontinuous moment, an inchoate period of societal and epochal hybridity. Hence, it is our contention that the contemporary world is in fact a shifting composite of *both* modern and 'post' modern features – which, for the sake of concision and clarity, we refer to as *late modernity*.

As criminologists of this transitional time, we seek to identify not just the changes underway but also the important continuities, for the contemporary period is clearly constituted from both. Accordingly, we need a criminology that is at once reflexive and progressive, modern and postmodern, drawing on theories and ideas from the past, embracing contemporary concepts and methods, and inventing new hybridizations of the two. As we have argued in the previous chapter, cultural criminology is just such an approach. It actively seeks to meld the best of our criminological past with newer theories and disciplines, to create a criminology that can not only situate crime and control in the context of culture, but demonstrate that contemporary cultural dynamics embody an intensification of existing trends.

What follows is a series of theoretical constellations that encapsulate some of cultural criminology's key facets. Often they are themselves hybrid forms, responses both to existing criminological theories and newer modes of interpretation. Always they offer ways of seeing crime and criminal justice – of 'reading' it, in terms of the previous chapter – mostly absent from orthodox criminological analysis. Together they sketch an emerging cultural criminology, a theoretical movement still coming into focus. Why coming into focus rather than sharply delineated? Because like other features of late modernity, ours is an iterative project, avowedly and inevitably a work in progress.

emotion, expression, experience

Criminology takes as its subject matter an area of social life that is the subject of heated conversation in the workplace and at the bus stop, a primary focus of cinema and television drama, the animated stuff of video games, the staple diet of the news media, and a central theme in a multitude of popular literary genres, from crime thriller to serial killer. It takes as its subject matter an act that is frequently charged with malice, thrill, and fear – an act which regularly galvanizes offenders, traumatizes victims, and outrages the general public. Criminology takes all this … and turns it into sanitized dross. As we will explore more fully in later chapters, both the phenomenology of crime and the fascination of the spectator are lost in the theory and methods of orthodox criminology – sometimes, it seems, intentionally so. Marcus Felson (1998: 3), for example, enjoins us to accept that the majority of crime contains precious little drama and is really 'not much of a story'. Indeed, he seems to celebrate the mundane nature of crime, reducing it to the other mass of events in everyday life. Yet, among other things, criminologists like Felson forget that everyday life is itself a site of frequent drama, tragedy, and joy, and that even the dullest of habits and routines are often sites of great intensity, scuttling escapes from existential fears, places of reassurance, and solace. The human condition is very much a story of intensity, we would argue, animated by joy and fear, passion and frustration, whomever the person, whatever the life.

In contrast to Felson and other orthodox criminologists, cultural criminology seeks to unearth and capture precisely this phenomenology of social life, and this *phenomenology of crime* (Katz, 1988) – its anger and adrenaline, its pleasure and panic, its excitement and humiliation, its desperation, and its edgework. Put in historical terms, cultural criminology is designed to attune not only to the phenomenology of crime, but also to the phenomenology of everyday life as lived in the late modern era. The search for excitement, the retreat into tedium, the tension of conformity – as we have already seen, all become more vivid and uncertain in late modernity.

Yet we are confronted at this moment by an orthodox criminology which is denatured and desiccated. Its actors seem to inhabit some arid theoretical planet where they are either driven into crime by social and psychological deficits, or left to make opportunistic choices in the marketplace of crime. They appear either miserable or mundane. They seem strange digital creatures of quantity, obeying probabilistic laws of deviancy; they can be represented by the statistical symbolism of lambda, chi and sigma, their behaviour captured in the intricacies of regression analysis and equation.

As we suggested in Chapter 2, and as we will confirm in the following chapters, we on the other hand understand human beings to be creative and culturally innovative, caught in circumstances not of their own making but making sense of these circumstances, making meaningful choices, and meaningful mistakes, nonetheless. In late modern circumstances of dislocation and structural uncertainty, such creativity and reflexivity becomes all the more apparent and important – and yet there is an irony: it is precisely in this culturally-charged period that a fundamentalist positivism has come to dominate orthodox criminology. Put bluntly, this constitutes a dangerous ahistoricism, a dumbing down of theory, and a deadening of reality – and so it is at this time that a cultural criminology must emerge as a counter.

cultural criminology vs rational choice theory

Currently two approaches to crime dominate orthodox criminological theory: rational choice theory (RCT) and positivism – the first stressing the mundane, the second the measurable. Both embody simple rational/instrumental narratives. For rational choice theory, crime occurs because of rational choice(s) – it derives from availability of opportunity and low levels of social control, particularly where individuals are impulsive and short-term oriented (e.g. Felson, 1998). Curiously – or perhaps revealingly – every intellectual attempt is made to distance crime from structural inequalities and social injustice. Instead, we are offered only calculative individuals, committing crime where possible, and on the other side the putative victims who, as likely targets, are only understood through their attempts to calculate their optimum security strategies.

In the second approach, that of sociological positivism, inequality, lack of work, community breakdown, and lack of social capital are to a certain extent recognized, but the analytic bridge from deprivation to crime, particularly violent crime, is not built but assumed (see Katz, 2002a). As with RCT, we are left with a desperately thin narrative, where intensities of motivation, feelings of humiliation and rage, even love and solidarity are all foresworn. If the first is the criminology of neo-liberalism, the second is that of mass social democracy, but in truth there is little to choose between them. They are even similar in their determinism: RCT might be better renamed *market positivism*, for between the determinants of poor character and opportunity for crime there is only a small space for the most pallid of market choices. Our critique of positivist social science and its attendant methodologies will be found in Chapter 6; here we'll examine cultural criminology as theoretically oppositional to the rational choice approach to crime.[1]

Though they have a much longer disciplinary history, RCTs of crime gathered traction during the 1980s (see Cornish and Clarke, 1986). As crime and recidivism rates spiralled upwards in the 1970s, many criminologists grew tired of traditional (dispositional) theories of crime based on notions of social deprivation. Their solution was to develop theories of crime based on allegedly fundamental principles of human behaviour associated with the 'classical school' of criminology. These 'neo-classicists' combined the utilitarian ideas of Beccaria and Bentham with more recent 'deterrence' theories (Gibbs, 1968; Zimring and Hawkins, 1973), and related economic theories of crime (Becker G, 1968; Hirschi, 1969).[2] The results were 'cost–benefit' constructs such as the *homo economicus* model of human action. This in turn led to the creation of a series of (deliberately) aetiologically-impoverished models of criminal behaviour where, as with classic control theory (Gottfredson and Hirschi, 1990), there is no special deviant or pathological criminality. Rather, criminal behaviour is simply understood as the result of calculative strategies aimed at utility maximization. Reaching their highest forms of abstraction in sophisticated algebraic expressions, contemporary RC theorists now test the efficacy of crime prevention initiatives by reducing the mind of the potential offender to a statistical formula: e.g. $Y_i = \alpha + \beta (XB_i) + \beta2 (Xc_i) + \varepsilon i$ (Exum, 2002). With rational choice theory, human meaning and criminal creativity are quite literally banned from the equation; criminality becomes a two-inch formula (Hayward, 2007).

Taken together with the commensurate and related rise of 'situational crime prevention', this supply-side approach to the crime problem did achieve some notable success in combating certain forms of economic/acquisitive criminality (see e.g. Farrell and Pease, 2001). Yet it also opened the door to a new 'criminology of normality' or 'culture of control', a strategy of crime control closely attuned to the fields of risk and resource management, and calculative governmental approaches regarding the containment and management of social problems (Garland, 1997: 190). Reducing crime and crime control to a managerial problem, reducing criminality itself to a set of exogenous factors, RCT forfeited any understanding of *internal* psychic-emotive processes, any analysis of structural inequality and injustice – and any hope of escaping the critical gaze of cultural criminology.

Set against the acquisitive/property crimes that are the stock-in-trade of RC theorists, for example, are the growing number of crimes that embody vivid emotional or 'expressive' elements – what elsewhere we've referred to as the crimes of the 'irrational' actor (Hayward, 2004). Clearly the situational/RC approach operates as a far less effective intellectual or 'managerial' tool when confronted with the chaotic, violent, and 'expressive' crimes that cause most late modern public distress and community disharmony (see Morrison, 1995; De Hann and Vos, 2003). Imagine, if you will, the intractable problems RC theorists would encounter when trying to explain, or contain, offences such as gang-related symbolic violence, stylistically-focused graffiti writing, hoax emergency service call-outs, hedonistic drug use, bar brawls, or drunken vandalism. Indeed, even within the rational choice camp, cracks are beginning to show. Exum's aforementioned test of RCT is particularly illuminating in this regard. Studying the effects of alcohol and anger on violent decision-making, he states that 'the [RC] perspective may not be the general explanation for crime it is proclaimed to be', concluding later that 'perhaps the model may only explain "cool-headed" behaviour but then *breaks down when individuals are in an emotionally charged state…*' (2002: 961, emphasis added).

It is precisely this 'emotionally charged state' that interests cultural criminologists, who suspect that subjective emotions and textured socio-cultural dynamics animate many crimes, *and increasingly so under late modern conditions*. Against the abstracted, mechanistic rational calculator, cultural criminology counterposes the naturalism of crime itself. The actual, lived *experience* of committing crime, of concluding a criminal act, of being victimized by crime, bears little relationship to the arid world envisioned by RC theorists. Indeed, the adrenaline rush of crime, the pleasure and panic of all involved, are anything but exogenous to the 'crime equation'. Crime is seldom mundane and frequently not miserable – but it is always meaningful.

Nor does acquisitive crime reduce itself to the instrumental payoffs that RCT would suggest (nor for that matter the deficit adjustments that sociological positivism would pinpoint). As the ex-con John McVicar (1979) once remarked, day labourers will always ultimately make more money than armed robbers – but of course that's often not the point. While bank robbers certainly receive 'instrumental economic pay off' from the completion of a successful robbery, they also reap considerable cultural and symbolic rewards from the act – something made clear in Katz's vivid account of the visceral dynamics involved in 'Doing Stickup' (1988). Even unsuccessful exponents are often fêted within the criminal fraternity and afforded high status and respect within institutional settings. Likewise, Richard Wright and Scott Decker (1994: 117) find that many burglars are committed not just to property acquisition but to the 'quest for excitement' and 'illicit action', even to the point of burglarizing occupied homes so as to amp the excitement; one of the adult property criminals that Ken Tunnell (1992: 45) studied similarly tells him that 'it's exhilarating … I get off going through doors'.

As the previous chapter showed, Al Cohen began to reveal this expressivity a half-century ago, showing that juvenile delinquents happily make mischief while in school, since 'the teacher and her rules are not merely something onerous to be evaded. They are to be *flouted*' (1955: 28). Or for a late-modern example consider binge drinking, one of the many phenomena allegedly 'manageable' through situational controls on urban incivility and crime. It's not just that binge drinkers only drowsily realize that they've passed the point of 'declining marginal utility' after they've passed it; there's the problem that the very basis of binge drinking is to 'unashamedly defy the normal injunction to think and act rationally' (De Haan and Vos, 2003: 45). Of course, it *could be* that drinkers rationally and systematically set out to stumble into door faces, projectile vomit, and pass out in the gutter (Hayward, 2007). Couldn't it?

These intensities of irrationality and emotion extend throughout the whole process of crime and its depiction, from the offender's momentary rage or later shame, to the gutted despair of the victim, the thrill of the police car chase, the drama of the dock, and the trauma of imprisonment. And circling all this, adding their own emotional charges: the outrage of the citizen, the moral panics of the media, and the fears of those in the streets and homes. We've said it before and we'll say it again: emotions 'flow not just through the experience of criminality … but through the many capillaries connecting crime, crime victimization and criminal justice. And as these terrors and pleasures circulate, they form an experiential and emotional current that illuminates the everyday meanings of crime and crime control' (Ferrell, 1997: 21). This is the naturalistic, even existential, counterpoint to the de-natured essentialism of rational choice theory and its cognate fields.

emotional metamorphoses

Acknowledging the importance of human emotions in crime, punishment, and social control is a first step in countering the mechanistic clank of orthodox criminology; understanding the workings of our shared emotional lives, and the sources of our emotional states, is the next. Emotions are complex and mysterious – yet we must attempt to understand them, and to investigate the emotive states that contribute to criminality.

While criminology hasn't paid sustained attention to the subject of emotions, other disciplines have, among them behavioural psychology, philosophy, the sociology of law, and consumer studies. Much progress has also been made by scholars in the new and diverse field of 'the sociology of emotions' (e.g. Kemper, 1990; Scheff, 1990; Barbalet, 1998; Bendelow and Williams, 1998; Williams, 2001). Yet, for all the intellectual energy, the subject of emotion within the social sciences and humanities remains enigmatic; theoretical consensus is hard to come by, even as regards fundamental questions concerning the source of emotions, or the best ways to study them. That said, the social construction and social significance of the emotions is now being recognized, and researchers are finally proceeding with a much clearer set of research questions. Additionally, there has been something of a convergence among scholars regarding the ontology of emotions, and their amenability to individual and social mediation. Increasingly, emotions are viewed as encompassing *corporeal* dimensions (the physical body), *cognitive* dimensions (mental processes, interpretations, and forms of reasoning), and *feeling*, or affect dimensions (how differentially socialized and socially located individuals experience the corporeal processes occurring within their bodies). For example, while most of us might well experience a rush of adrenalin when confronted by a group of football hooligans in a train carriage (corporeal dimension), we may impart different interpretative meanings to that response (cognitive dimension), in association with how we have come to respond to such experiences (the feeling dimension).

Even here, though, the precise workings of these three elements remains poorly understood – and perhaps that's not all bad. Commencing from a default position that recognizes emotional states as complicated and diverse can help researchers avoid the pitfall of analytic reduction. Consider, for example, the way emotions are approached within emerging criminal justice policy fields. Whether it's the narrow 'diagnostic' checklist that underpins the new wave of offender 'cognitive behavioural programmes', or the deracinated concept of emotions that props up various incarnations of restorative justice, the tendency is to downgrade the complexity and variety of emotions. Emotional states are not one dimensional or universal constructs, and so any approach that reduces them to a categorical listing not only fails us theoretically – it dehumanizes all involved. When it comes to the study of emotions, complexity serves as a buffer against reductionism and theoretical oversimplification.

Rather than distilling human emotion to a series of uniform 'emotive states', then, cultural criminology strives to understand the *phenomenological basis* of emotions, to locate emotions within the complexities of thought, consciousness, body, aesthetics, situation, and social interaction. As we've already seen, Jack Katz's (1988) book *Seductions of Crime* helped establish this phenomenological focus in cultural criminology; his more recent book, *How Emotions Work* (1999), can help develop this emotional dimension.[3]

Katz's starting point is unequivocal: emotions are enigmatic. At one level they appear 'beyond our control', as when we are wracked by guilt, overwhelmed by shame, or struck by something hysterically funny. At another level, emotions 'make up a part of our lives that is intimately *subjective*'. Individuals react differently to comic stimuli, for example, while we all own our particular guilt and shame. Katz (1999: 1–2) hence poses questions prescient for cultural criminology: when shame or rage flood through experience, where is the source of the inundation, where are the gates that let the rush of feelings come through, if they are not within? If we idiosyncratically own our emotions, why can't we fully own up to them?

Katz proposes a threefold answer to these questions:

1. Katz describes emotions as both *situationally-responsive* and *situationally-transcendent narrative projects*: 'What is the socially visible sense that a person is trying to make in the immediate situation of his action, and what is the current sense that the situation acquires within his awareness that his life reaches beyond the current situation?' (1999: 5). Analyzing a videotaped police interview with a killer, for example, Katz shows how the murderer's tears during his confession serve two purposes, aiding in his immediate dealings with the police interrogators, but also allowing him to grasp the implications of the interrogation episode for his quickly narrowing future.
2. *Interactional processes*. Katz is interested in how people shape their emotional conduct in relation to the readings and responses given to their emotions by others. At this point Katz stresses the bodily nature of many emotive states: 'In shaping emotional conduct, the subject also exploits resources for interaction that she finds in her own body … [we] see people creatively mining the resources they find at hand in order to shape the impressions that others take of their emotions' (1999: 6).
3. *Sensual metamorphoses*. As people move in and out of emotional states like shame, anger and rage, Katz argues, the sensual framework of their actions change. Again, this process may be embodied. Katz takes seriously 'what might at first glance seem to be hyperbole or surreal images. For example, I treat drivers' complaints that they have been "cut off" as literal descriptions; I then look for evidence of what in their corporeal experience was amputated' (1999: 6).

Katz's tripartite typology offers a useful starting point for cultural criminology's analysis of emotions. To begin with, as Katz himself suggests, it helps us overcome simplistic distinctions between the foreground experiences of the actor, on the one hand, and the other background factors like social class or education that typically preoccupy sociological analysis. In both *How Emotions Work* and a related article (Katz, 2002a), Katz amplifies a perspective he first developed in *Seductions of Crime*: that by starting with the emotional foreground of experience, we can arrive at 'background conditions such as power, gender, social class, ethnicity etc.' (2002b: 376).

Katz's analysis also helps in developing appropriate methodologies for understanding emotions. He argues that emotions cannot and should not be studied via questionnaires, or in laboratory experiments in which emotional responses are provoked or stimulated, since both methodologies distance researchers from the grounded phenomenology of emotional work. (When in Chapter 6 we discuss methodology, we'll show you a particularly absurd example of just this sort of research.) Instead Katz (1999: 17) prioritizes a more ethnographic approach, urging emotion scholars to study the way people construct their emotional behaviour in natural, everyday settings. As we'll show in this chapter's next section and in Chapter 6, cultural criminology has already developed methodologies for understanding the emotional experience of crime and crime control; Katz's work can help us refine these. As we'll also see, Katz's emphasis on the 'social interactive' dimensions of emotions, and their links to corporeality and transcendent performativity, complements existing cultural criminological perspectives on edgework and situated performance:

> It is exactly at the intersection of the situational and the transcendent that everyday life takes on its emotional force. Playwrights know this well, [and] … often focus on (1) situations of conflictual interaction that (2) carry transcendent significance and (3) are best conveyed when the audience is drawn to focus on how actors represent the conflict in idiosyncratic corporeal ways. (Katz, 1999: 77)

Of course, the drama of emotions is not always limited to situational dynamics amenable to ethnographic methods or phenomenological anaylsis. Within cultural criminology, for example, interesting work on the emotions engendered by mediated images and collective representations of crime is already well underway – work that Alison Young (2004, 2007) describes as a new 'criminological aesthetics'. Still, Katz's tripartite structure provides a useful platform for taking emotions seriously, and for considering criminality's emotive states.

edgework and transgression

Crime is an act of rule breaking, an act 'against the law'. It embodies particular attitudes towards these rules, assessments of their justness and appropriateness, and motivations to break them, whether by outright transgression or momentary neutralization. Crime is not, as in positivism, a situation where actors happen to cross the rules while mechanistically propelled towards some desiderata; it is not, as in rational choice theory, a matter of actors merely seeking holes in the net of social control, then ducking and diving their way through them. Rather, for cultural criminology, the act of transgression itself contains distinct emotions, attractions, and compensations.

We would point, for example, to the way poverty is *experienced and perceived* in an affluent society as an *act of exclusion* – the ultimate humiliation in a society defined by wealth and consumption. It is an *intense* experience, not merely of material deprivation, but of felt injustice and personal insecurity. Exacerbating this under late modernity is a shift in consciousness such that individualism, expressivity, and identity become paramount, and material deprivation, however important, is powerfully supplemented by a widespread sense of ontological deprivation. In other words, we are witnessing today a *crisis of being* in a society where self-fulfilment, expression, and immediacy are paramount values, yet the possibilities of realizing such individualized dreams are strictly curtailed by the increasing bureaucratization of work, indebtedness of everyday workers, and commodification of leisure and leisure time. In this context crime and transgression – even crimes of economy or acquisition – can be seen as a breaking of restraints, an illicit realization of immediacy, a reassertion of identity and ontology. In these and other crimes, identity and emotion are woven into the experience of rule breaking.

Within cultural criminology this analysis of transgression, identity, and emotion has been perhaps most fully developed in the research of Stephen Lyng (1990, 2005), Jeff Ferrell (2005; Ferrell et al., 2001), and others on *edgework*. In studies of individuals engaged in acts of extreme voluntary risk taking, such as advanced sky-diving, illicit motor bike racing, and illegal graffiti writing, researchers have found that participants are neither dangerously 'out of control' nor possessed of some self-destructive 'death wish'. Instead, they push themselves to 'the edge', and engage there in 'edgework', in search of 'the adrenalin rush', authentic identity, and existential certainty; they lose control to take control. Edgework functions as a means of reclaiming ones' life by risking it, a way of reacting against the 'unidentifiable forces that rob one of individual choice' (Lyng, 1990: 870).

Here, as suggested in Katz's analysis of emotions, the foreground of risk opens up to the background of law, power, and economy. Lyng's (1990) research, for example, has emphasized especially the way in which edgework allows participants to develop the very sorts of skills that the late modern economy of dumbed-down service work and temporary jobs takes from them. Moreover, these skills *matter* in distinctly dangerous ways, spiralling participants ever closer to an edge others can't know. After all, the more polished one's skills as a sky-diver or street racer, the more risk one can take – and the more risk one takes, the more polished those skills must become. Ferrell's (1996, 2005) research has discovered a similar dynamic, and one that links edgework directly to criminality, emotion, and criminal justice: if edgework sparks an addictive 'adrenalin rush' from its explosive mix of risk and skill, then aggressive law enforcement efforts to stop edgeworkers will only heighten the risk of their edgework, force them to further hone their skills, and so *amplify* the very adrenalin rush that participants seek and authorities seek to stop.

Edgework's original focus on prototypically masculine, high-risk pursuits has been criticized by a number of feminist criminologists (Howe, 2003: 279; Halsey and Young, 2006), who see it as further evidence of the essentially gendered nature of much risk research (e.g. Stanko, 1997; Walklate, 1997; Chan and Rigakos, 2002). Focusing on the extreme yet voluntary activities of street racers or graffiti writers, they argue, fails to take seriously the everyday, involuntary risks faced by women simply by virtue of *being* female in a patriarchal society – risks like domestic violence, sexual abuse, and public assault. While these are certainly valid criticisms of early edgework research, they do suggest the sort of dichotomization we've sought throughout this chapter to avoid. Even as first formulated, for example, the concept of edgework can help us understand gender and gender dynamics, including the considerable number of crimes that produce 'hegemonic masculinity' (Connell, 1995) from a mix of risk taking and embodied masculine emotion, to the detriment of women. Moreover, subsequent research (Ferrell et al., 2001) has found that women, both individually and collectively, often constitute some of the more skilled and esteemed members of illicit edgework subcultures.

The issue of edgework and gender can be approached from other angles as well. In her thoughtful response to Lyng's (1990) early formulation of edgework, Eleanor Miller argues that the edgework model is limited because of its too narrow focus on 'activities that are engaged in primarily by white men with an attachment to the labour force' (1991: 1531). But while she is right to be deeply critical of this and other aspects of Lyng's thesis, she does not dismiss them out of hand. Instead, she explores whether or not they can have utility for her own research on the risk-taking strategies of African-American female street hustlers, especially those involved in potentially dangerous 'street missions' and 'put overs'. Revisiting once again the tension between foreground practices and background structures, Miller sees the everyday circumstances of the 'underclass women' she studies as products of wider structural inequalities and racist ideologies, but acknowledges also that particular forms of edgework practice come into play 'among those who choose especially risky hustles'.

> In the case at hand, the sort of edgework engaged in by the members of these [underclass] groups should not be expected to resemble exactly the edgework described by Lyng; the structures of oppression to which it responds are unique. The resources of the members of the groups in question are usually fewer and different. However, experientially and in terms of social psychological impact, edgework might be functionally equivalent across these groups. Or, it might be different in ways that are sociologically important and interesting. But not looking forever dooms us to not seeing. (Miller, 1991: 1533–4)

Lyng has acknowledged as much, noting that the edgework model needs 'elaboration beyond its present empirical base' (1991: 1534) – and indeed in a recent edited collection on edgework (Lyng, 2005), he attempts just that, with chapters exploring the relationship between edgework and drug taking, the Victorian insurance and actuarial industries, youth delinquency, even anarchy. Most important in terms of our present concern, though, is Jenifer Lois's chapter, in which she explores the significant gender differences in edgework practices associated with voluntary mountain rescue teams. For example, she charts how trepidation and confidence emerge as gendered emotional strategies in preparation for edgework; how reactions to the 'adrenalin rush' vary by gender; and how major differences emerge in women's and men's management of fearful post-edgework emotions. She concludes that 'women's and men's gendered understanding of emotions influenced how they understood their "authentic" selves, and hence, their edgework experiences' (Lois, 2005: 150; see also Lois, 2001). Likewise, feminist criminologist Valli Rajah has recently developed a notion of 'edgework as resistance' in her study of poor, minority, drug-using women involved in violent intimate relationships. Rajah's work explores how 'edgework may be different across gender, class and race', and develops 'the resistance concept by specifying both when resistance is likely to occur and what the specific rewards of resistance may be' (2007: 196).[4] Most recently, Jeannine Gailey (2007: 1) has employed the notion of edgework to rebut essentialist or medicalized understandings of anorexia, showing instead how anorexic women employ precise skills to accelerate their anorexia and achieve 'intense emotive reactions'.

As this body of emerging research confirms, the concept of 'edgework' constitutes an invaluable intellectual model for exploring the interplay of emotion, risk, crime, and identity. And as Lyng argues (2005: 5), understanding this interplay will become only more crucial as the ethos of risk-taking increasingly circulates within the social and institutional structures of late modernity.

Edgework in the Streets

Elsewhere, we've sought to develop the relationship between expressive crime and edgework by situating the latter within a distinctly urban context (Hayward, 2004).

Conventional accounts of edgework often place participants on the mountain face, at the racetrack, or aboard the sky-diving plane. But what of those denied such opportunities, as many are? For some, run-down estates or unpatrolled 'problem' neighbourhoods become 'paradoxical spaces'. While they symbolize the systematic powerlessness so often felt by individuals living in these environments, they also become sites of risk consumption that provide numerous avenues for elicit edgework. Such spaces serve as 'performance zones', places in which displays of risk, excitement, and masculinity abound. In other words, 'many forms of crime frequently perpetrated within urban areas should be seen for exactly what they are, attempts to achieve a semblance of control within ontologically insecure life worlds' (Hayward, 2004: 165).

This notion applies especially to crimes with a strong 'expressive' element, crimes like joy-riding or 'car cruising' that offer both rich excitement and an illicit means of traversing, even momentarily escaping, the socially degraded neighbourhood. We might even categorize a whole host of crimes like graffiti writing and peer group fighting as 'urban edgework, attempts to construct an enhanced sense of self by engaging in risk-laden practices on the metaphorical edge' (Hayward, 2004: 166).

imagining a cultural criminology of the state

Cultural criminology is still developing – and one area we are keen to develop is a cultural criminology of the state. Cultural criminology has to this point tended to conceptualize and study culture more at the levels of criminal act, subculture, or media than at the level of the state. This is an oversight that we cannot afford; the cultural practices of the state are too important to ignore. So, while a thoroughgoing cultural criminology of the state would require a separate book, here we sketch some possible lines of inquiry, inviting your response and participation.

In February 2003, at the insistence of the Bush administration, the *Guernica* tapestry (a huge copy of Picasso's 1937 painting of the Nazi bombing of Guernica during the Spanish Civil War) was first covered, then removed, from the Security Room of the United Nations Building in New York City. Apparently it was no longer an appropriate backdrop for Colin Powell and other US diplomats to make media statements urging the case for the invasion of Iraq. What the neo-conservatives pulling the strings of the Bush administration knew only too well was that, when it comes to wielding power on the late modern global stage, image management is as important as the deployment of Apache attack helicopters. Or to put it another way: the play may be fatally flawed, but there's no excuse for not properly dressing the set.

Had he been around today, Guy Debord would surely have smiled. The guiding light of the insurrectionary Situationist International forty years ago, Debord declared then that, if capitalist accumulation was to continue unchallenged, it would require new forms of state control that held 'mastery over the domain of the image'. His argument was simple: as the state ramps up its involvement in the day-to-day lives of its citizenry through 'the colonization of everyday life', the control of images – especially via so-called 'perpetual emotion machines' like the television – becomes ever more vital to the maintenance of the capitalist social order. Yet this gives rise to a paradox: the more the state relies upon the image, the more it is vulnerable to image manipulation.

So back to today, to 9/11, the invasion of Iraq, and the war on terror. In an article on America's reaction to the attacks of 9/11, the Retort Collective argued that 'a state [the USA] that lives more and more in and through a regime of the image does not know what to do when, for a moment, it dies by the same lights. It does not matter that "economically" or "geopolitically" the death may be an illusion. Spectacularly, it was real. And image-death – image-defeat – is not a condition that the state can endure' (Retort Collective, 2004: 20). This is not simply a retreat to Jean Baudrillard's world of 'hyper spectacle' – something the Retort Collective are keen to avoid. Rather, it's a call for a clearer understanding of the geo-political interaction between the *symbolic* and the *material* – a line of inquiry that, no doubt, a radical interventionist like Debord would have welcomed. As the Retort Collective make clear, 'No one level of analysis – "economic" or "political", global or local, focusing on the means of either material or symbolic production – will do justice to the current strange mixture of chaos and grand design' (2004: 7). We must strive instead for modes of critique that merge these domains, combining images and analysis as tools to 'vulnerablize' the state and challenge its hegemony over the 'realm of the image'. Given today's multi-mediated world, this task becomes ever more central to any form of critical criminological analysis.

Enter cultural criminology, with its commitment to cross-disciplinary research, its interventionist sensibility, its championing of ethnography, and its call for criminologists to incorporate photography, documentary filmmaking, culture jamming, and other forms of symbolic inversion (Hayward and Presdee, 2008). Striking examples of this approach as a critical analysis of state culture are in fact already surfacing. Wayne Morrison (2004a, 2006) uses photographs and paintings to uncover the truth behind criminology's studied neglect of genocide and state crime in modernity. Bruce Hoffman and Michelle Brown (2008) employ digital filmmaking to highlight the continued 'spectacle' of US state executions. Tim Boekhout van Solinge (2008) mixes ethnography and photography to show governmental complicity in the illegal logging trade. Mark Hamm (2007) deconstructs in great detail the photos of Abu Ghraib prisoner abuse, revealing tell-tell signs of covert intelligence agency involvement.

While each of these studies suggests a way forward for future cultural criminological work on state culture, they are but the opening salvos in what must be a long and dedicated campaign. Our world is changing – largely as a result of the onslaught of state-approved neo-liberalism (Harvey, 2006) – and we need a criminology capable of understanding the social havoc this change causes. Perhaps more importantly, we need a cultural criminology that can investigate yet another paradox, this one involving late modern global capitalism and the nation state. While the global world becomes increasingly characterized by the erosion of cultural and political borders, the growth of information technology, the deregulation of financial markets, and the unfettered flow of goods – the sorts of late modern trajectories described at the start of this chapter – states and their bureaucracies are becoming more rigid and aggressive in their efforts at defining and maintaining sovereignty. Bryan Turner (2007: 288) explains: 'There is ... a profound contradiction between the economic requirements of flexibility and fluidity and the state's objective of defending its territorial sovereignty. In particular, with the growth of the global war on terror after 9/11, states, rather than becoming more porous, have defended their borders with increasing determination.' Turner describes this new phase as a 'parallel immobility regime' linked to the rise of 'global security systems' and the new 'enclave society' – and it's against this backdrop that we must imagine a new and unremitting cultural criminology of the state.

possibilities and provocations

So, to sketch some possibilities for a cultural criminology of the state:

It should include work on the state's new divisive territoriality, and its physical manifestations. We need more critiques of the bourgeois sensibilities propping up exclusive gated communities (Ferrell, 2001/2; Hayward, 2004: 128–44), more deep ethnographies of everyday life on either side of the steel barriers and security walls that increasingly separate 'respectable' parts of the city from the socially excluded wastelands of late modernity (Davis, 1990) – a virulently divisive process underway everywhere from Baghdad to Botswana, from the West Bank to West Hollywood.

It should develop an analysis of terrorism that traces its roots to entrenched cultural essentialisms as much as economic imperialism or 'blood for oil'. We must critique and overcome both the West's Orientalist view of the East as a place of violent, treacherous, and irrational populations, and the counter-discourse by which Eastern Occidentalism demonizes the West. As Edward Said makes clear, these and other stereotypical *imaginaires* 'correspond to no stable reality that exists as a natural fact' (2003: 63), and so must be unpicked and dismissed. Only then can we overcome the simplistic 'clash of civilizations' discourse (Huntingdon, 1993) and move towards more culturally-nuanced understandings of regional and national difference. Our analysis of terrorism must also strive to expose the misleading narratives of terrorism and counter-terrorism promulgated in the mass cultural script. As the major theme of television shows like *The Unit*, *24*, and *Spooks*, and video games like *Splinter Cell*, *Tom Clancy's Rainbow Six Vegas*, and *Shattered Union*, and as a pre-eminent trope of Hollywood's contemporary imagination, these narratives feed a Western culture of terror, fear, paranoia, and xenophobia (Jackson, 2005; Lewis, 2005; Furedi, 2007). Finally, we must understand terrorism and counter-terrorism as spectacle, a series of performances staged for enemies and other audiences.

It should promote a 'criminology of war' that forces mainstream criminology to include in its intellectual scope crimes associated with military action and state-sanctioned violence (see Jamieson, 1999; Green and Ward, 2004; Morrison, 2006). Imagine, for example, a cultural criminology of the Halliburton Corporation. Can't we do more to expose the grotesque profits Halliburton has made from the 'war on terror' and the 'neo-liberal shock therapy' associated with the post-invasion reconstruction of Iraq (Whyte, 2007)? Certainly information on the corrupt practices of Halliburton is available (CorpWatch Report, 2007), documenting everything from the overcharging of US taxpayers for spurious logistical military support to the double and treble counting of soldiers who use their mobile gyms and recreation rooms. But what is the corporate culture that promotes such scams? And by what cultural processes of 'disinformation', advertising, and news management are they masked? More generally, we must develop a criminology that looks beyond street crime, and to the hidden brutalites of war. We need to know the lives of combatants (see e.g. Wright, 2004) and non-combatants; we need to watch the videos they shoot, to read the poems they write.

This cultural criminology of the state should seek *to highlight within the public realm*, the inexorable rise of the modern penal archipelago in the USA

(2.2 million people in prisons and jails nationwide with an additional 4.7 million on probation or parole), in the UK (where the prison population is set to top 100,000 for the first time within the next five years), and elsewhere around the globe. Beyond exploring the reality of the prison–industrial complex (Schlosser, 1998) and its machinery of lobbying, marketing, and image, we must research and expose the full collateral damage of mass incarceration. For example, as Todd Clear explains in his book *Imprisoning Communities* (2007), in certain sectors of US cities imprisonment now exacerbates the very social problems it is allegedly intended to solve. With thousands of adult males removed from communities, neighbourhoods fall apart as they suffer from the dual erosion of the economic infrastructure and informal levels of social control. The result of this symbiotic relationship between the prison and the ghetto (Wacquant, 2002) is that social networks and families crumble, and further, in one of the crueller ironies of contemporary criminal justice, crime rates in these neighbourhoods actually increase. Meanwhile, codes of language, personal style, and self-presentation flow so rapidly between the prison and the neighbourhood that the culture of one becomes in many ways the culture of the other.

After the Floodwater: Blackwater

In the aftermath of Hurricane Katrina, polluted floodwater and violent gangs were not the only toxic threats coursing through the streets of New Orleans. Patrolling the streets alongside traditional law enforcement personnel and the US National Guard (at least what was left of it after mass deployments in Iraq and Afghanistan) were members of Blackwater Security Consulting, a private military contractor.

From a standing start a decade ago, Blackwater now have contracts with the US government totalling in excess of half a billion dollars, largely as a result of the privatization of the 'war on terror'. While Blackwater staff offer a wide range of paramilitary services, their primary role since 9/11 has been as a 'shadow army' of private mercenaries working alongside the US Army in post-invasion Iraq. During the height of the conflict, over 100,000 mercenaries were deployed in Iraq, but it was Blackwater operatives who caused the most controversy. Since 2004 Blackwater contractors have been involved in a series of illegal killings of Iraqi civilians, including most notably the 11 September 2007 incident in Nisoor Square, Baghdad, where, backed by their own helicopters, Blackwater staff indiscriminately opened fire on a large group of innocent Iraqis. Despite their woeful record, Blackwater has remained a nebulous target for prosecutors, both in Iraq and in the USA. Rulings by the former head of the US-led civil administration in Iraq, Paul Bremner, helped create a legal grey area surrounding privately contracted security forces, and as a result Blackwater has gone about its business with apparent impunity (Scahill, 2007). Moreover, Blackwater has lobbied aggressively to ensure they are not subject to the same forms of military law that apply to more traditional combat forces. As its public image has nonetheless been sullied, Blackwater have also worked to 'rebrand' itself through advertisements and corporate sponsorships.

> Blackwater is the creation of Erik Prince, an ultra-conservative Christian bank roller of the Republican Party. Using his powerful contacts, Prince has built a small private army of ex-military and intelligence operatives that he now hires out to the Bush administration whenever some under-the-radar muscle is needed – hence the presence of unmarked Blackwater vehicles on the streets of New Orleans following Katrina. With their flak jackets, desert camouflage combat gear, and automatic weapons at the ready, Blackwater operatives claimed to be in New Orleans to 'stop looters and criminals'. But with their lack of public accountability and their cavalier attitude to the rule of law, perhaps we should be asking ourselves: what was Blackwater actually there to stop? And who really poses the greater threat to civil liberties, the displaced population of a natural disaster or Blackwater's running dogs of neo-liberal capitalism?

The above are simply some suggestions and provocations, and we look forward to others' ideas on a cultural criminology of the state. Whatever form it eventually takes, though, one thing is clear: we must go beyond simply speaking to the academy. A useful cultural criminology of the state must link with the work of journalists, protest groups, and human rights organizations; it must build better relationships with prominent media figures; it must ask how it can be of help to the likes of Richard Sennett, Mike Davis, Robert Fiske, or John Pilger. We can no longer afford to limit our analyses to the confines of academic criminology; we must provoke criminological and popular cultural resistance. To do so, we'll need to fuse the many tools and methods of cultural criminology with the work of artists, writers, musicians, filmmakers, performance artists, documentarians, and others. We need the anti-war music of Steve Earle and Neil Young, the graphic art of Peter Kuper and Seth Tobacman (see Lovell, 2006), the documentary filmmaking of Clayton Patterson, David Redmon, and Ashley Sabin, the photography of Taryn Simon and The Innocents project (see Courtney and Lyng, 2007). Ultimately our goal is a transgressive one: to engage in acts of intellectual disruption.

We must not be held back by thinking this an impossible task. Other academics have achieved much by reaching beyond the constraints of their discipline, and here we can look to Pierre Bourdieu, C Wright Mills, Simone de Beauvoir and Jean-Paul Sartre, even Karl Marx in his more journalistic work. We mustn't shirk from the challenge ahead, for we are most certainly in a race against time. Unless we turn back the current course of geo-political imperialism cut with neo-liberalism, our current social order will slide into forms of chaos that will eventually bring the current era to a deeply destructive end. Around the world the signs are already there for those who want to see – signs of decay and signs of resistance. Protest riots over poverty and racial exclusion in Brazil, Bradford, and the French *banlieues*. Mass uprisings around the world in response to the rapidly escalating costs of staple foodstuffs. New wars in Africa and parts of the Middle East as climate change intensifies social conflicts over water supplies.

Add to this the social meltdown set to follow the collapse of the oil economy, and its clear: the only time we have left is now.

the criminology of everyday life

In his book *Soft City* (1974), Jonathan Raban contrasts two cities. One is the site of mass planning, rationalization, consumption, and production – the urban grid of neighbourhoods and zones, an iron cage in which humanity is channelled and pummelled. The second is the 'soft city', an alternate space where all sorts of possibilities are on offer, an urban theatre of dreams, an encyclopaedia of subculture and style. A similar sense of the city is offered by Michel de Certeau (1984), who contrasts the city of planners and rationalistic discourse, of quantitative data and demographics, with the 'experiential' city – a place of street-level interaction and inter-subjectivity that occurs beneath the interstices of plans and maps. Such accounts closely parallel Mikhail Bakhtin's notion of the 'second life of the people' (1984); as Mike Presdee argues, 'the only true site for the expression of one's true feelings for life ... where the irrational laughs and mocks the rational – where truth can be told against the cold-hearted lies of rational, scientific modernity' (2000: 8).

This analysis of urban space and its underlife runs throughout cultural criminology, and is in fact one of its key organizational concepts (see Ferrell, 2001/2, 2006a; Hayward, 2004). Consider, for example, how this approach underpins the sociology of deviance. Within this rubric, deviant action is understood not as some marginalized or abstracted concept, but rather as a meaningful nether world that bubbles just below, sometimes up through, the surface of appearances; Goffman's (1959) dramaturgical notion of institutions and their 'backstages' reflects a similar sensibility. Even as the bureaucratic, rationalistic order increasingly exerts its influence, then, it remains in some ways imaginary, the idealized construct of planners, politicians, and official spokespersons. It fails to fully comprehend, much less conquer, the existential fears, joys, and resentments of underlying everyday existence. Suffused by rule and regulation, the everyday world nonetheless remains a place where transgression occurs, where rigidity is fudged, where the rules are by turns bent or bowed down to. It is the world in which the imaginary of the powerful confronts the citizen – and is negotiated, internalized, or resisted by those it confronts.

Attention to this everyday struggle between rationalized surveillance and existential possibility – that is, to this *lived experience* of crime, transgression, and social control – animates much of cultural criminology. Theoretically, this focus suggests that rational choice theory and sociological positivism, with their affection for order and predictability, not only misunderstand the reality of crime but, collude in creating the bureaucratic cage that entraps human possibility. Politically, it critiques the notion that some future utopia can be achieved through increasing levels of security, situational crime prevention, and inclusion of the excluded in the existing order of rationalized work and commodified consumption. This, we would argue, mistakes the problem for the solution. For us as cultural criminologists, then, the everyday world is of such importance that we devote the following chapter to it. There we'll attempt to communicate something of the everyday and its importance – criminologically, theoretically, politically, and otherwise. There we'll also suggest that the everyday experience of crime and control under late modernity is in fact a cauldron of contested, even mediated, meaning. Dismiss it if you like – dip in if you dare.

exploring crime and the media

As the editors of *Cultural Criminology Unleashed* recently made clear, within late modernity an extraordinary inversion is all but complete. Images of crime and crime control are now almost as 'real' as crime and criminal justice itself – 'if by "real" we denote those dimensions of social life that produce consequences; shape attitudes and policy; define the effects of crime and criminal justice; generate fear, avoidance and pleasure; and alter the lives of those involved' (Ferrell et al., 2004: 4). A primary goal of cultural criminology, then, is to understand how mediated processes of cultural reproduction constitute the experience of crime, self, and society under conditions of late modernity (see Kidd-Hewitt and Osborne, 1995; Manning, 1999; Banks, 2005). In a world where media images of crime and deviance proliferate, where crime and control reflect off the shiny face of popular culture, cultural criminology means to make sense of the blurred line between the real and the virtual. Once again, this focus is political as well as theoretical. In late modernity, with power increasingly exercised through mediated representation and symbolic production, battles over image, style, and mediated meaning emerge as essential moments in the contest over crime and crime control, deviance, and normality.

Cultural criminologists therefore critically read the various mediated texts that promulgate the social 'story' of crime and crime control (e.g. Barak, 1994; Anderson and Howard, 1998; Bailey and Hale, 1998; Potter and Kappeler, 1998). Here, everything from televisual and filmic depictions of crime and criminality (Cheatwood, 1998; Fishman and Cavender, 1998; Schofield, 2004) to representations of crime and power in comic books (Nyberg, 1998; Williams, 1998), from crime and punishment images in artwork (Valier, 2000; A. Young, 2004) to news media imagery (Chermak, 1995; Barak, 1996; Chermak et al., 2003; Valier and Lippens, 2005) are examined for their cultural meanings and social effects.

In this late modern context, of course, the media is by definition not self-contained – and so other foci of cultural criminology also circulate in the mediated swarm. Subcultures can no longer be studied apart from their mediated representations; ethnography is no longer divisible from textual analysis. As regards earlier discussions in this chapter, the emotions that haunt the public imagination are likewise interlaced with media dynamics – something that Alison Young (2004, 2008) stresses in her work on the *affective processes* associated with crime representation.[5] Arguing that 'crime as image connects bodies', Young asks us to think about how visceral crime images affect us not only in terms of social policy or criminal justice practice, but bodily.

So critical is this holistic analysis of crime and the media that we dedicate the entirety of Chapter 5 to it. There we'll take you deeper into the media swarm, and show how cultural criminologists study not only images, but images of images, traversing as we do an infinite hall of mediated mirrors.

conclusion: reclamation and revitalization

In this chapter we've outlined both the wider backdrop of cultural criminology – late modernity – and some of our ways of engaging with the late modern situation. Our goal here, and throughout the book, is to develop a cultural criminology that is well equipped to understand, critique, and often counter the various transformations underway in current times. Our ultimate goal is a progressive cultural criminology that can help shape a better, more just world. As this and the previous chapter have shown, this criminology must first *reclaim the rich historical tradition of critical, sociological criminology*, and second, *revitalize and reinvent this tradition so as to meet the challenges and inequalities thrown up by the late modern social order.*

In the following four chapters we outline some of these new approaches, and suggest how they can help us make sense of current problems of crime and control. In particular, Chapter 6 highlights a suffocating irony increasingly facing sociological and criminological inquiry – and one that must be resisted and overcome: at the very moment that we must engage the late modern world and its crises, the tools that might help us with this task are under threat. Within the academy, the palpable lurch towards criminologies of simplistic crime reduction and pallid opportunity theory has largely excluded more thoughtful and critical approaches. As a result, the distance between the late-modern world and the academy has only grown, with most criminological analysis now confined to number sets and sanitized computer printouts. Widening this gap further is the subsuming of research within bureaucratic control, such that more engaged forms of research are stifled. Between the iron cage of the Institutional Review Board and the gentle pulling and pushing of government funding, the discipline changes its form, losing its critical edge and progressive direction. And it is in this context that we intend not only to develop a progressive and engaged cultural criminology, but to launch it as a criminological counter-attack on the cloistered institutional cowardice that afflicts us.

In developing this sort of cultural criminology, we hope that the various themes discussed in this chapter will serve as suggestions, not prescriptions; they're intended more as invitation than injunction. Much is still omitted, much left to be done, in this chapter, in the book as a whole, and within the larger project of cultural criminology.

notes

1 We recognize there is very little, if anything, to be gained by continuing or exacerbating the entrenched opposition that currently exists between the two 'sides' in the 'rationality versus emotionality' debate. Certainly, we would like to go on record here as stating that, when it comes to questions surrounding rationality and emotions within criminology, the situation is far more complex than this debate suggests. Ultimately, our goal as cultural criminologists is to produce analyses that can help transcend this delimiting explanatory bifurcation. Interesting in this sense is a forthcoming paper by Majid Yar (2009, forthcoming), in which he actively seeks to construct a path 'between these two criminological monsters' by 'reorganizing our understanding in terms of 'emotional reasons' and 'reasonable emotions'; that is to say, viewing emotions not as the other of reason and rationality, but one of its forms' (see relatedly Ekblom, 2007).
2 'The starting point of RCT is that offenders seek advantage to themselves by their criminal behaviour. This entails making decisions among alternatives. These decisions are rational within the constraints of time, ability and the availability of relevant information' (Pease, 2006: 339).
3 Katz's social psychology of the emotions is not without its critics (see, for example, the extended discussion of *How Emotions Work* in the 2002 special edition of *Theoretical Criminology* on emotions [especially Wouters, 2002: 369–74]). We hope that, just as cultural criminologists critically engaged with Katz's earlier *Seductions of Crime* and set about augmenting his analysis (Ferrell, 1992; Fenwick and Hayward, 2000; Hayward, 2001, 2004: 148–57 Young, 2003), a similar process will commence with *How Emotions Work*.
4 Rajah acknowledges, of course, that 'while edgework as a form of resistance to intimate partner violence may offer visceral rewards, it does not necessarily constitute a victory for women, and may even help to reproduce gender inequality' (2007: 210).
5 Alison Young is right, of course, to caution against the tendency within criminology to view 'affect' as somehow synonymous with emotion. As she points out: 'the term "affect" derives from the tradition of post-Deleuzean social theory, rather than using it to signal some lost emotional dimension within social theory' (Young 2009).

a selection of films and documentaries illustrative of some of the themes and ideas in this chapter

MINORITY REPORT, 2002, Dir. Steven Spielberg
Set aside the sci-fi hokum about the 'pre-cogs' and *Minority Report* is interesting in the way it turns around the notion of 'pre-crime'. In particular, it illustrates a shift underway from aetiological theories of crime and deviance to a control system based around risk and resource management. While we may seem a long way away from the film's Department of PreCrime, it's strange how many of the 'future' trends contained in the movie are either already with us or on the immediate horizon; everything from eye recognition software to a virtual CCTV 'scanscape', from the erosion of trial by jury to the concept of 'digital rule' – a grid of knowledge based on digital records.

No END IN SIGHT, 2007, Dir. Charles H Ferguson

A no nonsense documentary that focuses on the litany of mistakes and misjudgments made by the Bush administration in the two year period following the invasion of Iraq. With commentary from on-the-ground Bush staffers and military personnel, the film cuts through the political spin to present a harrowing story of neo-conservative over confidence and arrogance. *No End in Sight* makes a mockery of 'Mission Accomplished' and similar meaningless sound bites.

FIGHT CLUB, 1999, Dir. David Fincher

'Advertising has us chasing cars and clothes, working jobs we hate so we can buy shit we don't need. We're the middle children of history, man. ... We've all been raised on television to believe that one day we'd all be millionaires, and movie gods, and rock stars. But we won't. And we're slowly learning that fact. And we're very, very pissed off.' So speaks Tyler Durden, the central 'character' of *Fight Club*, an anarchic and controversial tale of anti-consumerism and masculine frustration. Depending on your point of view, *Fight Club* is either 'a witless mishmash of whiny, infantile philosophizing and bone-crunching violence' (Kenneth Turan, *L.A. Times*), or 'a wild, orgiastic pop masterpiece' (Bret Easton Ellis, *Gear Magazine*). The truth lies somewhere in between, of course, but whatever your view, it's not a film that can be easily dismissed. While critics have rightly pointed to its stylized nihilism, its 'microfascism' and its glamorised hyper violence – and certainly all these problematic aspects are apparent – it also makes some interesting observations on late modern alienation and the deadening pressure of boring, unfulfilling, precarious employment. In truth the film is a contradiction in celluloid – for example, it's at once a critique of consumer society and a commercial Hollywood blockbuster! We include it here not because we agree with its message or support its sentiments, but because of its ability to provoke debate and pose questions. See what you make of it.

THE WAR ON DEMOCRACY: A FILM BY JOHN PILGER, 2007, Dirs Christopher Martin and John Pilger

Countering George Bush's claims about 'exporting democracy', this film shows how US foreign policy in Latin America has actually stifled its progress. The film 'explores the disenchantment with democracy, concentrating on those parts of the world where people have struggled with blood, sweat and tears to plant democracy, only to see it brutally crushed' (www.warondemocracy.net). After producing over fifty TV documentaries, the veteran Australian activist and journalist John Pilger has produced a movie that vividly shows that the enduring principles of democracy are more likely to be found among the impoverished residents of the *barrios* of Latin America than they are among the shadowy figures that stalk the corridors of the White House.

SPARE PARTS, 2003, Dir. Damjan Kozole

A tragic tale of illegal immigration told through the lives of two Slovenian traffickers, *Spare Parts* sheds light on the desperate world of cross-border people smuggling.

towards a cultural criminology of the everyday

everyday crimes small and large

As we noted in the introduction to this book, cultural criminologists often focus their analytic gaze on those little situations, circumstances, and crimes that make up everyday life. Cultural criminology looks for evidence of globalization not only in the wide sweep of transcontinental capitalism, but amidst the most local of situations and common of transgressions. It finds the machinery of mass culture in even the most private of moments, discovers the residues of mediated meaning in even the smallest snippets of conversation. From our view, the essential subject matter of criminology – the manufacture of meaning around issues of crime, transgression, and control – remains an ongoing enterprise, an often unnoticed process that seeps into commonplace perceptions and saturates day-to-day interactions.

To understand the ways in which issues of crime, transgression, and control come to be animated with emotion, then, we certainly must pay attention to televised crime dramas and political campaigns – but we also must pay attention to the people around us, and to their constructions of experience and understanding. Most of all, in a world where information and entertainment swirl through everyday life, emanating from countless video screens and cell phones and digitized billboards, we can – we must – find mediated politics in personal experience. Watching people on the street, we can catch little shadows of last night's television crime drama, and all those that came before it; listening in on conversations in a pub, we can hear echoes of a politician's press conference at one table, distortions of the daily news at another. Encountering on the street or in the pub some commonplace crime, we can come to appreciate the extraordinary importance of crime itself.

As we also suggested in our introduction, cultural criminology's critics are aware of this focus on the everyday as well, but they see in it something more insidious. For them, the focus on everyday people and everyday crimes suggests that cultural criminologists are unwilling to take on larger, more important issues of crime and its political consequences. Martin O'Brien (2005: 610), for example, concludes his critique of cultural criminology by juxtaposing cultural criminologists' research into crimes like 'graffiti writing or riding a motorcycle recklessly' with the mercenary crimes of Mark Thatcher. The mollycoddled son of former British Prime Minister Margaret Thatcher, Mark Thatcher has indeed been accused of crimes ranging from racketeering and tax evasion to negligence, arms dealing, and an attempted coup d'etat – crimes that critics like O'Brien assume to be objectively and self-evidently of greater significance than more mundane forms of criminality.

Yet while we're certainly happy to judge the behaviour of a spoiled underling like Mark Thatcher to be morally odious, we're nonetheless left with a serious criminological question: By what terms can we judge his crimes to be more important, or more worthy of our analysis, than the crimes of the lesser known? Put differently, is it the exceptionality of a crime that should draw our analytic attention, or the banality? Is a father's abuse of his daughter more or less troubling, more or less revealing of power and its dynamics, than US soldiers' now well-publicized abuse of prisoners at Abu Ghraib prison? Anonymous Latino kids in America sent to jail or deported on trumped-up 'gang member' charges, African-American kids swept off the street by civil gang injunctions, British kids silenced or segregated by ASBOs, American marijuana users sent to prison under the 'War on Drugs' – are these often unnoticed, everyday occurrences more or less important to understanding and confronting injustice than the crimes of Mark Thatcher?

For cultural criminologists, *these aren't questions that can be answered definitively – they can only be interrogated culturally. The difference between one crime and another is negotiated, not innate – in the final analysis more a matter of contested meaning than inherent magnitude.*

In fact this negotiation of meaning, this fluid dynamic between the everyday and the exceptional, can be traced along any number of trajectories. As we and other criminologists have long documented, the criminalization process – the process by which new legal regulations are created and new enforcement strategies designed – can transform the most mundane of existing activities into major crimes, themselves made into the exotica of moral panic. Trash picking, idling about in public, searching for a place to sleep, dancing with friends, getting drunk or high – all of these have, at various times in recent British, European, and American history, been either matters of little consequence or manifestations of serious criminality. And if this criminalization process at times infuses otherwise little events with large significance, it regularly invokes larger patterns of political and cultural power as well, emerging as it does from media campaigns, staged political pronouncements, and the exercise of economic and ethnic inequality. In such cases, to study everyday transgression, or more specifically to study the *emergent and often amplified meaning* of everyday transgression, is to study the political economy of power.

If we return to the crimes of Mark Thatcher, we can catch a different sort of trajectory, and yet one that suggests a further dynamic linking mundane events and larger matters of meaning. Certainly a direct, cultural criminological analysis of Mark Thatcher's crimes, or for that matter those of George W Bush, would be useful and important. Such an analysis might explore the ways in which neo-conservative values of individual responsibility and personal acquisition in fact set the stage for personal misbehaviour among those who most publicly espouse them. It might examine the ways in which the political privilege of the parent begets the cultural privileging of the offspring, opening doors to inside deals and ensuring endless irresponsibility. It might even focus on the linguistic sleight of hand offered up by expensive lawyers and top-flight public relations consultants such that the misdeeds of the powerful can time and again be obfuscated, reinvented, ignored – and so *not* constructed as crime.

strategic and moral choices

To conduct this sort of analysis well, though – to actually get inside the gilded shadows that make up the world of Mark Thatcher, as opposed to relying on newspaper accounts and popular mythology – would require the sorts of money and connections that few of us have. It would perhaps require travelling in social circles that some of us find uncomfortable, if not repugnant. Most importantly, it would risk valorizing the very phenomenon we wish to analyze and critique – risk reproducing in our own research and writing, that is, the mediated gaze already fixed on the Mark Thatchers and George W Bushs of the world – as we focus too much of our attention on those all too well positioned to capture it. Again, and despite these pitfalls, such a study could make an invaluable contribution to our understanding of political and corporate crime and its consequences – but there is, we think, another way to conduct the study.

That way is to track down Mark Thatcher in the streets and alleys of everyday life, to document his crimes and their consequences in moments more readily available to us. When, for example, wealthy entrepeneurs like Mark Thatcher engage in racketeering and tax evasion, we can effectively explore the consequences of such crimes in the growing gap between the rich and poor of our communities, in decimated local economies and shuttered factories, in underfunded local schools and inadequate healthcare – and so in street-level drug markets and untreated drug overdoses, in everyday school vandalism and violence, and in the Mertonian strain towards theft or despair encountered by unemployed or under-employed folks all around us. When a global hustler like Mark Thatcher dabbles in the arms trade and in political upheaval, we and our colleagues in other countries can catch up to him at every orphanage, can see the consequences of his actions in a severed limb or a lost life. Like the great documentary photographer W Eugene Smith, who famously captured the horrific effects of systematic corporate mercury poisoning in the close-up deformities of one little girl, we can communicate the crimes of the powerful by way of their everyday consequences.

In this sense cultural criminology's focus on the everyday constitutes something of a strategic choice. For some cultural criminologists, the ethnography of everyday life has offered a do-it-yourself research method kept happily independent of university grant programmes, governmental funding agencies, and other outside influences likely to limit the critical scope of scholarly work. Hanging out on street corners, conducting interviews behind commercial buildings, calling up public officials or surfing company websites, researchers need ask neither for permission nor for money – and so they can follow their findings wherever they may go, unencumbered by funding concerns or official sanction. Certainly, critical scholarship can flow from any number of research strategies – but it flows with particular ease from methods that cast the researcher as an independent outsider. And if this sort of research keeps cultural criminologists outside the orbit of bureaucratic control, it also has the benefit of keeping them inside communities. Research on crime and transgression within everyday life tends to integrate the researcher into the local community, putting the researcher in touch with the lives of ordinary people, and yet offering often extraordinary insights into the dynamics of those lives and communities.

In this process of human engagement cultural criminology's focus on everyday life moves beyond strategic choice and towards moral and theoretical foundation. Attempting to understand the meaning of crime and the dynamics through which this meaning is manufactured, cultural criminology draws on a constellation of theoretical orientations attuned to everyday experience. Among these are symbolic interactionism, with its emphasis on the daily transactions by which individuals create, sustain, and contest shared meaning; phenomenology, with its attentiveness to the intricate and distinctive features of everyday experience; and ethnomethodology, fine-tuned to the reflexively 'elegant knowledge' (Mehan and Wood, 1975: 117) that animates commonplace situations and events. Certainly, these rich theoretical models merit more than these few lines (Lindgren, 2005), but for present purposes we can derive from them a shared insight: *the social world cannot be understood apart from the agency of those who occupy it*. While of course working within profound limitations of political and economic exclusion, everyday people are nonetheless neither 'judgmental dopes' (Garfinkel, 1967: 67) nor calculating machines; they are agents of social reality, active interpreters of their own lives. Watching television crime news, fearing for our own safety, deciding whether to fix that broken backdoor lock, we make do as best we can – and as we do, we continue to make sense of the world around us, and so to contribute to its collective construction.

Cultural criminology's focus on everyday life becomes in this way also a form of moral politics that we might call *critical humanism*. By 'humanism', we mean simply a scholarly and moral commitment to inquire into people's lived experiences, both collective and individual (see Wilkinson, 2005). By 'critical' we mean two things. First, critical humanism signifies a willingness to critique that which we study, to unpack even the most dearly held and elegantly argued of assumptions. Put differently, a commitment to engage with people on their own terms does not mean that those terms need be uncritically accepted; appreciating the human construction of meaning, we may still judge that meaning to be inadequate, not in terms of some moral absolutism, but out of concern for what harm that constructed meaning may cause others. Second, and relatedly, critical humanism denotes an inquiry into human experience within a larger project of critique and analysis. As already suggested in the case of Mark Thatcher, we intend for cultural criminology not only to give voice to everyday accounts seldom heard, but to gather those voices into a chorus of condemnation for broad structures of violence, inequality, and exploitation. Again, the hope is to overcome the dualism of agency and structure, to link the ordinary and the exceptional, and to discard the false dichotomy between crimes large and small.

Through this work we hope also to affirm the possibilities for progressive social change within the practice of everyday life. Those eager to distinguish large crimes from small are often eager as well to distinguish large-scale political engagement from the less consequential politics of daily life. For them, Mark Thatcher matters more than other criminals precisely because he and his mum matter more politically. And indeed they do – but sometimes they don't. Sometimes progressive social change does indeed emerge from the ballot box or the mass movement, from utilizing millions of voters or millions of marchers to confront structures of social injustice. But sometimes progressive social change percolates in the little moments of everyday experience, as one small act of resistance to the daily routine, to the micro-circuits of social control, sets the stage for the next. Our tendency, then, is to believe that the future remains unwritten, to remember that revolutions often explode when least expected, and so to celebrate progressive moments where we find them. If the everyday remains a primary site for the enforcement of injustice, it remains a place of hope and resistance, too.

a day in the life

What follows is true fiction – a compilation of everyday situations and events extant in the contemporary world, here fictionalized into a single, integrated narrative. It's also a test, of you and of us. If we've managed so far to communicate some sense of the everyday and its importance, some sense of how transgression and control animate everyday life, the following account should glow with meaning as you make your way through it. In it you should discover many little windows into the unnoticed politics of day-to-day crime and control, and more than a few clues as to what shape a cultural criminology of everyday life might take. But in case we've failed so far, or in case you're about to, we'll even provide a guide. Each time you see an italicized phrase in the following narrative, you can be sure that there's more to be said about the situation it describes – and before we do say more later, you might consider for yourself what importance some inconsequential moment, some simple situation of everyday constraint or transgression, might have for a cultural criminology of our lives.

'Ah, man', he says to himself. 'I gotta get those damned curtains fixed.'

The alarm's not set to go off for another twenty minutes, and the daylight streaming in the window where the curtains hang loose has awakened him. Waking up, it still seems more like a dream for a moment, what with the morning light coming in between the decorative *black iron burglar bars*, filling the room with long shadows like some late modern *film noir*.

Hell, he figures, I'm awake. I may as well get up. Switching off the security system, he opens the front door and heads out to pick up the morning newspaper, only to find that the *Guardian Home Security System sign* planted in his front yard has been knocked over. He stoops over to get the paper, stoops again to right the sign, and heads back inside.

Since the divorce he doesn't bother much with breakfast, so after a quick bath and a cup of coffee, he gets into his business suit and heads off for a brisk walk to catch the train into the city. Arriving at the platform, realizing he left his newspaper at home, *he uses his credit card to buy another paper* and a second cup of coffee and heads to the platform. Head buried in the morning paper, reading the crime news, waiting for the train, it's just a morning like any other. He doesn't notice the *CCTV cameras* mounted on either end of the platform, or the two middle-aged fellows *trainspotting* on the platform across the way.

When he gets tired of standing and retreats to one of the few benches on the platform, though, he does notice something. *Didn't these damn benches used to be more comfortable?* Crossing and uncrossing his legs, moving from side to side, he can barely keep from sliding off as he reads the paper and waits for the train.

Once on the train it takes a minute or two to find a seat; the coach section is crowded with other morning commuters. Finding a seat, settling in, looking up, he notices across the aisle a young woman, half his age, maybe mid-twenties. When she catches his glance he looks away, but he can't help but look back. *She's dressed in a Middle Eastern-style head scarf, sleeveless Che Guevara T-shirt, long shiny necklace, short black skirt, torn fishnet stockings, and knee-high hiking boots; her arms are covered in Maori tribal tattoos. He finds her as much curious as he does attractive; now looking back at her a third time, he even finds himself a bit uneasy.* And when she catches his glance once again, frowns and shifts in her seat, he's uneasier still.

Turning to look out the train window he's able to avoid further embarrassment, but not further discomfort. The train's getting nearer the city, and the sprawl of graffiti writing on the low walls bordering the tracks is increasing. He's noticed this before, he remembers, but he still doesn't understand it: *all this wildly unreadable graffiti along the tracks, sometimes even on the bridges and control towers above the tracks.* Maybe it's the graffiti, or the girl in the odd outfit, or the crime news in the newspaper, but he's feeling unsettled, unsure of himself, even a little angry.

Turning back from the window, he's careful not to look over at the young woman, but no need; she got off the train while he was looking out the window, at the previous stop, the one just a quarter mile before his.

In fact, by now she's already made her way through the train station and out into the street. As she walks towards her job she's a bit annoyed herself, thinking about the jerk on the train, the one who kept staring at her, but she smiles when she thinks about the cylinder necklace swinging from her neck as she walks. It's her favourite, the one her boyfriend gave her for dealing with guys like the one on the train: the *Pepperface Palm Defender pepper spray necklace.* Really, she'd have been happy with the plain silver one, or even the 18-carat gold version, but it was her birthday and he wanted to impress her, so he got her the top of the line: the one encrusted with Swarovski crystals. And besides, it looks cool with the Che shirt.

Since she started working at the *Starbucks* last year, she's walked this route hundreds of times, and to fight off the boredom and the dread of getting to work, she's made a game of seeing how many different graffiti tags she can spot. She's seen some of them so many times, on so many walls and alleyways, she feels like she knows the writers who leave them. *Scanning one alley for tags as she cuts through it, she notices two broken second-floor windows and laughs to herself – side by side like that, with the big jagged holes in each one, they look like two big bloodshot eyes staring back at her.* And come to think of it, *after last night's binge drinking session down at the pub,* her eyes are probably a little bloodshot, too; once she gets to work, she tells herself, she'll grab a coffee while the manager isn't looking.

She checks her watch, afraid she'll be late for work again, and picks up her pace. Problem is, she used to have *a couple of shortcuts* – through the park by the school, and then through the little passageway between the grocery store and the mobile phone shop – *but now the park gate stays locked most days, and somebody has planted a prickly hedge between the two shops.*

By the time she gets to work – ten minutes late – the guy from the train has already been at his desk for twenty minutes, having grabbed a cab out front of his train station. He's hard at the first task of the day, the first task of every work day: clearing emails from his inbox. *Pornographic come-ons, African money transfers, spurious bank requests for credit card information* – the company's spam filter isn't working very well. But what the hell he thinks, while checking out a couple of the porn websites and deleting emails, *the company monitors employee keystrokes as a way of checking up on productivity,* so for all they know I'm working. What he doesn't know is that *the company also monitors and tracks web usage,* and as the corporate data log shows, this isn't his first visit to a porn site on company time.

Not that he really cares. Since the company began downsizing operations and exporting positions overseas, he's figured it's only a matter of time until his position goes away as well. It's bad enough to sit in front of a computer all day, *bored out of your mind*, without having to worry about whether you'll be back to do it tomorrow. Deep in debt as well, he's starting to feel a little lost. No wife, one of these days no job, nothing but bills to pay – makes a man miss the good times, *like that last holiday they had before the divorce, when the two of them flew to Spain, and the tour guides kidnapped them and marched them into the mountains of Andalusia.*

Daydreaming about Andalusia and deleting unsolicited emails kills off the first hour of work, filling out the online forms for the company's upcoming internal audit kills another, and now it's time for a mid-morning coffee break. Before the downsizing started, there was always a pot of coffee down in the break room; you put a few coins in the donation jar and got yourself a cup of coffee, maybe had a chat with a colleague.

These days he goes to the Starbucks across the street from the office, but just for a change, he decides to walk to the Starbucks a block over. Bad decision, since the young woman in the Che T-shirt works behind the counter there – except that she too has clocked out for a quick mid-morning break. No Starbucks coffee for her – she needs something stronger. She's looking for Cocaine.

'Hey', she says to the clerk in the little convenience store in the next block, walking back towards the check-out counter from the cold case. '*Where's the Cocaine?*'

'We're out', he tells her, his accent betraying his Iraqi heritage. 'Since they had it on *The Daily Show* we can't keep it in stock. Should have some tomorrow. Sorry.'

'OK, well, thanks', and she's headed back to work – may as well just sneak another cup of company coffee.

His trip to the Starbucks hasn't gone any better. Sure, he got his usual – double decaf latte – and it was as good as the one he gets at the other Starbucks. Identical, in fact. But then he went over to the little park across the street to sit and enjoy it, and ... *Damn it, another ball-buster of a bench. Is there no decent place to sit left in this city?*

Then, shifting uncomfortably on the bench and slurping his latte, all hell breaks loose. *This guy in a car tosses some fast food out into the street. A female bike courier grabs the food and tosses it back in, yelling 'don't litter in my neighbourhood'. He jumps out, throws two coffees at her, and now he's stomping on her bike and they start scuffling. Some guys come off the sidewalk and pull him off of her. Meanwhile another dude with a camera just keeps shooting – but when he tries to photograph the car's licence plate, the guy from the car opens the trunk, grabs a baseball bat, and charges him.*

Christ, he thinks to himself, the whole damn world is falling apart. It's like that film with Michael Douglas, you know, that American actor who was in *that other film where the woman tries to kill him. But in this one he's lost his job and people are messing with him and trying to rob him and ... what's the name of that film?*

Back at the office he Googles for awhile, trying to track down the film title – more internet misuse for the company log. Giving up, he begrudgingly gets back to the audit forms, which drag him through the afternoon in a sort of slow death march towards quitting time.

At the Starbucks, a steady stream of latte and espresso orders has dragged her through the afternoon as well, but with at least a bit of excitement. Around three o'clock she got suspicious of these two girls lingering near the counter; one of them had an open book bag, and it looked to her like they were trying to shoplift the newest Starbucks music CD. *So she and the assistant manager went out from behind the counter, smiling and asking the girls if they could help them with anything, and then kept chatting with them until they left the store.* And as the girls left, she noticed something else: *a little black orb attached to the book bag.*

Work day over, she's walking back to the train station when she notices that *the FCUK (French Connection UK) clothing store has changed its display window since she walked past this morning. It now features skinny female mannequins, dressed in the latest FCUK designs, shoving and throwing punches at each other.*

Backing away from the window to get a better look at the tableau of stylized sex and violence, she bumps into someone behind her and turns around.

Son of a bitch, it's that jerk from the train this morning! The FCUK window fresh in her mind, scared and mad that maybe he's been stalking her all day, a bit embarrassed for bumping into him, she reaches for her Pepperface pepper spray necklace, fumbles with it for a moment, gets her finger on to the spray button – but by this time he's backpedaling, arms out, palms up, saying, 'sorry, sorry' – and in a flash he's disappeared into the crowd on the sidewalk.

Disappeared into the crowd indeed – he couldn't be more mortified. To be honest, yeah, he'd been fantasizing a little while looking at those sexy mannequins in the FCUK window, and then all of sudden that girl from the train – a real girl, the real girl he had checked out on the train this morning – was right in his face. Very weird moment, very scary, very embarrassing – and it wasn't the first odd moment on the walk back to the train station from work. *There was also that bus stop shelter with the big speech bubbles pasted over the advertisements – or were those part of the ads?*

Calming down, getting to the train station, checking his electronic organizer, he's reminded that Friday is his ex-wife's birthday; their daughter lives with her, so he still likes to stay in touch. Early for the train, he dips into the Hallmark card shop in the arcade next door. Browsing the cards, he can't find one he likes, but then he spots a card that, well, just seems perfect for her, for their fucked up relationship, and for the day he's had. 'So, anyway, I'm standing in line to buy a freakin' birthday card', the cover of the card begins, 'and the line is like seventeen billion people long....'

After a few more verses of this, the cover concludes with 'and I just really hope you like this card'.

Plate 4.1 FCUK shop window, Canterbury, England
Credit: Photographs Jeff Ferrell and Keith Hayward (2006)

And then when you open the card, inside it says, *'Cause I stole it. Happy Birthday'.*

That gets him laughing a little, and on the train ride home he relaxes and realizes he's hungry, so he buys a prawn sandwich and a Coke – but, he thinks to himself, I'd better not let that vegan punk daughter of mine know about the sandwich. *According to her, even a damn prawn sandwich is a crime.*

So when he gets off the train at his local station, he's careful to toss the uneaten half of the sandwich and the Coke can into the station trash receptacle – and *not five minutes later one of the many dishevelled folks who hang around the station is just as careful to extricate from the trash the half sandwich, the Coke can – and a brand new designer scarf.*

On the walk home he's still thinking about his daughter – worrying about her, that is. *It's bad enough she got that ASBO slapped on her last year for yelling animal-rights slogans at the McDonald's assistant manager; now she's in trouble at school as well. Last month, the school counsellor advised him and his ex-wife that his daughter* seems driven to take risks, to push her own limits, to test herself and her teachers. The counsellor even told them that the school psychologist had diagnosed his daughter as suffering from *ODD, Oppositional Defiant Disorder*, a pathological disregard for school and parental authority. Wait a minute, he thinks to himself, maybe that explains the girl on the train, the one who confronted him in front of the FCUK window – maybe she has ODD, too. But back to his daughter: after he heard all this from the school counsellor, he got so concerned that he bought his daughter a new cell phone, one with a GPS device so he could track her movements. But that only ended up worrying him more – one time he tracked her down across town at some sort of illegal street race. One of these days, he worries to himself, I'm going to find her with *that bunch of damn 'chavs' that hangs out down at the end of the road*.

Home now, he heats some leftovers and plops down in his big easy chair, surfing TV channels while he eats. *It's the same old stuff – CSI: Crime Scene Investigation, Law and Order: Criminal Intent, Cold Case, Without a Trace* – but it keeps him occupied for a couple of hours, anyway.

He's still thinking about his daughter, though, worried about her ODD, so before bed he gets on the Web. That first site that comes up, ADD ADHD Advances (http://addadhdadvances.com/) is run by Anthony Kane, MD, who notes that he is an author and lecturer on such disorders, and 'the parent of several children with ADD ADHD and Oppositional Defiant Disorder'. The website looks promising. It asks 'Is Your Child's Bickering, Tantrums, and Defiant Behaviour Embarrassing You, Destroying Your Home, and Making You Feel Like a Failure as a Parent?' and 'Who Else Wants to *End* Their Child's Fighting, Arguing, and Talking Back Once and for All?', and offers an answer: Dr Kane's treatment programme, 'based upon universal principles of human nature. It doesn't matter what country you live in.' Better yet, while he's scrolling through the site, a pop-up ad appears: 'Congratulations. You Are Invited To Enroll In A Free Course, How To Control Your Defiant Child.'

He's reassured; maybe there's hope for his daughter after all. So after taking two of those sleeping pills they advertise on TV, reactivating the home alarm system, setting his bedside alarm, and falling into bed, he's able to drift off to sleep easily enough. But then the nightmare comes. It's not that half-awake *film noir* moment he had this morning; its worse, a surreal mashup of a day in the life. It's some kind of funeral, with everyone sitting around the coffin on tiny, hard benches. Fast-food wrappers and coffee cups cover the ground, cover the feet of the mourners, crawl up their legs. And there's his daughter, away from everyone else, dressed in a head scarf and a long shiny necklace, kneeling before some sort of coffee cup memorial. But wait a minute, now he's the memorial, he's covered in coffee cups, and he's in the coffin, his head split clean in two by the blow from a baseball bat. And the girl from the train, she's dead too, lying next to him in the coffin.

Except she's not dead. She made it home just like he did, and now she's asleep next to her boyfriend. They went to bed early. Just out after doing six months on a marijuana possession charge, he has to make an 8 am appointment with his parole supervisor, and she has her 9 am cultural criminology class at the university. She's majoring in criminology, and helping to pay tuition with the Starbuck's job – though she's still managing to run up one hell of a student loan debt.

In fact, she's dreaming too, her dream mixing her boyfriend and her major. *In the dream she's reaching for him, trying to pull him through some sort of wall, but she can't keep her grip and he fades away, receding into the innards of the American penal gulag, disappearing into the crowd of two million other prisoners for whom a day in the life is something very different indeed.*

interrogating the everyday

Just another day in the life of two people making their way between home and work; a little unpleasantness here and there, some petty criminality – but nothing of any importance, no real violence, no crimes of politics or passion, no big police crime sweep through a dangerous neighbourhood. So to tell such a story, and to pay attention to it, is to stay safely away from the big issues of crime and social control, tucked securely inside the cultural minutia of the mundane.

Or is it? A cultural criminology of the story – that is, an interrogation of the story in search of meaning – reveals something more. Carefully considered, this story – constructed, it will be recalled, only from existing everyday events – in fact reveals global shifts and historical trends monumental in their meaning. If we look carefully, we can see the ways in which transgression increasingly comes to be commodified and contained within late capitalist economies. We can see something of social control, and the way in which contemporary mechanisms of social control are morphed, masked, coded, and reinvented. We can notice that these forms of social control, already troublesome in their insidiousness, are in turn cut and mixed with emerging patterns of legal containment and surveillance – and then, for good measure, marketed to the public under the guise of public safety, even freedom of choice. If we look carefully enough we may even see the future – and decide, as have others, to confront it.

Black iron burglar bars

Guardian Home Security System sign

From the view of cultural criminology, burglar bars and home security systems provide more than a hardened home target; they offer evidence of the pervasive, politically useful late modern fear of victimization by outsiders and invaders. They also provide everyday evidence of the billion-dollar home security industries that promote, and profit, from precisely this fear (Hayward, 2004: 128–137).

Home security signs, burglar bars, high fences, and other domestic fortifications also become signs in another sense, constructing the home as a text to be 'read' by neighbours, passers-by, and potential intruders. The 'angry lawns' and armed homesteads that Mike Davis (1990) documents betray the modernist mythology of domesticity, of the home as a pleasant refuge from the dislocated stress of everyday life.

And yet even fear and fortification are not without their aesthetics. In the USA, home security businesses seldom advertise 'burglar bars'; instead, they advertise and sell *decorative* burglar bars that can, as one real estate website notes, 'enhance, or at least not detract from, the appearance of the home' (www.real-estate-agents.com).

Film noir

The deeply unsettled years following World War II saw the emergence of new cinematic forms that presented the promise of a 'good society' ambiguously at best. In Europe and Great Britain cinematic neo-realism emerged as a stark counterpoint to romantic film traditions. In the United States, *film noir* ('black film') offered its own sort of realism: a disturbingly blurred vision of crime and justice. While uncertain morality and unclear identity pervaded the films' plots, the shadowy spaces and dark corners of *film noir*'s cinematography also suggested something far more sinister than the old-fashioned search for truth and justice. In more than one scene, stark outside light cuts through Venetian blinds to cast long, sharp shadows around the film's protagonists – shadows symbolizing *film noir*'s sense of existential entrapment and social claustrophobia. This aesthetic stylization of crime, and this particular *sensibility* about crime, continues as a reference point for filmmakers, artists, and writers.

He uses his credit card to buy another paper

Under the coordinated corporate conditions of late modernity, the simplest of credit card purchases adds information to a massive, integrated web of databases harbouring information on consumer preferences, population movement, and personal habits. Significantly, such databases not only enable corporate surveillance of individuals, but accumulate information tapped by legal authorities as part of the 'war on terror' or other social control campaigns. As Katja Franko-Aas (2006) has shown, even the human body becomes a source of information and surveillance under such conditions, what with DNA databases, biometric passports, and mandatory drug testing.

Nathan Garvis, vice president of government affairs at Target, one of America's largest retailers, recently offered an unusually candid account of the logic underlying this surveillance process. Assigned by Target to explore possibilities for helping the criminal justice system become more efficient, Garvis came to realize that tracking criminals 'was really an inventory-management problem'. So, tapping into Target's already widespread affiliations with law enforcement, the company donated 'tracking technology and database translation', and began to take 'a lead role in teaching government agencies how to fight crime by applying state-of-the-art technology used in its 1,400 stores'. Today, the company also 'donates' its employees to law enforcement agencies, provides money to prosecutor's offices, coordinates police undercover operations, and does extensive pro bono work for local, state, federal, and international law enforcement agencies. Much of this work occurs at the company's own state-of-the-art forensics lab – 'one of the nation's top forensics labs', according to FBI Special Agent Paul McCabe. Target likewise runs a 'Safe City' programme that 'uses video and computer equipment to help police patrol neighbourhoods by remote control, coordinated with security workers at participating businesses' (Bridges, 2006: A1).

Seamlessly interweaving inventory control with social control, Target translates both the ideology and technology of corporate consumerism into the practice of late-modern policing. And just as distinctions between product and person are lost, so are the rights of the accused and the presumption of innocence, with Target apparently feeling no compulsion to make similar donations to defence attorneys, public defenders, or databases tracking the wrongly convicted. 'Fascism' isn't a word we use lightly – but certainly this is late-modern fascism, consumer fascism, an incestuous integration of corporate control and political authority in the interest of tracking individuals and constructing cities safe for consumption.

Soon, perhaps Target's databases will even be able to make the consumers run on time.

CCTV cameras

The United Kingdom is the undisputed leader in urban closed-circuit television provision, or CCTV (see Wakefield, 2003), with more surveillance cameras in the UK than in the rest of Europe combined. As a result, many people in the UK accept the intrusion of panoptic camera technology into everyday life. With CCTV seeping into virtually every aspect of day-to-day life, though, a cultural transformation is taking place; surveillance is becoming not just commonplace and acceptable, but cool, fashionable, even aspirational. CCTV is now used by everyone from artists (see, for example, the surveillance-inspired works of Julia Scher and Marko Peljhan) to advertisers (a recent jeans promotion asked, 'You are on a video camera ten times a day. Are you dressed for it?'), restaurant and bar designers, and prime-time TV shows like *Big Brother* or *Real World*.

Here we see an emerging relationship between society and surveillance, a relationship that transcends the 'feel good' sensations of safety and reassurance associated with established security products, while consigning civil liberty anxieties to the obsolescent register of early modernity. This is a world where *Big Brother* is only ironic and *Real World* just unreal, a world where non-stop surveillance becomes a source of pleasure, profit, and entertainment (Hayward, 2004).

Yet while cameras may add a sense of voyeuristic or performative satisfaction to the 'lifestyle' social environment, they alone cannot build closely-knit communities or vibrant, pluralistic public spaces. On this point it is interesting to reflect on the differing approaches to CCTV in the UK and continental Europe. In the UK, CCTV is typically the first step in attempting to 'galvanize' run-down communities, an approach that illustrates the extent to which regulation has been resituated as 'community', or more accurately a form of sanitized inclusion. Meanwhile in countries like Italy and Spain, where community and family ties remain strong in regional towns, the demand for surveillance is almost non-existent.

Trainspotting

In Great Britain, and to a somewhat lesser extent in the United States, 'trainspotting' – hanging around train stations, recording and compiling the specifics of various locomotives as they move about the country – has long been a hobby associated with a certain middle-brow, mundane lifestyle. With the release of the 1996 British film *Trainspotting* (Dir. Danny Boyle) – a film exploring the lives of Edinburgh heroin addicts – the term took on another layer of meaning, and perhaps a certain ironic caché.

Now, amidst the 'war on terror', new layers of political and criminal meaning have been added. In the UK, trainspotters have been identified as a security risk, and in some cases removed from train platforms. In contrast, United States officials have attempted to enlist trainspotters in the war on terror, utilizing their penchant for watchfulness as yet another form of everyday surveillance.

Didn't these damn benches used to be more comfortable?

Yes, they did. As part of the CPTED (Crime Prevention Through Environmental Design) strategy in the United States, and similar strategies of spatial crime-control in the UK and elsewhere, public spaces are regularly remade as less comfortable and less welcoming to those who might linger, or loiter, or fail to consume, or commit a public offence. These strategies include rebuilding public seating in ways that disincline long-term sitting and prevent reclining. In this way ideologies of control, surveillance, and exclusion come to be built, quite literally, into the everyday environment.

She's dressed in a Middle Eastern-style head scarf, sleeveless Che Guevara T-shirt, long shiny necklace, short black skirt, torn fishnet stockings, and knee-high hiking boots; her arms are covered in Maori tribal tattoos. He finds her as much curious as he does attractive; now looking back at her a third time, he even finds himself a bit uneasy

The liquidity of late modernity, the global flow of production and consumption, can be glimpsed in the bricolage of styles that constitute everyday 'fashion', and especially 'street fashion' as invented and displayed in large metropolitan areas.

Under such conditions, meaning comes loose from its original moorings; specific styles and images re-emerge as free-floating references to be re-sewn into individual and group style. Che Guevara, the 1950s Latin American revolutionary, has long since been reborn as cultural icon and fashion accessory; along London's trendy Kensington High Street in the 1980s, the *Che* clothing shop sold the latest in mass-marketed apparel, and today *The Che Store* (www.thechestore.com) markets T-shirts and berets 'for all your revolutionary needs'.

This late modern mélange of meaning is not without its consequences. In what remains the definitive analysis of such stylized displays, Dick Hebdige (1979: 90) cautions us not to 'underestimate the signifying power of the spectacular subculture ... as an actual mechanism of semantic disorder: a kind of temporary blockage in the system of representation'. So while her outfit evacuates the political meaning of Latin American revolutionaries or Maori tattoos, it nonetheless retains the power to cause uneasiness, even upheaval, for those who witness it – or attempt to police it.

Still, those Maori tattoos do constitute, on closer inspection, a particularly spectacular fraud. They're actually not tattoos at all, but rather part of custom clothing marketed by Canadian fashion designer Susan Setz. 'Blending funky fashion with traditional and modern art', she has invented a line of sheer mesh tattooed shirts and sleeves whose invisibility fools the observer into thinking that their wearer is indeed tattooed.

Criminologist Wayne Morrison (2004b: 76) would be particularly amused by these ersatz Maori tattoos, dislocated from the Maori and even from the skin itself. As he has shown, Cesare Lombroso, founding father of criminological positivism, had already stolen away their meaning 125 years before, reducing them to 'the true writing of the savage' and equating them – erroneously – with common criminality.

All this wildly unreadable graffiti along the tracks, sometimes even on the bridges and control towers above the tracks

Graffiti is surely one of the most pervasive and visible crimes of late modernity, decorating and defacing walls, buildings and bridges throughout the USA, South America, Great Britain, Europe, the Middle East, and elsewhere. Its forms are as varied as the subcultures of those who write it. Looking out a train window in New York City, or London, or Amsterdam, a passenger might well see the angry graffiti of neo-Nazis, the political graffiti of anti-gentrification activists or the anti-globalization movement, love-struck marks of personal affection, symbolic threats issued from one gang to another – even the 'reverse graffiti' of those who write on city surfaces by selectively wiping accumulated soot from them. Entangled on walls and buildings, these various forms of graffiti make for yet another mélange of uncertain meaning, encoding urban space with the pluralism of late modern life. But amidst this swarm of signification, a few things are likely, though not certain:

If our train passenger found the graffiti particularly unreadable, it was probably hip hop graffiti ('graff'), a highly stylized form of public painting through which graffiti 'writers' compete and communicate.

If the graffiti was written on a bridge or tower high above the tracks, it was likely a residue of 'tagging the heavens', a hip hop graffiti practice of writing graffiti in high and highly inaccessible spots so as to gain visibility and status.

If our passenger did get a bit angry or uneasy upon seeing graffiti, that was likely mostly the result of mediated anti-graffiti campaigns that work to define the *meaning* of graffiti by intentionally confounding gang graffiti with other graffiti forms, and by associating graffiti with violent assault and rape (Ferrell, 1996).

And if our passenger thinks, as some do (Halsey and Young, 2006: 293), that graffiti writers 'are not edgeworkers' and ready lawbreakers – and moreover, that this argument *against* cultural criminology can be made by actually *incorporating* many of its key findings (Ferrell, 1995, 1996, 2001/2) without acknowledgement – we'll simply say that, among graffiti writers, stealing someone's style is called *biting*.

And we'll add a closing comment from Earsnot, 'a big, black homosexual' as his friends describe him, out and proud, and a founding member of top New York City hip hop graffiti crew IRAK – a crew name that plays on the graffiti slang for stealing ('racking'), and of course on a certain Middle East situation. 'One of the things I always say', says Earsnot, 'is that a really good graffiti writer will make a good shoplifter – someone who's used to breaking the law fifteen or twenty times a day' (in Levy, 2007: 4).

Then again, as we'll see in the next chapter, all that track-side graffiti could just as well be corporate advertisement.

Dazed and confused

We might hope that the authors of criminological textbooks devoted to the scholarly analysis of juvenile delinquency would clarify distinctions lost in the media-induced confusion over the types and consequences of youthful graffiti. Put differently, we might hope that students of criminology would come to know more about urban graffiti than the average train rider or newspaper reader. In most cases, that hope would be unfounded. In fact, far from addressing such issues, many juvenile delinquency textbooks perpetuate the confusion – and display their confusion on their covers for all to see.

One 1990s textbook presents on its cover what appears to be an image of early hip hop graffiti, circa 1980 or so – but it's difficult to know since hip hop graffiti doesn't appear in the table of contents, text, or index (Jensen and Rojek, 1992). Bynum and Thompson's mid-1990s (1996: 288–90, 473) *Juvenile Delinquency: A Sociological Approach* likewise offers the student a cover apparently composed of computer-generated graffiti-style markings; inside is a short section dealing only with gang graffiti, and a glossary entry that defines 'graffiti' exclusively as 'the distinctive language/ symbolism of street gangs...'. By the seventh edition a decade later (Bynum and Thompson, 2007), a new, more stylish cover reproduces a section of a hip hop graffiti mural, the book's front page shows another sophisticated mural, chapter introductions and summaries repeat these hip hop images – and the errors of the text and glossary remain unchanged. The fifth edition of Bartollas's (2000) *Juvenile Delinquency* features as its cover an aesthetically stunning wall of multi-coloured hip hop graffiti murals and tags – and no mention whatsoever of hip hop graffiti in the table of contents, text, glossary, or index. The more recent seventh edition (Bartollas, 2006: 112, 134) has replaced this cover with a drawing of young man holding a spray can and painting a wall of non-specific graffiti. Inside, the book includes a photo of a young man painting hip hop graffiti, as an illustration of 'destruction of property' and Cohen's 'reaction formation', another uncaptioned photo of a young Latina holding a gun in front of a wall covered in assorted tags and markings – and still, no mention of hip hop graffiti in the table of contents, text, glossary, or index.

Other recent textbooks replicate this discordance between cover and content. An image of non-specific graffiti adorns the cover of Regoli and Hewitt's (2006) *Delinquency in Society*, and is repeated as a background image inside the book, yet the book neither explores nor indexes youthful graffiti. The covers of both Struckhoff's (2006) *Annual Editions: Juvenile Delinquency and Justice* and Burfeind and Bartusch's (2006) *Juvenile Delinquency* present a young man with a spray can in front of hip hop-style graffiti, but neither manages to integrate an analysis of hip hop graffiti into the book itself. Schmalleger and Bartollas's (2008) *Juvenile Delinquency* comes with a cover featuring a darkly atmospheric photograph of hip hop graffiti murals painted on trains. From the look of the trains and the graffiti, it might be New York City or Philadelphia in 1980, maybe London five years later, but we'll never know – the book omits graffiti from its table of contents, text, and index. Most dramatically, Whitehead and Lab's (2006: 125) *Juvenile Justice* wraps a spectacular example of a hip hop graffiti mural around both its front and back cover, literally encasing the book in an explosion of hip hop style and colour, and then fails spectacularly to engage with its own image. Out of its 472 pages of text, the book dedicates five lines to graffiti, under the heading 'Gang Behavior and Types of Gangs'.

We well understand that textbook cover decisions are made as much by publishers as by authors; as Burns and Katovich (2006: 111) noted in their study of melodramatic images in introductory criminal justice texts, 'the highly competitive textbook market ... influences textbook design'. Yet these graffiti covers, when affixed to books that consistently fail to address the complexity of graffiti forms – that in many cases fail to address youthful graffiti at all – constitute a form of intellectual fraud. It's not only that the books fail to deliver what their covers promise; in many cases, by juxtaposing hip hop graffiti images with discussions of gang graffiti, they reinforce the very misperceptions we might hope they would dispel. Ironically, while the repeated use of such covers tacitly acknowledges the aesthetic power of hip hop graffiti to startle and engage, the texts turn away from this engagement, ignoring the most publicly visible and aesthetically meaningful form of juvenile delinquency. Having mischaracterized graffiti in both image and analysis, Bynum and Thompson (1996: 228; 2007: 347) note that 'an understanding of graffiti is very important to law enforcement officers...'.

It's very important to students, too.

Pepperface Palm Defender pepper spray necklace

'We've heard all the stats about rape and other violent attacks', writes Alyson Ward (2006: 3G) in a recent newspaper article breathlessly endorsing the new Pepperface Palm Defender, 'But how many of us are really carrying around a clunky canister of pepper spray?'

The solution is the Palm Defender. Its manufacturer, Ward explains, 'is turning personal safety into fashion … In fact, it hopes we'll start to think of it the way we think of our cell phones or MP3 players – as a useful *and* pretty necessity we carry everywhere.' Best of all, 'one shot will incapacitate an attacker for at least half an hour. Which gives you a chance to run, girl'.

Of course, if Ward had *really* read the stats, she'd remind her readers that the most important place to wear the Palm Defender would be around the house, since women remain far more likely to be victimized by acquaintances or intimate partners than by strangers. But no matter – the real issue here is the aesthetic consumption of crime prevention. No unsightly bulges from clunky cans of pepper spray or large concealed weapons – the stylishly hardened target prefers the Palm Defender, or maybe one of the smaller, sleeker handguns that American weapons manufacturers now market to women, the 'smaller, lighter, jazzed up guns for girls' that sport fine detailing and 24-carat gold gilding (Ulrich, 2006).

Coming soon to a shop near you: the new line of ultra-slender stilettos for the stylish woman – and we don't mean high heels.

You go, girl.

Starbucks

A cultural criminology of Starbucks would require a book of its own; here we'll offer just a sketch.

As a key player in the homogenization and globalization of American consumer culture, Starbucks undermines local economies and undercuts the vitality of locally-owned coffee shops; as such, it abets the larger globalizing process by which local economic autonomy is eroded, and through which distinctive neighbourhood cultures are replaced by marketed ideologies of convenience and predictability. Moreover, as Steve Hall and Simon Winlow (2005; see also Winlow and Hall, 2006) have shown, this process of corporate encroachment weakens traditional urban communities, leaving them more vulnerable to unemployment, absentee ownership, and predation among those disaffiliated from long-standing social bonds. Not surprisingly, then, anti-globalization and human rights activists target Starbucks outlets for protest, and in some cases symbolic vandalism. In addition, the Industrial Workers of the World (IWW) – a militant union known a century ago for organizing low-wage and itinerant workers – has now begun organizing a new generation of young, low-wage, transient Starbucks' workers. While the IWW has employed tactics of direct, disruptive action inside Starbucks outlets, and has successfully filed complaints with the US National Labor Relations Board (NLRB) over unfair labour practices, it has also confronted Starbucks on the turf of corporate image-making. 'We're going to escalate our outreach to workers', says 27 year-old IWW organizer Daniel Gross, 'and pierce the socially responsible image that the company has so skillfully promulgated around the world' (in Maher and Adamy, 2006: B6).

Weakened local communities, protests and vandalism, NLRB cases and unfair labour practices add up to a question or two. Is Starbucks criminogenic? And when you buy that overpriced latte at your 'local' Starbucks, are you also buying into a pattern of corporate globalization that victimizes communities and, as the IWW might say, undermines your 'fellow workers'?

Scanning one alley for tags as she cuts through it, she notices two broken second-floor windows and laughs to herself – side by side like that, with the big jagged holes in each one, they look like two big bloodshot eyes staring back at her

Actually, she shouldn't be laughing – at least not according to one popular criminological model.

Perhaps the most politically prominent approach to crime over the last few decades has been Wilson and Kelling's (2003 [1982]: 402–4) 'broken windows' model of crime causation. Utilized as the scholarly reference point for a range of reactionary, punitive public policing strategies since its emergence in the 1980s, 'broken windows' is often seen as a straight-ahead, no-nonsense approach to crime control. In reality, it is a deeply *aesthetic* analysis of crime's etiology – and a deeply flawed analysis as well. According to this model, broken windows and similar public displays of neglect and petty criminality function as symbolic invitations to further criminality, in that they 'signal that no one cares', or perhaps 'seem to signal that "no one cares"'. Likewise, 'such otherwise harmless displays as subway graffiti' communicate to subway riders 'the "inescapable knowledge that the environment … is uncontrolled and uncontrollable …"'. In such cases, Wilson and Kelling argue, 'residents will think that crime … is on the rise', potential criminals will perceive these signs of inattention as encouragements to accelerated misbehaviour, and a downward spiral of disorder will be set in motion. Claiming in this way to engage issues of image, public display and perception, 'broken windows' stands or falls on its aesthetic analysis of crime.

It falls.

A useful justification for the conservative clampdown on everyday 'quality of life' crimes like graffiti writing and panhandling, a pseudo-theoretical pretext for aggressively policing marginalized urban populations the model is decidedly less useful as an aesthetic of crime. Imagining the contours of symbolism and perception rather than investigating them, the model constructs a series of abstract, one-dimensional meanings that it arbitrarily assigns to dislocated images and idealized audiences. In fact, as any city-dweller knows, the symbolic texture of the urban landscape is far more ambiguous and complex. To the extent that 'broken windows' function as symbols, for example, they may symbolize any manner of activities to any number of audiences, depending on situation and context: community resistance to absentee ownership, a long-standing personal grudge, the failure of local code enforcement, or the illicit accommodation of the homeless. Likewise, depending on particularities of content and context, gang graffiti may symbolize a neighbourhood's intergenerational history, suggest changing patterns of ethnic occupation or conflict, or even enforce a degree of community self-policing. A proliferation of hip hop graffiti in place of gang graffiti (a distinction ignored by Wilson and Kelling) may likewise suggest a *decline* in criminal violence – that is, it may lead some neighbourhood residents to understand that gang crime is on the decline – and in fact may harbinger a less violent social order now negotiated through the very symbols that Wilson and Kelling so tellingly misrepresent (Sanchez-Tranquilino, 1995; Ferrell, 1996; Phillips, 1999; D. Miller, 2001; Snyder, 2007).

So a man on a train may find a display of graffiti perplexing, a woman on the way to work may find alleyway graffiti intriguing or broken windows amusing, and others will engage still different perceptions of the urban environment. As cultural criminologists, our job is to investigate this environment and these perceptions, to explore these various meanings – not, as with Wilson and Kelling, to impose our own constipated perceptions in the service of the state.

After last night's binge drinking session at the pub

In recent years 'binge drinking' has emerged as a powerful force in the modelling of a transgressive British stereotype (Hayward and Hobbs, 2007). While press and politicians have been quick to taint drunken kids as 'binge drinkers', less has been made of the wider economic imperative behind so-called 'beer towns' and the 'Nighttime Economy' more generally (Hobbs et al., 2005). Recent governmental policies have facilitated the expansion of local nighttime economies based almost exclusively on the commodification of hedonism and alcohol-related excess. In a bid to 'regenerate' flagging post-industrial cities, the government has encouraged the drinks industry to restructure city centres by compressing alcohol outlets, increasing licensing capacity, and re-zoning areas into 24/7 operations. At the same time, the drinks industry has dramatically changed the way it markets alcohol, switching its focus to younger drinkers and drawing on motifs from the 'dance' and 'rave' scenes in a bid to tap into new psychoactive consumption styles. As Measham and Brain (2005: 266–76) point out, this new willingness to experiment with altered states of intoxication represents a new and distinct 'postmodern alcohol order', characterized by a penchant for increased sessional consumption and a desire for liminal experimentation.

While governmental ministers dreamt of a sophisticated nocturnal café society, they unintentionally created monocultural urban spaces comprised of homogeneous theme bars, branded pubs, and fast-food outlets. Within these environments aggressive hedonism and disorder were rife, with violent 'hot spots' found among concentrations of late-night bars. Rather than blame their own policies, though, the government blamed the 'binge drinker'; after all, pointing the finger at the consumer was easier than examining the government's morally dubious relationship with the UK drinks industry, or endangering the immense tax revenues that that industry generates. So, desperate to keep the drinks industry satisfied and the revenues flowing in, the government has transformed hundreds of town centres into dystopian drunk-fests: brutal, instrumental urban sites of alcohol-driven excess and violence (Winlow and Hall, 2006).

Not to worry, though: with town centres awash in drunkenness and violence, local governments are responding by rolling out CCTV cameras at unprecedented rates – so at least the next time someone projectile vomits on your parked car, or shoves a fist in your face, it will be seen on videotape by a poorly paid rent-a-cop in a control bunker five miles away! This slice of late-modern culture represents 'the perfect image of the ruling economic order, ends are nothing and development is all – although the only thing into which the spectacle plans to develop is itself' (Debord, cited in Hayward and Hobbs, 2007: 443).

A couple of shortcuts … but now the park gate stays locked most days, and somebody has planted a prickly hedge between the two shops

In the late capitalist city, public spaces – parks, city squares, play areas – are increasingly privatized in the interest of economic development and social control; as Randall Amster (2004) has shown, even city sidewalks are made private, and so made unavailable for public activity. Similarly, that new prickly hedge wasn't the gardener's idea; it was most likely suggested by the environmental design security consultant or the neighbourhood police officer. Among today's environmental strategies for regulating human movement in urban areas is 'barrier planting' (Ferrell, 2001/2: 5–6) – the planting of shrubs and bushes with the potential to impale those who might seek out shortcuts. As it turns out, the politics of the everyday are present even in the flora.

Pornographic come-ons, African money transfers, spurious bank requests for credit card information

The sociologist Gary Marx (1995) has noted that 'new telecommunications technologies require new manners'. With each new advance in the technology of mediated communication, a new *culture* of communication must emerge as well, a new set of interactional codes and symbolic manners appropriate to the technology. The structural grammar of the written letter gives way to the casual speed of email; the expectation of response generated by the phone message differs from that of an email message; the symbolic codes of the instant message compress and abbreviate in relation to the compressed size and speed of the technology itself.

New technologies require new crimes as well, and new crime cultures. A mailed letter offering easy cash offers one kind of enticement, an email message promising an African money transfer another. With the email and its attachment, the recipient's information can be phished more deeply and more quickly – if only the sender can utilize appropriate symbols and markers so as to convince the recipient of honest intentions, or emergency need. Of course the intended victims of such crimes themselves learn new manners, new safeguards against identity theft or consumer fraud, from their own experience and from each other.

We might even say that every technology gets the crime it deserves.

The company monitors employee keystrokes as a way of checking up on productivity … the company also monitors and tracks web usage

New technologies spawn new forms of control, too – forms of surveillance today built into advancing communication technologies as surely as spatial controls are built into the reconstructed social environment. Among these are hard-drive searches, keystroke monitors, 'spyware', and screen-view software, enabling remote viewing of a computer screen in real time. 'However, as with all forms of surveillance', Richard Jones (2000, 2005) notes, 'the more knowledgeable the person (potentially) under surveillance is about the surveillance practices likely to be used against them, the more strategies they can employ to try to evade surveillance.'

Bored out of your mind

As we've documented elsewhere (Ferrell, 2004a), boredom seems one of the definitive experiences of late modernity; kids complain of it, workers hunker down and endure it, and activists of all sorts cite it as the condition against which they agitate and organize. Built into the assembly line and office cubicle as surely as the fast-food outlet and the school curriculum, boredom pervades the everyday operations of a rationalized social order. Even those avenues that promise an escape from the tedium of the everyday – televised entertainments, new music releases, theme parks and adventure tours – themselves quickly become routine, ultimately little more than predictable packages of commodified experience.

In this sense boredom calibrates, second by awful second, the experience of drudgery in the late modern world. As a cultural artifact, it likewise measures the gap between the late modern promise of fulfilling work and the reality of a deskilled service economy, the gap between the breathless marketing of individual excitement and the delivery of fast-fried McEmotions. From a Mertonian view, boredom emerges from strain, from human expectation and experience straining against the false promises of late modernity. And as Merton (1938) would predict, this strain – this desire for desire, to paraphrase Tolstoy – can lead to all manner of illicit adaptations.

Like that last holiday they had before the divorce, when they flew to Spain, and the tour guides kidnapped them and marched them into the mountains of Andalusia

Playing on the romanticized mythology of the nineteenth-century Spanish *bandolero* (bandit), Bandeloro Tours offer full-day or half-day kidnappings, in which tourists pay to be kidnapped, taken into the Andalusia mountains, and there 'regaled with legends about great *bandeleros*' (Abend, 2006: V2) before being returned. The cost is 100 euros for a full-day kidnapping, 50 euros for a half-day.

Likewise, Mexico's Hnahnu Indians offer a *caminata nocturna* – a nighttime hike – for tourists wishing to replicate the experience of illegally crossing the Rio Grande river into the United States (Healy, 2007). Complete with pursuit by *faux* Border Patrol agents and a substitute river, a *caminata* is a bargain in comparison to a *bandelero* kidnapping, at just 200 pesos ($11 US).

Where's the Cocaine?

A new entrant in the growing, youth-oriented 'energy drink' market, Cocaine comes in red cans with the drink's name written in what appear to be lines of white powder. Name and can alike in this way reference both the drug cocaine and the drink Coca-Cola, or Coke. But whereas Coca-Cola/Coke did in its early years contain significant amounts of cocaine, Cocaine the energy drink doesn't. Instead it contains 280 milligrams of caffeine, more than enough to contribute to the growing phenomenon that doctors label youthful 'caffeine abuse'.

According to the company's website (www.drinkcocaine.com), 'the question you have to ask yourself is: "Can I handle the rush?"'. We have some other questions. Is the product's provocative name mostly a matter of marketing commodified transgression to kids? (Yes.) Has the subsequent controversy, in which 7-Eleven has pulled the product from its shelves, further helped promote the drink and cement its outlaw image? (Yes.) And how is it that Coke, a drink that in fact did once contain cocaine, is now the sanitized soft drink of choice for mid-America, and Cocaine, a drink that never has contained cocaine, is now the edgiest of drinks for the young and the restless?

Damn it, another ball-buster of a bench. Is there no decent place to sit left in this city?

Probably not, unless you're willing to pay for it. The privatization of public space and the hardening of the urban environment serve not only to control the movement of urban populations, but to herd them into commercial consequences should they desire even the most basic of human amenities: a drink of water, a place to sit, a toilet.

This guy in a car tosses some fast food out into the street. A female bike courier grabs the food and tosses it back in, yelling 'don't litter in my neighbourhood'. He jumps out, throws two coffees at her, and now he's stomping on her bike and they start scuffling. Some guys come off the sidewalk and pull him off of her. Meanwhile another dude with a camera just keeps shooting – but when he tries to photograph the car's licence plate, the guy from the car opens the trunk, grabs a baseball bat, and charges him

This incidence of urban conflict exploded in Toronto's crowded Kensington Market area in January 2006. Happening on the scene, photographer Adam Krawesky began shooting photos of it – but that was only the first turn in a spiral of crime and culture. When he posted the photos to the CityNoise website (Krawesky, 2006; www.citynoise.org), thousands of responses began to pour in, and in no time the photos and the story had been picked up by countless other websites and blogs. Meanwhile a daily newspaper, the *Toronto Star*, published three of the photos without Krawesky's permission as part of a feature article on the street conflict, the photos, and the web responses to both (Powell, 2006). By this time Krawesky was getting calls from national and international media, working with another daily newspaper, and, as he told us, learning about the power of mediated images to mislead and mythologize (Krawesky, 2007). After all, he emphasized, he hadn't even been able to photograph the entire incident – and yet people around the world were now sure they understood it, sure of their opinions about it, sure they could make sense of it by referencing street justice, or gender conflict, or similar scenes in the Hollywood film *Crash* (Dir. Paul Haggis, 2004).

Plate 4.2   An image of urban conflict
Credit: Adam Krawesky (2006), by permission

But in this one he's lost his job and people are messing with him and … what's the name of that film?

The name of that film is *Falling Down* (1993), directed by Joel Schumacher, and starring Michael Douglas and Robert Duvall. **That other film where the woman tries to kill him** is *Fatal Attraction* (1987), directed by Adrian Lyne, a film widely criticized for its demonization of women and back-handed valorization of traditional marriage. If nothing else, films such as these capture something of the late modern vertigo that plagues the once-secure middle classes; perhaps they exacerbate that vertigo as well.

So she and the assistant manager went out from behind the counter, smiling and asking the girls if they could help them with anything, and chatted with them until they left the store

Jeff Ferrell recently scrounged a *Gap Loss Prevention Manual* from a trash bin behind a Gap clothing store. The manual emphasizes to employees that 'customer service' is the best guard against shoplifting and other theft-related 'shortage', since 'great service keeps our customers coming back and shoplifters from coming in'. The manual offers specific suggestions for customer service as crime prevention – 'extend a warm hello to customers and offer your assistance' – and even suggests scripts: 'Hello, are you shopping for yourself or for a gift?' 'How do you like our new fall colours?'

Should this preventive strategy fail, employees are advised to use 'recovery statements' to reclaim shoplifted merchandise. 'Role-play different scenarios with your managers', they're told. 'Practice using APPROPRIATE, NON-ACCUSATORY, SERVICE-ORIENTED Recovery Statements'. Specific statements are again suggested, including 'That dress is really cute. I bought one for my niece the other day.'

This management of verbal interaction is matched by the management of emotion (Hochschild, 2003). 'Remember to remain positive!' when making recovery statements, the manual urges; even when responding to a store alarm, 'do not accuse the customer or allow the conversation to become confrontational'. Under guidelines for the hectic holiday sales season, employees are urged to call the Loss Prevention Hotline if they suspect internal problems at the store (all calls confidential, reward of up to $500), but in the next line encouraged to 'Have fun!!! The holidays are a perfect time to "choose your attitude!!"'. Further emotional support is provided by Loss Prevention Contests, with employees rewarded with gift certificates or movie passes for knowing loss prevention procedures.

If those two girls in the story are up to nothing more than shoplifting a Starbucks CD, these sorts of soft control, customer-service-as-crime-prevention techniques may succeed. But what if the girls are part of the Yomango underground? Yomango emerged in 2002 in Spain, the name being Spanish slang for 'I steal' and a play on 'Mango', a Spanish chain store. Now a growing phenomenon, Yomango embraces the notion that shoplifting – 'liberating products from multi-national companies or big chain stores' – can function as 'a form of civil disobedience and a survival technique' (www.yomango.net; Adbusters, 2005; see Edemariam, 2005).

Plate 4.3   San Precario, transgendered patron saint of the precarious and a '*detournement* of popular tradition' (Tari and Vanni, 2005)

Credit: chainworkers.org after an image by Chris Woods

More broadly, illegal everyday practices like Yomango, squatting, and fare-dodging train travel are practised as part of a new 'precarity' youth movement that confronts the precarious conditions of late modernity. Practitioners argue that the fluid, globalized dynamics of late capitalism – 'flex scheduling', part-time service employment, outsourced work, temporary jobs *sans* benefits or long-term assurances – leave more and more people, especially young people, with nothing but emotional and economic uncertainty. Yet this very uncertainty – this very precariousness – creates a new sort of commonality, maybe an amorphous social class, where 'immigrants, mall workers, freelancers, waiters, squatters … an immigrant worker and a downwardly-mobile twenty-something' (Kruglanski, 2006) together drift through the anomie of late modernity. So precarity itself replaces the job site as a place to organize the disorganized, to find some slippery common ground – and those navigating this slippery ground even invent San Precario (Saint Precarious), the playful patron saint of late-modern uncertainty.

After all, if for an earlier generation 'a job was an instrument for integration and social normalization', today jobs are only temporary 'instruments we use to obtain the cash we need in order to live and socialize with the least humiliation possible' (Kruglanski, 2006). And yet the minimum-wage cash from a part-time job is never enough, and the humiliation only increases – recall those young Gap workers, forced to mimic the manual. 'Smiling is working – where does my real smile begin?', Kruglanski (2006) asks. 'Whether your friendliness is tainted by the shade of networking, or shaded by "Hello, how are we today? My name is Rob and I'll be your server"'. And so, with the social contract effectively voided by the fluid predations of late capitalism, the smiling clerks and servers turn on the very situations that entrap them.

But wait a minute; how can these young shoplifters beat the mall security system, avoid the surveillance cameras, elude the loss prevention strategies of The Gap and Starbucks? Oh, that's right – *they've read the manual*; it's their orchestrated smiles and scripted greetings that constitute the front line of loss prevention in the first place.

A little black orb attached to the book bag

The black orb is ExisTech's new high-fashion surveillance accessory: a sophisticated camera, not unlike the spherical ones you see scanning suspects in department stores, but here utilized by advocates of a process known as 'Sousveillance'. From the French 'sous' (below) and 'veiller' (to watch), sousveillance challenges the ubiquitous surveillance practices of late modernity. It draws on the 'detournement' practice of 'reflectionism' – that is, 'appropriating tools of social controllers and resituating these tools in a disorienting manner' (Mann et al., 2003). Sousveillance not only allows the watched to do some watching of their own – as Mann and his colleagues found out in a series of Research Performances – it also greatly unsettles surveillance agents and security guards.

In one case, sousveillance practitioners donned 'invisibility suits' – wearable computer systems linked to flat-panel monitors worn as backpacks – that project images from a small head mounted video camera. The wearer's back becomes a 'window' and gives the impression of actually seeing right through the wearer. While this type of public display brings sousveillance practitioners into conflict with security staff, 'the wearer argues that the motivation for wearing the camera is to provide protection from being seen by surveillance cameras. Thus the surveillance agent's objection to the

sousveillance camera becomes an objection to his own surveillance camera'
(Mann et al., 2003: 355).

*The FCUK (French Connection UK) clothing store has changed its display
window since she walked past this morning. It now features skinny female
mannequins, dressed in the latest FCUK designs, shoving and throwing
punches at each other*

Unsurprisingly, a retail clothing chain whose name plays on the naughty titillations of sexual slang also displays its apparel amidst a stylized tableau of
female violence and victimization. Here transgression is commodofied twice
over, first 'branded' into the very identity of the retailer, then reconfirmed in
the violent poses frozen in the shop window.

Meanwhile, along New York City's exclusive Madison Avenue, a dealer in fine
European antiques files a $1,000,000 suit against three homeless men whose
transgression consists of sitting on the sidewalk in front of his display window.
According to the suit, the dealer 'spends large sums each year in carefully
preparing the displays appearing in the storefront window showcases', and by
their homelessness, the three men distract customers from proper apprecia-
tion (Burke et al., 2007).

Following the lead of FCUK, he might consider instead allowing the three to
set up residence just *inside* the storefront window, maybe throwing a punch or
holding up one of the antiques now and then.

*Son of a bitch, it's that jerk from the train this morning! The FCUK window
in her mind, scared and mad that maybe he's been stalking her all day, a bit
embarrassed for bumping into him, she reaches for her Pepperface pepper
spray necklace, fumbles with it for a moment, and gets her finger on to the
spray button – but by this time he's backing away, arms out and palms up,
saying, 'sorry, sorry' – and in a flash he's disappeared into the crowd on the
sidewalk.*

This sort of accidental, ambiguous swirl of emotion marks many everyday
episodes of transgression, whether accomplished or only momentarily
considered. Intentions are read and misread, emotions more or less managed, flickers of aggression amplified or redirected, and all of this amidst
the seductive urban semiotics of corporate signage, crowded sidewalks, and
symbolic identities.

As we discussed in Chapter 3, the rational choice perspective, on the other
hand, would have us believe that such moments unfold along a linear sequence
of rational decision-making. According to Cornish and Clarke (2006: 19–21),
the accidental collision, her act of reaching for her pepper spray, even his
retreat away from her, each involved 'a sequence of choices made at each stage
of the criminal act – for example, preparation, target selection, commission of
the act, escape, and aftermath'. So desperate are such theorists to maintain the

mythology of individual rationality that they find such choices – even when 'made quickly [and] revised hastily', even when made 'in a fog of alcohol and drugs' – to remain 'rational, albeit imperfect'.

In a late modern world suffused with the celebration of irrationality and spontaneity, this claim is serious business – and a serious mistake. In fact, if most contemporary crime, and fear of crime, can't actually be reduced to rational calculation, then rational choice theory begins to appear less an explanatory theory of crime and more what it is: a sycophantic adjunct to the apparatus of criminal justice, orchestrated in the interest of punitive 'policy-making' and narrowly-conceived crime prevention. In this sense, those moments of transgression that punctuate everyday life – and more precisely, the *meaning* of those moments – carry political stakes that couldn't be higher.

There was also that bus stop shelter with the big speech bubbles pasted over the advertisements – or were those part of the ads?

The Bubble Project (www.thebubbleproject.com) is a form of guerrilla media whereby ex-advertising agency worker Ji Lee (2006) and others paste empty, cartoon-style 'speech bubble' stickers over advertisements at bus stops and other public places. The empty speech bubbles invite passers-by to fill them in with dialogue or critique, and once filled in the bubbles are photographed and archived. As its manifesto argues, 'the bubble project is the counterattack' and 'the bubbles are the ammunition' in a battle to take back public spaces – bus stops, train stations, subways, public squares – that have been 'seized by corporations to propagate their messages solely in the interest of profit'.

In this way The Bubble Project operates as a form of *invitational vandalism* – an act of illegal defacement that invites further defacement. A process of illicitly interactive street communication, The Bubble Project recalls the newspapers pasted to walls during the political upheavals of Paris 1968 – newspapers that eventually became 'difficult to read ... so covered over are they with critical comments' (Star, 2001: 66) – or more recently the work of the graffiti artist Banksy (2005: 50–5), whose illicit 'This Wall is a Designated Graffiti Area' stencils successfully invite further graffiti. The Bubble Project also recalls, once again, the concept of *detournement*, the 'theft of meaning', whereby activists subvert everyday messages by undermining their meaning. 'Once placed on ads', The Bubble Project argues, 'these stickers transform the corporate monologue into an open dialogue'.

'Cause I stole it. Happy Birthday'

One afternoon Jeff Ferrell was dumpster diving behind a drug store/chemist's when he found this and hundreds of other discarded retail greeting cards. The front of the 'Cause I Stole It' card was eye-catching; instead of the usual flowers or poetry, it featured this long rant, printed in a cut-and-paste 'ransom note' style and adorned with oversized fingerprints like those left at a crime scene.

Wow – this suggested a whole new area of cultural criminology. We all know that crime gets packaged and sold back to us as entertainment, what with cop movies, reality television shows, video games, and gangsta rap. But here was crime packaged as a birthday greeting! And of course we've all heard the debates over whether cartoons, popular songs, movies, and television shows are criminogenic – whether they promote criminality or cause 'copy-cat' crimes among those who consume them (Hamm and Ferrell, 1994). So was this a criminogenic birthday card? In some oddly reflexive way, was it promoting its own theft, like Abbie Hoffman's (1971) classic *Steal This Book?* How weird would it be if somebody saw this card in some store, read it, and decided to steal it – just so they could tell the intended recipient, 'Dude, I *really did* steal it! No kiddin'!'

According to her, even a damn prawn sandwich is a crime

And maybe it is.

As Martin O'Brien (2006: 6) has shown, the prawns (shrimp) in that sandwich are the result of a global system of large-scale prawn production and distribution that produces at the same time 'murder, abuse, exploitation, theft and environmental destruction'. Global consumer culture not only distances the consumer from the process by which an item of consumption is produced; it distances the consumer from the criminal abuses inherent in that process as well. From Mardi Gras beads (*MardiGras: Made in China*, Dir. David Redmon, 2005) to Christmas figurines (Ferrell, 2006a: 165–6), cultural criminologists attempt to traverse that distance by linking everyday consumer objects to the conditions of their globalized production. As with Dick Hebdige's (1988: 77–115) brilliant deconstruction of the Italian motor scooter, we look for the currents of meaning embedded in the materials of everyday life.

Not five minutes later one of the many dishevelled folks who hang around the station is just as careful to extricate from the trash the half sandwich, the Coke can – and a brand new designer scarf

The vast economic inequality that haunts late modernity is confirmed each time an impoverished scrounger reaches into a trash bin, digging for survival amidst the discards; the highs and lows of late capitalism both occupy that moment.

On the high end, the hyper-consumerism that drives late capitalist economies produces astounding amounts of waste among those privileged enough to afford the next designer suit or computer. A century ago, the great sociologist and economist Thorstein Veblen (1953 [1899]) began to notice patterns of 'conspicuous consumption' – consumption predicated not on the satisfaction of physical need but the attainment of status. A century later, as advertising saturates daily life with the mythology of the perpetually 'new and improved' product, this sort of consumption is pervasive, with consumers endlessly purchasing goods for the sake of lifestyle and status. But of course these consumer goods accumulate, lose their conspicuous luster, and so are discarded to make room for the next wave of consumption. Trash bins overflow with discarded goods, many of them unused and unworn, but now unworthy (Ferrell, 2006a).

On the low end, as we saw in the previous chapter, the same economic system that spawns widespread consumption and waste also spawns widespread poverty and homelessness. The economic circumstances of those 'precarious' part-time retail clerks and flex workers seen earlier are precarious indeed; with low wages and no guarantees of ongoing employment, they remain always on the brink of joblessness, in or near poverty, in many cases one paycheck away from homelessness. For more and more women, single parenthood or the demise of a bad marriage leaves them likewise vulnerable to loss of income or housing – and so we see homeless shelters filling with women and their children. Add to this the steady destruction of low-cost housing in the interest of 'urban development', the corporate 'downsizing' and 'outsourcing' that define the late modern global economy, and it is little wonder that more and more homeless and unemployed people – and 'under-employed' minimum wage workers – find themselves sorting through the waste of others' consumption.

Against all odds, such folks salvage not only cans and clothes but a modicum of dignity, sharing scrounging techniques and inventing moments of do-it-yourself resourcefulness. Others mix trash with do-it-yourself autonomous political activism. The group Food Not Bombs scrounges discarded food, cooks it, and serves it free of charge to the homeless. Projecting the do-no-harm ethic of a vegan diet into the realm of consumption, 'freegans' reject retail shopping for the dumpster diving of food and clothing 'so as to give no economic power to the capitalist consumer machine' (http://freegan.info/; see Clark, 2004; Greenwell, 2006). Around the United States, college students also engage in activist dumpster diving. Wesleyan University students hold dumpster-diving workshops, scrounge the trash of Ivy League schools, and are even making a film, *Operation Ivy: Dumpster Diving at Elite Colleges*, to serve 'as a propaganda vehicle to develop colleges' recycling programs' (Kimes, 2006: 13).

So that dishevelled scrounger digging in the train station trash bin might well be hungry and homeless, but might also be a minimum wage worker, a political activist, a found-object artist, or a committed college student. That scrounger is almost certainly a criminal as well – that is, almost certainly violating one of the many contemporary legal statutes that prohibit urban trash scrounging. In many cities Food Not Bombs activists are likewise denied permits to feed the homeless, then ticketed or arrested for feeding the home-less without a permit; Las Vegas and other American cities now go further, banning any provision of food to the homeless in downtown parks. As urban economies come to rely increasingly on the high end of late capitalism – on upscale retail consumption within sanitized environments – urban authorities readily criminalize those who, by living from the excesses of that consump-tion, might somehow interrupt it (Ferrell, 2001/2).

And this dynamic of consumption and waste isn't confined to the relative afflu-ence of the United States, Britain, and Western Europe. In India many of the destitute live from urban trash dumps, in some cases even growing vegetables in the composting waste. In the Gaza Strip, Palestinians scrounge scrap metal from abandoned Israeli settlements. Mexican peasants weave purses and belts from candy wrappers and cookie packages; Brazil's poor collect and sell trash in the tradition of the *garrafeiro*, or 'bottle collector'. As shown in the Academy Award-nominated documentary *Recycled Life* (Dir. Leslie Iwerks, 2006), generations of impoverished Guatemalans have mined Guatemala City's landfill, the largest in Central America. The *cartoneros* ('cardboard people') who scavenge for card-board and scrap paper in Buenos Aires, Argentina, even ride their own stripped-down 'Ghost Train' to and from their nocturnal work in the city-centre. Meanwhile, in Guiyu, China, 60,000 people work amidst toxic metal and acid runoff as they disassemble old computers – a task, and risk, they share with thousands of inmates in US federal prisons, who earn as little as 23 cents an hour for disassembling electronic equipment (see Bloch, 1997; O'Brien, 2008).

It's bad enough she got that ASBO slapped on her last year for yelling animal-rights slogans at the McDonald's assistant manager

ASBO stands for Anti Social Behaviour Order, a peculiarly British phenome-non that emerged in 2003 in an attempt to 'clamp down' on the anti-social activities associated with so-called 'yob culture'. Unhappy with the existing legal definition of *anti-social*, as set down in the Crime and Disorder Act of 1998, the Labour government began to proscribe hundreds of activities as 'anti-social', including the throwing of fireworks, begging, shouting and swear-ing, discarding condoms and letting down car tyres (see Presdee, 2005: 192–8). Despite the fact that ASBO activities are generally already covered by existing laws, the government's policy continues unabated, with everything from operating a crack house to illegal parking now part of the ASBO compass. Add to this the fact that since coming to power in 1997 the Labour govern-ment has created more than 3,000 new criminal offences – one for almost every day it has been in power – and it would seem that Stan Cohen's (1979: 346) prophesy for the future of social control (i.e. 'thinning the mesh and widening the net') has proved an accurate one.

The school counsellor advised him and his ex-wife that his daughter seems driven to take risks, to push her own limits, to test herself and her teachers

As you've seen in previous chapters, cultural criminological theories suggest some explanations for the daughter's behaviour, and the counsellor's perception of it. Like her father, she may be responding to boredom – to the boredom that the school enforces through dress codes, attendance requirements, and curricula generally drained of critical thought. Like Cohen's (1955) delinquent boys, she and her friends may be delinquent girls, inverting and resisting the standards by which they are judged. Or, as we saw in the previous chapter, she may be one of the many girls and women now engaged in edgework, and so looking for the sharpened sense of self that the rationalized school denies (see Garot, 2007b).

ODD, Oppositional Defiant Disorder

The meaning of crime and transgression can be made in many ways – even medically. From the earliest days of the American juvenile justice system, constructions of 'juvenile delinquency' mixed legal constraint with models of medical treatment and moral rehabilitation. Today, we see the ongoing medicalization of childhood activities, with most any inattentiveness or opposition to adult authority defined as a psycho-medical condition: attention deficit disorder, attention deficit hyperactivity disorder, oppositional defiant disorder. Such definitions of course encode adult authority over children with the legitimacy of medical science – and manage to sell a few billion dollars in behaviour-modifying drugs along the way. As labelling theorists were well aware, meanings such as these can even be made retrospectively, such that a girl on a train can be seen to have ODD not when first encountered, but when later remembered (Rossol, 2001).

That bunch of damn 'chavs' that hangs out down at the end of the road

Another British phenomenon is the 'chav', a pejorative label given to white youth who engage in minor forms of unruly behaviour in and around town centres and fast-food outlets. 'Chavs' are allegedly identifiable by their love of designer sports apparel and ostentatious jewellery, a penchant for alcohol and promiscuity, and their sneering attitude towards the police and other authorities. Almost unheard of before 2002, the term 'chav' has emerged as a ubiquitous British epithet for everyone from unwed teenage mothers to high-profile celebrities such as Posh and Becks.

As we've argued elsewhere, the mediated emergence of 'chavs' must be understood within broader socio-economic processes of marginalization (Hayward and Yar, 2006). Given that late modern identity is now forged primarily through consumerism, the popular media increasingly construct marginality and social deficit not in terms of flawed relations to *production*, but by purportedly pathological class relations to the sphere of consumption. Indeed, we found that the rise of the term 'chav' and the decline of 'underclass' discourse in the UK were not unconnected; instead of vilifying an underclass that fails to 'work hard' and adhere to established relations of economic production, we now vilify the chav because of 'inappropriate' consumer choices. The chav is guilty of excessive consumption in areas stigmatized as aesthetically bankrupt; the chav's problem is consumption deemed vulgar by superordinate consumer classes. The chav phenomenon nicely exemplifies the dynamics of late modernity, with its convergence of consumption, identity, marginality, and social control; in the 'chav' we see that consumption practices have become the locus around which exclusion is configured and the excluded identified and managed.

It's the same old stuff – CSI: Crime Scene Investigation, Law and Order: Criminal Intent, Cold Case, Without a Trace

So large is the market for death that it transcends death itself. 'We're really seeing the day of the zombie', says book publisher Don D'Auria. 'As a monster, it's speaking to people' (St John, 2006: 1). We'd guess that it's saying something about apocalyptic anxiety, and an overblown sense that danger lurks always amidst the everyday. But in any case, as zombie films, novels, and video games proliferate, so do the opportunities to read of humankind stalked by a terror that doubles death back on itself, to watch as the undead eat out the brains of the soon-to-be-dead. No longer do we go gentle into that good night; now we hype the journey, and return to carry others along with us.

The roaring popularity of CSI (Crime Scene Investigation) television programmes pushes this death culture deeper still into everyday life. Here, the long process of criminal justice is lost in the pseudo-scientific moment, and the drama of death is in the details – torn and severed flesh, flecks of blood, entry and exit wounds, all to be analyzed in slow-motion close-up (Cavender and Deutsch, 2007). Contemporary cultural artifacts confirm the extent of this American tele-death festival: seven of the top-ten TV shows in August 2005 are CSI, Law and Order, Cold Case and their spin-offs; again in 2007, these make up seven of the ten most-watched TV shows, with a combined audience of some 70 million, and emerge as 'the most lucrative thing on television' (Trend, 2007: 98). If mediated violence is pornographic in its objectification of pain and victimization, these shows are hard-core pornographic snuff films: close-up shots of bullet-on-flesh action or body parts gnawed by rodents, all designed to titillate even the most satiated consumer of televised death. Indeed, it seems we're addicted to the culture of death, dancing every day with violence and morbidity, and inventing as many zombies, serial killers, terrorists, and multi-fatality car wrecks as necessary to keep us, well … happy.

Can it be any surprise, then, that a society hooked on the happy indulgences of televised forensic pornography – a society that finds in televised gore and violation a sad sort of existential succour – wishes only the most painful and punitive consequences for those who traffic in *actual* criminality? This love/hate relationship is less a contradiction than it seems – more two sides of the same titillation. The criminal must be constructed and punished as 'the other' to successfully serve the viewer's voyeuristic escape from the everyday; the escapist love of the televised criminal and the punitive hatred of the actual criminal are both acts of distancing, of exclusion, and so both necessary safeguards for the consumer of crime news and entertainment. A sadomasochistic marriage of fear and fascination is consummated, and with it a thin line indeed between love and hate.

And by the way: What might we think of a society where seven of its ten most popular television shows portrayed and endorsed the tenets of fundamentalist religion? Would we be concerned about a media-abetted theocracy? If seven of our most popular shows featured hardcore *sexual* pornography, might even the most liberal among us worry that citizens were just a bit preoccupied with sexual gratification, to the exclusion of other matters? So, with seven programmes oriented towards the most graphic of death depictions, with the culture of the zombie ascending like a corpse from the grave, what now? A thanatocracy, a commercialized zombie culture consumed by its own death wish (Jarvis, 2007)?

In the dream she's reaching for him, trying to pull him through some sort of wall, but she can't keep her grip and he fades away, receding into the innards of the American penal gulag, disappearing into the crowd of two million other prisoners for whom a day in the life is something very different indeed

More and more occupants of the late modern world find themselves extricated from the usual rhythms of the everyday, in some cases by the criminal violence they have given or received, in others by the inequitable machinery of contemporary criminal justice as embodied in mandatory and differential sentencing, racial profiling, impoverished public defender programmes, and 'wars' on drugs, gangs, and terror. As we showed in Chapter 3, this incarceration machine now imprisons more than two million Americans, with millions more under the ongoing state surveillance of probation and parole.

And yet this carceral madness has spawned its own critique, has birthed a scholarly Frankenstein more than ready to turn on its creator, and in so doing to reveal the real monster. Emerging from the experiences of those who have transformed their own incarceration into informed critique, *convict criminology* mixes inside exposé, qualitative research, and critical theory to produce a damning critique of mass incarceration. Left with little choice but to 'spend considerable amounts of time observing the culture of today's prison and their impact on staff and convicts' (Austin et al., 2001: 20), these convict criminologists likewise marshal ethnographic immersion and theoretical sophistication to construct a critical, cultural critique of 'managerial' prison research that offers 'little empathy for prisoners' and 'disregards the harm perpetrated by criminal justice processing of individuals arrested, charged, and convicted of crimes' (Richards and Ross, 2001: 177).

A collective act of intellectual courage, convict criminology might be considered the cultural criminology of the everyday life that no one cares to notice.

a selection of films and documentaries illustrative of some of the themes and ideas in this chapter

TRAFFIC, 2001, Dir. Steven Soderbergh
Traffic is a gripping, multi-layered film that explores the intricate interconnections of the illegal drug trade in contemporary America. Broad in scope, the film's storyline cross-cuts various aspects of the drug trade, from the internal dynamics of drug cartels to the problems faced by Drug Enforcement Agency officers, from the political hypocrisy surrounding the 'war on drugs' to the drug habits of the middle classes. See also the 1990 British Channel 4 series *Traffik* (on which the Hollywood film *Traffic* was based).

FALLING DOWN, 1993, Dir. Joel Schumacher
At one level, a formulaic Hollywood shoot-em-up; at another level, a more problematic story of metropolitan meltdown, as Michael Douglas's character 'D-Fens' psychologically unravels during a cross-LA odyssey. Importantly, *Falling Down* should not be read only as a metaphor for late modernity or, for that matter, ontological insecurity. Rather, it is a parable of alienation and maladaption; a tale of a man out of time. D-Fens is a disillusioned and unstable man who can no longer function or make sense of a more complex, pluralized social order – as a result adopting disturbing measures to achieve his warped version of the American Dream.

MARDI GRAS: MADE IN CHINA, 2005, Dir. David Redmon
Vividly illustrating the inequities and ironies of global capitalism, David Redmon's documentary exposes the link between the consumer excesses of the New Orleans Mardi Gras and the harsh realities of Chinese female factory workers. The film 'reveals the glaring truth about the real benefactors of the Chinese workers' hard labor and exposes the extreme contrast between women's lives and liberty in both cultures' (Meredith Lavitt, *Sundance Film Festival*).

RECYCLED LIFE, 2006, Dir. Leslie Iwerks
Recycled Life is a sobering and ultimately touching short documentary about the generations of families who call Guatemala City's garbage dump home. Abandoned by their government, thousands of Guatemalans are today forced into a daily survival struggle as they eek out a living by recycling consumptive waste. Leslie Iwerks film exposes this hidden world and sympathetically documents what it's like to live in the foothills of Central America's largest and most toxic landfill mountain.

Brick, 2006, Dir. Rian Johnson

Late modern *film noir* for the Y Generation, *Brick* is the story of dysfunctional teenagers in an anonymous Californian high school. All the classic components of *film noir* are in evidence here – *femmes fatales*, fast-paced expositional dialogue, and double-crossing – only this time they're re-energized by their location among high school drug-dealing subcultures. Of interest here is the way young people are adultized, while the actual adult world is marginalized to the point of insignificance.

media, representation, and meaning: inside the hall of mirrors

There is nothing more to explain … as long as words keep their meanings, and meanings their words.

Alphaville, dir. Jean-Luc Godard, 1965

Times are tough when things have got no meaning.

'Stand By Me', Oasis, 1997

Cultural criminology's sense that the meaning of crime and crime control is always under construction comes into especially sharp focus when we consider our contemporary world of media festival and digital spectacle. For many of us it is a rare day indeed when we don't interact with the late modern 'mediascape' (Appadurai, 1996: 35), that bundle of media that manufactures information and disseminates images via an expanding array of digital technologies. In this enveloping world of the 'Mediaopolis' (De Jong and Schuilenburg, 2006), meaning is made in motion. Pervasively popular forms of contemporary communications now constitute the primary gauge by which we assess the value and importance of current events – from the most serious to the most banal. Pop culture blurs with news media reportage, images of crime and war are repackaged as entertaining digital escapism, and unreal 'reality TV' moments shape moral values and social norms. In this world the street scripts the screen and the screen scripts the street; there is no clearly linear sequence, but rather a shifting interplay between the real and the virtual, the factual and the fictional. Late modern society is saturated with collective meaning and suffused with symbolic uncertainty as media messages and cultural traces swirl, circulate, and vacillate.

These are the conditions that symbolic interactionists and labelling theorists anticipated decades ago, with their sense of transgression as a sequenced negotiation of unsettled social identity (see Chapter 2). Only now the situation has intensified. Enter the theorists of the so-called 'postmodern', that *Boulevard*-wise ensemble of predominantly French intellectuals who sought to understand the fluctuating socio-cultural and epistemic transformations associated with the 'mediascape'. While Jean-François Lyotard, Michel Maffesoli, and Paul Virilio have all had their say about this fluid, mediated epoch of 'disengagement, elusiveness, facile escape and hopeless chase' (Bauman, 2000: 120), it was the self-styled 'intellectual terrorist' Jean Baudrillard who gathered most traction. Simply stated, Baudrillard argued that society is now constituted around reflexive 'signs' and 'codes' that have little or no referent to a 'reality' other than their own. Hence his world of 'hyperreal' simulation – a media-saturated environment of 'connections, contact, contiguity, feedback and generalized interface … a pornography of all functions and objects in their readability, their fluidity, their availability … their performativity … their polyvalence...' (Baudrillard, 1985: 126–34; also 1983, 1996).

Heady intellectual stuff indeed – but if one of the goals of cultural criminology is to move beyond the insightful, yet now dated, interactionist analyses of the 1950s and 1960s, it is also reluctant to embrace uncritically this postmodern sensibility; while Baudrillard may inhabit a 'void-like world of empty signs and unfilled desires', many others find crime to be painfully tangible and immediate in its impact. Yet while many criminal acts retain their sensual immediacy, the *culture* of such acts increasingly resembles not so much static entity or domain as *flow*, a flow that carries with it the contested meanings of crime and criminality. To paraphrase Marshall McLuhan, it's this movement that in many ways is the message; this constant flow of collective meaning is itself meaningful, itself a circuitry of meaning, opening possibilities of social control and social change unavailable under more solid circumstances. Abuses of legal and political authority defy direct confrontation, slipping away just as we might catch them out, circulating and escaping through skilfully spun press releases and photographs lost and found. Resistance to such authority is no sure thing either, always in danger of becoming the medium through which it is carried out, or even that which it resists – and yet this very uncertainty offers new possibilities for a politics of subversion, for a 'semiotic guerrilla warfare' that fights and falls back (Umberto Eco, as quoted in Hebdige, 1979: 105). Criminals and the crimes they commit likewise seem always on the move, criss-crossing the contradictions of a globalized political economy, other times tangled up in their own mediated representations. The terms of cultural and political engagement, the meaning of crime and resistance and control, remain endlessly unsettled.

If our aim is the development of a critically engaged cultural criminology, we must account for this cultural motion, must imagine ways to track meaning as it moves through the politics of crime and social control. We certainly cannot forget the experiential consequences of crime, nor surrender our critical stance to the seductions of cultural uncertainty. But we can't forget the swirling dynamics of culture, either; a photograph, a freeze frame, can catch a moment in an emerging process, but ultimately, neither substitutes for a moving picture of the process itself. We must conceptualize the flow of collective meaning, must immerse ourselves in it – and immersing ourselves, perhaps discover ways to move this cultural fluidity towards progressive ends.

One of the tasks of this chapter, then, is to introduce and analyze some of the ways in which the meaning of crime circulates within the late modern mediascape. After all, while notions of cultural 'motion' or 'flow' imply instabilities of collective meaning, they needn't suggest that this motion is random, or that this flow is unfettered. Far from it – political economies of contemporary culture regularly set meaning in motion, and at least initially, set the terms and parameters of its movement; just as often emerging technologies invent new channels through which mediated perceptions can move, or be confronted. Even in motion, collective meaning leaves traces of influence and understanding, offers up trajectories amidst all the movement.

Fact or fiction?

In September 2007 Jeff Ferrell is being interviewed for a story on urban scrounging by a friendly, decent-minded Senior Investigative Producer for a local television station. After the interview they're chatting amicably, and the producer says, 'Hey, do let me know if you have any ideas for local crime stories. We have all those *CSI* [Crime Scene Investigation] and *Cold Case* [police detective] shows from 9 to 10 pm, and we like to use them as lead-ins to crime stories on the 10 pm newscast'.

crime and the media: the well-trodden path

Much of the existing scholarship on 'crime and the media' relies on relatively formulaic readings of crime's presentation in the media, or alternatively, the effects of this presentation on attitudes and behaviour. In our experience, though, these existing formulas for assessing the link between crime and the media don't adequately address the mutating world of the late modern mediascape. From our view, new approaches are badly needed – approaches more expansive and holistic in tracing the contemporary flow of meaning between crime and the media.

Others have eloquently summarized and critiqued existing scholarship on crime and the media (see, for example, Ericson, 1995; Kidd-Hewitt and Osborne, 1995; Reiner, 2002; Carter and Weaver, 2003; Jewkes, 2004; Greer,

2005, 2008; Trend, 2007). Here, in preparation for outlining an alternative vision of crime and the media, we'll only encapsulate the major existing approaches.

Content analysis. Based on a communications model of the mass media, content analysis treats media content – words, paragraphs, pictures – as discrete texts to be analyzed. This method focuses on assessing the amount (and to a lesser extent form) of crime, violence, and control present in the media. Typically, work in this area proceeds from a quantitative, social scientific perspective, with the objective of isolating and measuring 'message variables' via an 'objective' analysis of media forms ranging from crime news to fictional depictions of crime in comic books, television shows, and film. While considerable doubt has been cast on the claim that content analysis can proceed 'objectively', this body of work has unearthed some important findings: exaggerated levels of serious violent crime in the mass media, for example, and sympathetic portrayals of the criminal justice system (see, for example, Felson, 1998: 3–6; Cavender and Deutsch, 2007).

Simply quantifying visual crime events or codifying crime messages, however, leaves us only able to examine media as a product. Hence the emergence of more theoretically-inspired, qualitatively-oriented content analysis, concerned with understanding the processes by which crime stories and images are produced and understood. Here the emphasis is on 'the use of language, the forces and constraints that shape media production, or the wider influence of the economic, political, and cultural environment' (Greer, 2005: 159; Altheide, 1987, 1996). We'll explore the value of these more fluid approaches to media content analysis when we consider the methods of cultural criminology in Chapter 6.

Media 'effects' research. As the name implies, this body of work is concerned with identifying causal linkages between media representations and subsequent human thoughts and behaviours. While an inestimable amount of time and money has been expended in testing this link, no hard conclusions have been drawn – and as a result the 'media effects' debate endures in the social sciences and elsewhere. As with content analysis, this is in part a result of methodology and its limitations.

A 50 year-old body of research, for example, has sought to substantiate a direct correlation between violent imagery and violent behaviour in the real world, often by way of a controlled experiment in which subjects are exposed to aggressive stimuli – a battery of criminal images or a violent film – and then monitored to see if their behaviour and attitude have been affected by what they have experienced (see Bandura et al., 1961, 1963; Paik and Comstock, 1994) Such studies – and there have been thousands – have been employed to substantiate various causal explanations of violent behaviour, from 'social learning theory' (Bandura, 1973, 1977) to psychological theories of 'disinhibition' and 'desensitization', and have likewise been employed as part of campaigns for moral conservatism or censorship (Ferrell, 1998).

Such 'laboratory' experiments have been roundly criticized by scholars who doubt that behaviour exhibited in artificial contexts will be replicated in real-world settings, and who understand that short-term media effects fail to consider long-term sociological, psychological, and cultural influences (see Livingstone, 1996; Gauntlett, 1998). As a result, we've recently seen the emergence of more sophisticated attempts to gauge the deleterious effects of violent images – attempts that no longer simplistically strive to identify some pure, causal media effect. These approaches affirm that 'media images affect people, who are not passive recipients but active interpreters, in a complex process of interaction with other cultural and social practices' (Reiner, 2002: 399). We concur, and attempt to explore precisely this culturally interactive context of effect in this and other chapters.

A second version of existing 'effects' research is the tradition of so-called 'cultivation analysis'. This tradition argues that television's overemphasis on 'anxiety-inducing' violent crime stories causes those who view 'too much television' to develop an overly anxious, fearful view of the larger society (Gerbner and Gross, 1976; Signorielli and Morgan, 1990). Or, to put it another way, 'scary TV cultivates scared people'. Yet while this 'cultivation effect' allegedly explains excessive fear of crime within society, other 'effects' must be considered amidst the late modern swirl of mediated crime as news, entertainment, and escape. Lynn Chancer (2005), for example, argues that high-profile violent crimes often evoke not fear but rather a 'symbolic politics' of political division and racial conflict. And as we will argue later in this chapter, when crime comes to be stylized and commodified in the media, it is as likely to induce pleasure, or titillation – or shopping – as it is fear (see Lupton and Tulloch, 1999; Lowry et al., 2003).

Media production observation. A more recent body of work considers the underlying ideological factors that influence the selection, production, and circulation of crime stories, especially crime news stories. Rather than measuring media content or testing media effects, studies on the media production process examine how ideology and power are articulated through various organizational and professional decisions and processes. Two theoretical models dominate.

First, the so-called *liberal pluralist* perspective asserts that, while much media is owned and even 'steered' by certain powerful individuals and conglomerates, any influence exerted from 'on high' is more than offset by the professional integrity of journalists and the gritty on-the-ground necessities of the newsgathering process (see Gans, 1980; Starky, 2006). Yet while famous cases like Woodward and Bernstein's scoop reporting on the 1972 Watergate political scandal are often presented as exemplars of this sort of journalistic corrective to power (see Alan J Pakula's 1976 movie *All The President's Men*), Pulitzer Prize-winning journalists are rare indeed, and in fact many crime reporters don't have the time or resources to do much more than hang around courthouses and pick over police press releases. Moreover, many crime journalists conform to a rigidly formatted crime reporting template (Cerulo, 1998; Yanich, 2001) – and changes in general news content often drive parallel changes in crime reporting, making it difficult for journalists to defy editorial control and produce stories that go against the popular grain. For example, the media's overall fascination with 'celebrity' tends to marginalize routine crime stories in favour of those crimes made more newsworthy by the sprinkling of celebrity gold dust.

This sense of newsworthiness brings us neatly to the second perspective: the more *radical* tradition of media production observation as influenced by the work of Karl Marx, the Frankfurt School, and Antonio Gramsci. For propaganda analysts such as Noam Chomsky and Ed Herman (Chomsky, 1989; Chomsky and Herman, 1994), the banal narratives of today's celebrity-obsessed mass media are simply the latest example of global communication conglomerates and 'informational capitalists' (Castells, 1996) manipulating news and entertainment content so as to 'manufacture consent' among the masses, thereby ensuring the stable social and political conditions needed for capitalism to flourish. Put bluntly, the more people are interested in celebrity crimes and indiscretions, rather than critical political news analysis, the less likely they are to pose crucial questions about the injustices of the prison–industrial complex or the growing worldwide disparity between rich and poor. For Chomsky and other 'propaganda analysts', then, the role of journalists is marginal at best when compared with the political and ideological agenda of cultural elites.

A less conspiratorial but no less radical analysis is the 'hegemonic model' of news production. This model sees the relationship between the 'dominant' and 'subjective' classes as one of constant *contestation, renegotiation, and reinforcement*. As regards the nexus between crime and media, the hegemonic model sees newsrooms as sites of contestation, places where ideological struggles take place and power dynamics are reinforced. Hence, much is made of the 'institutionalization' of crime reporters, and in particular their over-reliance upon information supplied by police contacts and other 'normalizing' agents of the state apparatus (Chermak, 1998). It is through such 'symbiotic relationships' that the mainstream media frames the debate about crime and punishment so that any critical dissent from the standard crime narrative as promulgated by the dominant, conservative elite is marginalized (see Macek, 2006). Between the dependence on accounts of crime sourced directly from formal criminal justice agencies, and the unflinching adherence in newsrooms around the world to the classic, money-making mantra of 'If it bleeds, it leads', a one-dimensional 'story of crime' emerges within the public consciousness – a story that rarely prioritizes the crimes of the powerful, whether governmental or corporate in origin.

Certainly each of the approaches just considered has a place within cultural criminology, what with cultural criminology's concern for understanding mediated representations of crime, their effects within individual and collective behaviour, and their connections to power, domination, and injustice. Yet none of these approaches seems sufficient for untangling the complex, non-linear relationships that now exist between crime and the media in our increasingly media-saturated world of global satellite television and duelling websites, YouTube and Facebook, MySpace and Metacafé. What is required now are new modes of analysis that utilize aspects of the above approaches without reproducing their old formulae and outdated dualisms: too much or too little media content regarding crime, effects or no effects of violent imagery, media coverage of crime that is democratic or elitist. As Carter and Weaver (2003: 16) make clear, the only way forward is to radically rethink 'the terms of a debate that has become intransigently binaristic'. The goal of cultural criminology, then, is to 'intellectually reorient' and 'radically repoliticize' the study of crime and the media, to explore the fluidities of meaning by which the crime – media dynamic 'socializes and directs our thinking and actions in a range of hierarchical, complex, nuanced, insidious, gratifying, pleasurable and largely imperceptible ways' (Carter and Weaver, 2003: 167).

loops and spirals: crime as media, media as crime

For the cultural critic Paul Virilio (1986, 1991), an axiomatic feature of late modern life is what he calls 'the logic of speed'. Virilio's various writings on so-called 'speed culture' turn around the insight that the speed at which something happens ultimately dictates its nature. Consider as an example 24-hour rolling news. In this hyper-competitive broadcast environment it's obvious that 'that which moves at speed quickly comes to dominate that which is slower'. For Virilio, then, it is the speed of movement, or more accurately the velocity of circulation, that dictates what he describes as our postmodern 'logic of perception'. We agree with Virilio – at least when it comes to understanding the remarkable velocity of information in the contemporary mediascape. However, what is perhaps more important is the nature of the circulation itself – that is, the extent to which fast-moving mediated images and bits of information reverberate and bend back on themselves, creating a fluid porosity of meaning that defines late modern life, and the nature of crime and media within it, more than does speed itself.

How Fast is Fast?

Even the temporal immediacy of the 24-hour rolling news format is now under threat from the interplay of high-speed digital communications and user-generated websites. Long before news stations had any viable footage of the Virginia Tech University shooting in 2007, for example, students trapped in university buildings were posting digital phone video footage of the shootings on the university's 45,000 member Facebook site. By this time, of course, the shooter had already taken the initiative of mailing a videotape to the national television media. And in the aftermath of the shooting, news stations gathered information about the victims from the online tributes posted in student user groups.

From this view, contemporary culture can be conceptualized as a series of *loops*, an ongoing process by which everyday life recreates itself in its own image. The saturation of social situations with representation and information suggests that the linear sequencing of meaning is now mostly lost, replaced by a doppelgänger world where the ghosts of signification circle back to haunt, and revive, that which they signify. Peter Manning (1995, 1998) describes a social world of screens and reflections, and specifically a televised world of 'media loops' whereby one image becomes the content of another; elsewhere we've described a mediated 'hall of mirrors' where 'images … bounce endlessly one off the other' (Ferrell, 1999: 397). No matter the metaphor, each catches something of the same process: a circulating cultural fluidity that overwhelms any certain distinction between an event and its representation, a mediated image and its effects, a criminal moment and its ongoing construction within collective meaning. Importantly, this looping process suggests for us something more than Baudrillard's postmodern hyper-reality, his sense of an 'unreality' defined only by media images and cultural obfuscation. Quite the opposite: we mean to suggest a late modern world in which the gritty, on-the-ground reality of crime, violence, and everyday criminal justice is dangerously confounded with its own representation.

If this sense of cultural looping constitutes a starting point for making sense of contemporary meaning, it marks a starting point for cultural criminology as well. The fluidity of contemporary culture not only carries along the meaning of crime and criminality; it circles back to amplify, distort, and define the experience of crime and criminality itself. Within such circumstances crime and culture remain hopelessly confounded – and so any criminology meant to make sense of contemporary crime and control, and to move these circumstances towards progressive possibilities, cannot do so by artificially segregating that which is intimately and inevitably intertwined. Instead, we would argue, a useful criminology of contemporary life must be, if nothing else, *culturally reflexive* – that is, self-attuned to image, symbol, and meaning as dimensions that define and redefine transgression and social control.

And when it comes to crime, transgression, and control, this looping circularity offers up dynamics that interweave the ludicrous with the malicious. Consider, for example, *Cheaters*, an American reality TV programme that exposes extramarital affairs. In one episode, the producers contrive and film from numerous angles a confrontation between an estranged husband and his cheating wife. Stepping outside her workplace to phone police about problems with her husband, she is restrained by a *Cheaters* security guard and confronted by her husband, who, by confronting her, violates a protective order and finds himself charged with third-degree felony assault. A domestic violence expert subsequently argues in the local newspaper that the programme has 'revictimized' the wife; the husband's lawyer counters that 'the videotape doesn't show an assault, in my opinion'. Meanwhile, more *Cheaters* videotape – this time of the wife consorting with her lover – leads to problems for the lover; he's demoted and suspended from his job ... as supervisor of the police department's criminal investigations division (Boyd, 2005a, 2005b; Branch and Boyd, 2005).

In other news – this time from the world of celebrity – the British supermodel Kate Moss sees her career stock ebb and flow at warp speed as her cocaine proclivities are churned through the spin cycle of the world's tabloid press. The resulting interplay of shock, moral indignation, enticement, and ultimate normalization says much about contemporary society's ambiguous, and mediated, relationship to drug use. Moss and her supermodel peers have long made a living pedalling corporate products that trade on edgy notions of the forbidden: perfumes like *Opium, Poison,* and *Obsession,* Lolita-like sexuality, anorexic aesthetics, allusions to illicit sex and sadomasochism, and the infamous 'heroin chic' aesthetic. Yet it's not until Moss is secretly filmed snorting cocaine that the media turn on her. With stills from the hidden camera footage splashed all over the Sunday papers, Moss is publicly pilloried, and most of her corporate sponsors drop her like a set of hot curling tongs, claiming her drug-taking image is now inconsistent with the drug-laced messages they purvey to their youthful customers. And the mediated loop of sex, drugs, and commodities fizzes on. Moss enters rehab, like a waifish penitent to a late modern nunnery – and spurred on by the newsworthiness of her publicized contrition and her 'personal battle against drugs', her flagging career is quickly regenerated. A host of multinational corporations now fall over themselves to sign the new and improved 'outlaw' Moss – an odd but marketable embodiment of edgy, street savvy, and redemptive.[1]

Criminal justice likewise stumbles over its own image. For a while now we have been treated to the spectacle of dashboard-mounted squad car camera footage, a window on crime that turns police officers into performers and traffic stops into vignettes available for the nightly news or later prime-time compilation shows such as *World's Wildest Police Videos* and *Police, Camera, Action.* Along with shows like *COPS,* this form of entertainment claims to represent the 'reality' of everyday policing, and has become so popular that it now constitutes its own genre: the so-called 'criminal vérité' format. Yet while *COPS, Top COPS,* and similar 'reality' shows have become television staples – *COPS* alone has been running for eighteen years and 600 episodes, grossing more than $200 million in the process – the reality they portray is in fact a looping process constructed in conjunction with television cameras and local police departments.

To start with, programmes like *COPS, To Serve and Protect, Cops with Cameras, RCMP* and *LAPD: Life on the Street* inevitably record the ways in which the presence of their cameras alters, and exacerbates, the reality of encounters between police and suspects.[2] While lauding the show's supposedly unfiltered realism, the founding producer of *COPS*, for example, admits 'it's like a casting call. We look for the most proactive, interesting cops.' One cop featured on the show argues that 'what you see is what's happening out there ... [people] know exactly what we go through every day', while adding that 'the only problem I had was ... the sound guy kept giving me the signal to keep talking' (Walker, 1999; Mayhew, 2006; Woodson, 2006). Police chases likewise unfold as interactive made-for-television movies; following one deadly chase, in which a cameraman in the squad car's back seat video-records himself urging the cop to 'Go get him!', a wrongful death suit is filed based on the video-recording (Vick, 1997). More worrying still is the way these programmes shape popular views on policing, and so the mindsets of citizens, voters, and police academy recruits. As Richard Rapaport (2007) suggests, both the police and the policed now believe that 'appropriate law-enforcement correlates with high-speed chases, blocking and tackling, drawn weapons, and a shoot-first, think-later mind set'.

Meanwhile, in court, American jurors increasingly expect evidence to match that fictionalized in popular *CSI* (*Crime Scene Investigation*) shows; in response, prosecutors regularly refer to television programmes in their opening statements, alter their presentation of evidence, and attend acting classes (Dribben, 2006). Criminologists have even begun to investigate a specific 'CSI effect' – 'jurors who rely too heavily on scientific findings and, conversely, are sceptical about the potential for human or technical error or fraud ... jurors ... who demand that prosecution provide the same type of irrefutable evidence they see on TV' (Mopas, 2007: 111) – despite the fact that many of the forensic techniques employed on *CSI* have been dismissed as 'blatant hokum' (Roane, 2005, cited in Cavender and Deutsch, 2007). In the courtroom as elsewhere, reality and representation blur.

And it's not only jurors who get confused, For example, during the trial of rapper ODB (Ol' Dirty Bastard – real name Russell Tyrone Jones) on charges of illegally wearing body armour, his defence attorney argues that 'due to how famous he is, he's at risk of his life. He's been in gun battles and that's why he was wearing body armour'; the deputy district attorney counters by suggesting that ODB 'heads a street gang named Wu-Tang Clan'! In cases such as these, and even more so in high-profile cases like that of O J Simpson, we witness yet another looping dynamic: that of 'cultural criminalization' (Ferrell, 1998), where mediated publicity trumps legal proceedings in constructing perceptions of guilt and criminal identity.

spirals

At times loops such as these remain relatively self-contained, playing out as little episodes that bend back on themselves; more often they emerge within larger processes of collective meaning, as but one twist or turn in an ongoing *spiral* of culture and crime. In this sense the notion of 'loops', while certainly catching something of contemporary culture's fluid reflexivity, sometimes offers only a few frames from a longer film. After all, as Stan Cohen (1972) documented decades ago, the collective meaning of crime and deviance is made not once but time and again, as part of an amplifying spiral that wends its way back and forth through media accounts, situated action, and public perception. Spiralling in this way, the next loop of meaning never quite comes back around, instead moving on and away to new experiences and new perceptions, all the while echoing, or other times undermining, meanings and experiences already constructed. As with Cohen's mods and rockers, today's spirals of crime and culture continue to wind and unwind – only faster and more furiously.

Mad Max meets the Mods and Rockers

It's March 2005 and Keith and Jeff are in Canterbury, England, rolling out of town for an early Sunday morning bicycle ride. Waiting at a traffic light, we notice a procession of thirty or so motorcyclists turning left in front of us, riding an assortment of scooters, choppers, and Japanese racers, heading out for their own jaunt in the countryside. And here's the funny thing, at least to us: they're all heading for Margate, a seaside town some ten miles away.

What's funny about that? Well, for us, it's not just ten miles to Margate – its forty years since Margate, and apparently a long way from what Margate once meant. As we saw in Chapter 2, forty years before Stan Cohen (1972) had written *Folk Devils and Moral Panics: The Creation of the Mods and Rockers*, showing how nationwide moral panic and on-the-ground police responses emerged over the mythically bloody violence between scooter-riding mods and motorcycle-riding rockers on the beaches of Margate and other seaside towns. And now forty years later we watch a placid group of middle-class motorcyclists, heading out to the beaches of Margate, a motley mix of mod-reminiscent scooters and retro-rocker motorcycles, *sans* blood, violence, or the old manufactured meanings. Are they even aware of that old moral panic, or of the historical irony that rides with them as they make their way to Margate? Or has that panic long since passed, to be replaced by the next and the next? Damned if we know – it's tough to ride a bicycle fast enough to catch a group of motorcyclists for questioning.

A month later, back in the States, another anniversary ride comes together – but there's no doubt that this one is indeed steeped in cultural awareness. It's been twenty-five years since the release of *Mad Max 2: The Road Warrior* (Dir. George Miller, 1982) – the film where Mel Gibson leads an assemblage of motorcycles and scooters, not to mention armed automobiles and a sand-filled tanker truck, around an apocalyptically damaged Australian outback – and so some of the film's more devoted American fans decide to stage a re-enactment. Surrounding an old tanker truck with motorcycles and other vehicles, arming themselves with fake machine guns and real knives, twenty-five costumed fans assemble at a Boerne, Texas, motorcycle dealership and head down the highway for San Antonio.

They don't get far.

'People were freaking out', a San Antonio police officer later tells local television station WOAI. 'They see these guys with machine guns, they're getting on their cell phones, exiting the highway'. Ultimately, police arrest eleven members of the Mad Max convoy, nine for obstruction of a highway, two on that charge plus a charge of 'possession of a prohibited knife' – all of which strikes Chris Fenner, the convoy's organizer and a collector of Mad Max costumes, as unfair. He can't understand how 'anyone would confuse the costumed crew re-creating a scene from *Mad Max 2: The Road Warrior,* set in a post-apocalyptic wasteland, with a real threat' – apparently forgetting for a moment the post-apocalyptic ecology of the highway that runs from Boerne to San Antonio. 'To me what we were doing wasn't so crazy', he adds. 'I think the response was crazy' (www.woai.com, visited September 2005; Associated Press, 2005).

As crazy as the response to the Mods and Rockers? Apparently not, since while the Mad Max arrests made the news, they didn't generate the same sort of moral panic as did the Mods and Rockers forty years before. After all, times have changed, and new sorts of folk devils have been constructed – not so much Mods and Rockers, or mobile movie fans, but maybe inner-city gang members, or illegal immigrants, or drug users. As Angela McRobbie and Sara Thornton (1995) note, something else has changed as well. Perhaps panics have become all but predictable, and in such a culturally cluttered climate those people constructed as 'folk devils' are sometimes not only victims of inequitable representational practices, but appreciative recipients of free publicity. Hell, maybe they even conspire in some sense in their own devilish degradation, aware as they are – aware as we all are these days – that even negative media attention is media attention nonetheless, and so a sort of public affirmation.

Karl Bartoszynsk understands this irony. In 2003 he created a website dedicated to costumes from the *Mad Max* films – but he'd been involved with *Mad Max* long before that. In fact, on his website he provides an ascending chronology of his life as a *Mad Max* devotee. He first became a fan back in 1990, after seeing *Mad Max 2: The Road Warrior.* By 1999 he had moved to Melbourne, Australia, and proudly taken personal tours of *Mad Max* filming locations. And then came 2005, and the apex of his journey into the *Mad Max* experience.

'Attended RoadWar 151 in San Antonio', he writes in his online blog.

'Met Vernon Wells', one of the stars of *Mad Max 2.*

'Got arrested with eleven others for obstruction of highways and made international news' (www.madmaxcostumes.com).

Some of the loops already noted can themselves be reconsidered as spirals. When the cameras of 'reality' television programmes like *COPS* alter the very reality they record, when police officers play to the camera and producers proffer instructions and advice, when all of this is framed and edited and broadcast as the unmediated 'reality' of everyday policing, this is only the beginning. From there, 'best of' reality television programmes and for-purchase compilations are cobbled together from programmes already aired – with still other television programmes claiming, in ironic counterpoint, to expose the growing black market in fake reality video footage. As already suggested, lawsuits for wrongful death or invasion of privacy or false arrest are filed, with video footage offered up as evidence and counter-evidence, and of course full media coverage of the trials themselves. Police departments and police officers in turn utilize such programmes as recruiting tools, and as informational devices to keep up with developments in other police departments; one officer even reports that he uses *COPS* as 'a training thing. It helps me to refer to situations when I'm out on the street' (Woodson, 2003, 11F). Rapaport (2007) further documents how the latest popular permutations of 'criminal vérité' – police SWAT (Special Weapons And Tactics squads) shows like '*Kansas City SWAT*', '*Dallas SWAT*', and '*Detroit SWAT*' – have served to 'culturally consecrate activities that have historically been the province of military engagements in places where the Bill of Rights do not apply'. Such shows, he argues, 'invite us to celebrate the Heckler and Koch machine pistols, Parker-Hale Model 85 sniper rifles, flash-bang grenades, armoured personnel carriers, and other paraphernalia of what is essentially infantry war-fighting transferred to American streets…'.

When rappers like ODB are put on trial, when district attorneys confuse a multi-platinum selling rap group with a street gang, this is likewise no one-time collision of music and law. It is but one more turn in a now decades-old dance between rap artists, record companies, local prosecutors, and moral entrepreneurs, all of whom find both problem and potential in the intermingling of 'gangsta rap', gangs, and criminal history. For the record companies and the rappers, a carefully crafted outlaw image, even a criminal record, moves product; for local prosecutors and religious conservatives, high-profile public campaigns against such images move product as well, if of a somewhat different sort. For an attorney representing an accused killer, this spiral can even become a defence. When Ronald Howard was convicted of killing a Texas state trooper, his defence attorney recalled his failed defence strategy: not guilty by reason of rap music. 'He grew up in the ghetto and disliked police and these were his heroes, these rappers … telling him if you're pulled over, just blast away', said attorney Allen Tanner. 'It affected him. That was a totally valid, serious defense.' And indeed, just before he shot the state trooper, Howard was listening to a Tupac Shakur rap – the one about shooting a cop and remembering the video of Rodney King (Graczyk, 2005).

Two other spirals are also worth noting for their tragic integration of mediated loops, representational spirals, and concrete consequences. In the first, Andrea Yates drowns her five children in the family bathtub, and at trial the prosecution, seeking to ensure a conviction, calls on psychiatrist and forensic analyst Park Dietz. A 'frequent expert witness' in such cases and a consultant on the NBC television drama *Law and Order*, Dietz is employed to bolster the prosecution's contention that Yates developed her murder scheme from watching particular episodes of *Law and Order* that fictionalized actual cases of mothers killing their children. When his professional credentials are challenged by the defence, Dr Dietz responds by outlining in some detail the very episode of *Law and Order* that provided Yates with the perfect script for her actions – except that such an episode never existed. As it turns out, Dr Dietz had confounded 'the facts of three child-murder cases on which he had worked and the two *Law and Order* episodes based on them'. Because of this, Andrea Yates's murder conviction is overturned on appeal, and a new trial is ordered; no word yet on whether Dr Dietz will help convert this second trial, or the first, into an episode of *Law and Order* (Wyatt, 2005).

The second tragedy is of considerably longer duration, spiralling downward for decades now. As with the criminalization of marijuana in the 1930s (see Becker, 1963), the contemporary war on drugs in the United States has from its beginning spun image and ideology in such a way as to construct the very problem it claimed to address – and yet, shaped in this way, the 'problem' has continued to spiral back into the campaign that constructed it. As we noted years ago, the criminalization of drugs creates criminal consequences, consequences that call forth aggressive enforcement and further criminalization (Young, 1973). As Clinton Sanders and Eleanor Lyon (1995) have documented, police officers and prosecutors working under the pressure of contemporary anti-drug campaigns come to define most all murders as 'drug deals gone bad', most all assaults as fights over drugs, most all perpetrators as drug users. As Ferrell (2004b) has shown, drug users in such circumstances sometimes do endanger the public, especially when the police are pursuing them at high speed as public dangers. And so, as the flow of drugs and drug panic becomes self-confirming, fabrications of 8 year-old heroin addicts win the Pulitzer Prize (Reinerman and Duskin, 1999), faked drug mule documentaries harvest international awards, World Health Organization officials suppress reports on marijuana's relative harmlessness, and the spiralling process so constructed continues to put people in prison and politicians in office.

To speak of such loops and spirals is to imply perhaps a certain smoothness of motion, a soft trajectory as the meaning of crime and criminal justice circulates through popular culture. But of course trajectories can change, and dramatically; spiralling movements of meaning can be made to alter course and serve new political masters. Amidst the political rubble of the World Trade Center attacks, for example, the spiral that is the war on drugs was spun in a new direction. Playing to public fears, sensing that one war might be made to flow into another, the keepers of the drug war now engineered a cultural confluence of drugs and terror. The White House-based National Youth Anti-Drug Media Campaign produced a series of print and video ads that coupled recreational drug use with violent terrorism – creating, as Michelle Brown (2007: 13) says, 'linkages by which, semiotically, to chain individuals to the structural concerns of criminality, violence, and terror'. The spiral described by Reinarman and Duskin (1999: 85) – whereby ongoing anti-drug campaigns 'forge a public prepared to swallow the next junkie stereotype and to enlist in the next drug war' – had now been turned hard right again, this time towards a new war and a new set of stereotypes.

'rappin', 'retromacking', and the reconstitution of reality: thinking differently about [media] 'signs' and [street] 'codes'

Language, as a cultural code, relates to a world of meanings. All knowledge and language are culturally coded. Thus, knowledge or even a consciousness about delinquency is a social product. It is precisely here in the realm of knowledge that ideologies are contested, resisted, or accepted. (Visano, 1996: 92)

Charis Kubrin (2005) has recently documented how 'gangsta rap' music has become a 'constitutive element of contemporary black urban culture'. In doing so, she's also opened up some interesting possibilities for thinking about mediated loops and spirals in relation to crime and transgression.

Kubrin begins with the established body of ethnographic work on the way structural conditions in black inner-city communities give rise to cultural adaptations that become embodied within a 'code of the street' (Anderson, 1999). According to this body of work, a local, hyper-masculine order develops within disadvantaged black communities, with its own codes and rituals of authenticity: a willingness to use violence in reputation-building, a valorization of sexual promiscuity and conquest, conspicuous consumption as a means of establishing self-image and gaining 'respect', and a pronounced antagonism towards the police and other authorities. Kubrin's aim is simple: to examine the extent to which this 'code of the street' is present not only at street level but also in rap music.

In brief, gangsta rap music originated in a combination of the 'hustla' lifestyle associated with 1970s 'Blaxploitation movies', the 'retromack' (pimp) culture of East Oakland, and the violent street gang wars of South Central Los Angeles (Hayden, 2004). As Kubrin explains, standard scholarship approaches gangsta rap as an expression of a classical subcultural order, with the existing street code serving as inspiration for rap lyrics, which then reflect this code. Kubrin's approach, though, is more nuanced; she views the culture/music/identity nexus from a 'constitutive' perspective. Gangsta rap, she says, should be understood as an 'interpretive resource', a way of 'organizing' or perhaps more accurately *reconstituting* reality, whereby 'rappers' accounts … reflexively accomplish a sense of reality – for themselves and for others'. Rap in this sense 'creates cultural understandings of urban street life that render violence, danger and unpredictability normative' (Kubrin, 2005: 366, 376).

Rather than trying to isolate any pure 'media effect', then, Kubrin shows how media influence operates alongside related cultural and social practices in a complex process of exchange and interaction. And as regards gangsta rap, other loops and spirals abound as well. Eric Watts (1997), for example, notes the dozens of high-profile rap artists who've been perpetrators or victims of criminal activity – from Snoop Dogg's involvement with Long Beach street gangs to the murder of Tupac Shakur – and so confirms that, in gangsta rap, crime and its representation are irrevocably intertwined. But Watts is more interested in a *material* analysis of rap, exploring how consumerism functions as an interpretive schema for defining and clarifying the relations among hip hop culture, gangsta rap narratives, and the interposition of an expanding rap industrial complex.

Watts focuses on a classic 'old school' rap song/video: Ice-T's 1991 'New Jack Hustla'. Here we are presented with a familiar slice of rap imagery – Uzi-wielding rappers extolling their commitment to violence as an expression of ghetto power – and so seeming confirmation of rappers as vulgar, barbaric, and nihilistic. Careful analysis, though, reveals something more and something different: clues to the close symbiosis between rap and consumer capitalism.

Superficially, 'New Jack Hustla' appears to offer a straightforward validation of Kubrin's thesis that the 'code of the street' gets integrated into rap music, with the song's lyrical boasts about instrumental violence, weapons, bitches, and money. Ice-T's Hustler is justifying his way of life, clarifying his self-image, and most importantly validating his chosen 'Hustla' lifestyle. Yet Watts argues that this portrait of 'nihilistic bravado' is not all it seems. In other moments the song offers a peek behind the rapper's 'mask of invincibility'; in fact, a closer lyrical analysis reveals another psyche for the Hustler.

Along with the drive bys and shoot outs, Ice-T is keen to articulate what he calls his 'capitalist migraine'. Not for him life working at 'Micky Ds', broke and broken, he assures us. And the solution? His own warped version of the American Dream, where 'the ends justifies the means, that's the system', where 'I had nothing and I wanted it/you had everything and you flaunted it/turned the needy into the greedy/with cocaine my success came speedy …'. Watts explains:

> Since the Hustler's being is constituted through the pressures of a street code, and since it seems to be a foregone conclusion that one will meet with some kind of untimely death in the ghetto, poverty represents a kind of living nothingness. … [G]angsta rap articulates an important perspective on the sad stasis of discharged personhood – the cultivated refusal by a cannibalistic consumer society to own up to its inability to meet its fabulous promises for livelihood. And so, the Hustler is a spectacular façade whose public performances both refute and sustain his status as a glamorous image. (Watts, 1997)

Or, as Ice-T asks, while posing the central paradox of rap and consumer society: 'Got me twisted, jammed into a paradox … is this a nightmare or the American dream?'

Lyrics like these offer moments of 'textual revelation'. Originally, Ice-T's Hustla could only make sense of the world through an internalized code of the street. But as the song continues, a dawning awareness transcends the posturing: caught in the economic claustrophobia of mainstream materialism, the street code makes for a losing game, a trap, and some bad politics to boot. Just as importantly, while this paradox is apparent in Ice-T's 1991 song, it seems now to have evaporated from commercial rap music. In many of today's rap videos, as we'll see shortly, consumerism and the American Dream are roundly embraced – and advertising, marketing, and consumerism are displayed with a sort of knowing self-awareness.

In this way, contemporary rap music embodies the evolving fusion of crime and consumerism, of transgression and popular art. But the commodification of crime isn't limited to rap or hip hop; the corporate colonization of crime and violence today pervades popular culture as a whole.

'kill this dumb fuck': the commodification of violence and the marketing of transgression

People had been working for so many years to make the world a safe, organised place. Nobody realised how boring it had become. … Nobody had left much room for adventure, except maybe the kind you could buy. On a roller coaster. At a movie. Still, it would always be that kind of faux excitement. … And because there's no possibility of real disaster, real risk, we're left with no chance for real salvation. Real elation. Real excitement. … The laws that keep us safe, these laws condemn us to boredom.

Chuck, Palahnuik, *Choke* (2000: 59)

The grainy surveillance camera cutscene dissolves into a wide shot. Scrawled on the wall in front of the central protagonist, the former death row prisoner James Earl Cash, are the words 'Kill this dumb fuck'; an on-screen arrow points towards an unwitting member of one of Carcer City's ultra-violent street gangs. Cash moves in quickly, applies the wire guillotine, administers a series of powerful blows to the face and then, with a deft flourish, snaps the gang member's neck like a chicken bone. Cash is in a hurry; he needs to kill quickly if he's to satisfy Lionel Starkweather, the twisted mastermind behind Valiant Video Enterprises, America's leading producer and distributor of 'violent, visceral, underground snuff movies'.

Welcome to the digital netherworld that is *Manhunt*, Rockstar Games' 2003 hit 'first person shooter' video game. Along with similar games like *Grand Theft Auto IV, Scarface, 50 Cent: Bulletproof, The Warriors*, and *True Crime: Streets of LA, Manhunt* is of considerable interest to cultural criminologists. Interesting enough is the way that the game was caught up in a moral panic when it was erroneously linked to the brutal murder of a 14 year old (BBC News, 2004). More interesting is the way such games exemplify the broader trend towards the commodification of violence and the marketing of transgression.

It is a notable irony that the more Western governments attempt to control the youth crime problem by imposing a series of external controls – everything from curfews to exclusion orders to Public Disorder Acts – the more they engender within young people not compliant rationality but heightened emotionality. Hence an interplay in which the 'irrational responses' of young people to state control provoke ever more punitive measures from the state, with youth culture thus becoming at once the site of excitement, contestation, and experimentation. That this is the case is not surprising. The transgressive nature of youthful cultural practices has long provoked indignation among politicians keen to curry favour with the 'moral majority' by vilifying the perceived immorality of the young. Whether lowering the age limit for the imprisonment of children or siding with schools in banning snowball fights, the government turns the screw on the young, subjecting not only their oppositional pleasures to increasing state sanction, but also their legitimate cultural practices and everyday round.

All the while, the market feeds into this dynamic, contributing to it and commodifying it. As we have seen, moral panics unfold today in a far more complex series of loops and spirals than was the case when Stan Cohen (1972) first articulated the concept. Now another twist: a decent dose of moral outrage on the part of older authorities can constitute the acid test of a truly oppositional, and therefore worthwhile, youthful endeavour. And as McRobbie and Thornton (1995) make clear, even this response is often co-opted and incorporated, as corporations use manufactured moral panic – threat of censorship, suggestion of sexual scandal – for their own profitable ends. In fact, panic-inducing images of crime and deviance are now prime marketing tools for selling products in the youth market. At one level, there is nothing inherently new about this; the compellingly salacious nature of certain criminal acts ensured a ready audience for crime throughout the twentieth century. What has changed, however, is the force and range of the illicit message, and the speed at which it loops and reverberates. Crime and transgression are now packaged and promoted as fashionable cultural symbols, with transgression thus emerging as a desirable consumer decision (see Fenwick and Hayward, 2000). Here, within consumer culture, crime becomes an aesthetic, a style, a fashion – and so the distinction between the representation of criminality and the pursuit of stylized excitement, especially youthful excitement, evaporates.

Recall our discussion of rap music and its immensely popular mélange of street gang iconography, retromack style, and urban transgression (Miller, 1995). Add to this the murders of major rap artists like Tupac Shakur and the Notorious BIG as part of East Coast/West Coast rap feuds, and the 'flagging' of gang symbols and signs in rap videos, and it becomes clear that, in gangsta rap at least, musical commodity and street life are ever more intertwined and indistinguishable. But to fully understand this commodification process, we must recall and rethink Watts's focus as well: the way in which consumer culture now dictates the terms of the dynamic.

While brands have long featured in rap culture, recently the stakes have risen. Once hardcore artists like Ice-T or Tim Dogg rapped about $60 Nike trainers and 40 oz bottles of Colt 45; today giants of corporate hip hop, like P Diddy and Jay-Z, extol the virtues of Louis Vuitton luggage, Cristal champagne, and the new Porsche Cayenne.[3] As De Jong and Schuilenburg (2006) suggest, so long as 'the street' and 'the urban' remain referenced for their symbolic authenticity, the rap and hip hop industry can move high-end product, even as the genre retreats from the impoverished lifeworlds where it originated. In the video for Snoop Dogg and Pharell Williams' hit 'Drop It Like It's Hot' (2004), for example, luxury cars and jewel-encrusted accoutrement seem intended to function as signifiers of both consumerist success and urban life, with transgressive stance and self-worth now conflated in simple commodity codes, as interpretable as a Nike 'swoosh' or a Gucci monogram (Hayward, 2004: 181).[4]

With its inherently transgressive dimensions, rap music – not unlike punk rock, hard house, and death metal – perhaps seems an obvious place for the selling of crime, and for the confounding of illicit identity and consumer status. More remarkable and revealing is the way violent transgression is now emerging within more mainstream areas of consumerist cultural production. Crime and punishment now feature as regular tropes in major advertising campaigns – again, not an entirely new phenomenon, but one defined by a qualitative shift in the range and tone of advertiser-appropriated violence. While this area remains woefully under-researched within criminology, one US-based study is useful in this regard. In 2000 Maguire and associates analyzed 1,699 commercials televised between 1996 and 1997, concluding that, while violence in television advertisements was 'generally tame' and innocuous in nature, there had been a '100 per cent increase in violent content in television advertisements in 1997 compared to 1996' (cited in Carter and Weaver 2003: 120). The limitations of this type of research not withstanding, it is interesting to note that a decade after the Maguire et al. study, this tendency has accelerated, with advertisers regularly alluding to crime and criminality in their campaigns.

As we have demonstrated elsewhere (Hayward, 2004: 171), car stereo ads now feature images of street riots – with car ads referencing 'joyriding', reckless driving, extreme sports, and pyromania – while other mainstream advertising campaigns feature vandalism, drug references, and political rebellion. The advertising industry has likewise long relied upon explicit sexuality and patriarchal gender stereotypes to move product (Berger, 1972: ch. 7; Williamson, 1978; Goffman, 1979; Jhally, 1987), but now women are increasingly portrayed as victims of, or passive accomplices to, crime and violence. In Chapter 4 we saw the FCUK shop window and its display of women violently victimizing one another; Kilbourne (1999) highlights similar cases of violently misogynistic marketing, with men pointing guns at women's heads, or attacking a woman in a jeans ad with the tag line 'Wear it out and make it scream'. A Baby-G watch advertisement on the side of a bus similarly depicts a naked women tied up with giant watches (Carter and Weaver, 2003: 126).

Recently, über-trendy fashion house Dolce and Gabbana were forced to withdraw newspaper ads following a public outcry over their violently sexist content. In Spain, an ad showing a woman held to the ground by a half-dressed man was condemned by Labour Ministry officials as an offence to women's dignity and an 'incitement' to sexual violence. In Britain, the Advertising Standards Authority moved to ban another Dolce and Gabbana ad that featured, much like the FCUK window, bloodied women with knives. Such images may or may not directly 'incite' violence in the tradition of the media effects model, but they do clearly contribute to the cultural normalization of violence against women, to a sort of 'epistemic socialization' (Bennett and Ferrell, 1987) whereby viewers and consumers learn to see women as victims-in-waiting. With dippy fashionistas like Dolce and Gabbana ignoring the larger meaning of their advertisements, with companies making deals to place their consumer products in misogynistic rap videos, a particular interplay of crime, media, and profit is made manifest: the willingness of mainstream corporations and their advertisers to portray women as passive, emotionless ciphers on the receiving end of transgressive violence.

Predatory Media?

In the United States, Dateline NBC's *To Catch a Predator* television programme pays the vigilante group Perverted Justice to set up online chats with potential child sexual predators, then orchestrates and televises the scenes in which the potential predators are subsequently confronted, and arrested. Through this 'formula' for creating sensational, viewer-friendly programming, NBC closes any remaining distance between media, crime, and criminal justice, intertwining in one programme the dynamics of entrapment, criminal intent, policing, news coverage, and entertainment. In one recent case, as police cars and television cameras surrounded the house of a man caught up in the programme's net, he chose to commit suicide rather than face the swirl of public exposure and enforcement. His sister later claimed that the programme had in fact 'ended his life' (Bauder, 2007: 2B) for him; Dateline NBC responded by promoting and airing the episode, and the suicide, during the high-profile television 'sweeps week' in February 2007. (See, relatedly, Karen Schofield's (2004) insightful work on the commodification of child sexual abuse).

bumfights and televised beatdowns

The violent titillation doesn't stop there, of course – far from it. Surf late night satellite TV and you'll experience a whole new televisual sensation: the expanding world of self-styled 'extreme television'. Here the emphasis shifts from rap narratives or advertised misogyny to embodied moments of visceral transgression: broken bones, concussions, lacerations. Unfettered by prime-time censorship restrictions, this new genre of youth TV constitutes a storehouse of illicit excitement, a ready resource for the voyeuristic consumption of pain and transgression. The popular TV show and film series *Jackass*, and its many derivative shows now available in the United States and the UK, mix pop nihilism, pervasive hedonism, and extremes of self-destructive violence (self-inflicted cuts, self-administered pepper spray) to create profitable mainstream entertainment. Meanwhile the proliferation of cable networks and broadband downloads ensures that lightly censored 'extreme TV' is global in range, with each country quick to cash in with its own version of *Jackass* (e.g. Britain's *Dirty Sanchez* and the Finnish show *The Dudesons*). Better yet – or worse yet – is the fusing of extreme 'reality' TV with the *CSI* genre. Now available are explicit crime 'documentaries', such as Bolivia's hyper-violent *Telepolicial* and the Russian prime-time offering, *Criminal Russia*, both of which include graphic crime-scene footage of real crimes – street and gangland slayings in the case of *Telepolicial*, and infamous serial killings (both solved and unsolved) in the case of *Criminal Russia*.

But for real extremes of mediated violence, forget television. Bubbling under the media surface is a netherworld of uncensored DVDs, websites, and Podcasts that present brutally real crimes as illicit entertainment. In Chapter 1 we highlighted the case of Michael G Jackson and his illegal *Agg Townz Fights* video series. Yet this was no one-off occurrence; there exists a veritable mass market for this kind of real-life violence, all bought and sold on the internet. From fairly innocuous 'Happy Slapping' compilations to hardcore 'caught on camera' schoolyard beatdowns and street fight downloads, so much of this material now circulates that 'producers' have begun to stratify their product in a bid to meet niche demands. Alongside standard fare like the *Agg Townz* schoolyard/street fights, or the eBay favourite *Beatdowns and Scraps*, consumers can now select DVDs or downloads that feature fights between recently released US Federal prisoners (*Felony Fights, Volumes 1–5*), organized street gangs (*Urban Warfare: Gangs Caught on Tape*), and 'all girl' protagonists (*Spotlight Honies vs. Worldwide Honies: Good Girls Gone Bad, Extreme Chick Flicks*, and *Queen of the Hood*).

And then there are the infamous *Bumfights* – the undeniable inspiration for most, if not all, of the above titles. Here the premise is simple: find some homeless folks, maybe drug addicts or alcoholics, persuade them to fight each other for booze or cash, videotape the confrontations, synchronize the blows and pratfalls to a cool skate punk soundtrack, and package the whole thing into a series of stylish video releases. Think consumption of this sort of staged barbarism is confined to a few social outsiders? Think again. It's estimated that over 600,000 copies of the various *Bumfights* videos have been sold worldwide, making the four Las Vegas high school filmmakers who hatched the original plan wealthy men indeed. Needless to say, authorities in both California and Nevada have reacted; but while the *Bumfights* founders have been the subject of a number of lawsuits (including one requiring them to cease distribution of the videos), *Bumfights* merchandise – including everything from the DVDs to branded beanie hats – is still available on their up-scale website.

One thing's for sure: the *Bumfights* producers certainly know the profit potential of commodified violence. Their latest offering, *Terrorists, Killers and Middle
East Wackos*, sees them tapping into the post-9/11 mindset and making a fast
buck out of footage that's loosely based around the themes of international
terrorism and political violence. No insights into the world's geo-political
problems here, by the way; this is little more than a crypto-snuff movie, a compilation of brutal torture scenes, political killings, and gruesome executions.

And it's not just bottom feeders like the *Bumfights* team that realize there's
money to be made from selling war-themed shock footage. While some media
consumers may tire of nightly news images of Iraqi suicide bombings and
Taliban fire fights, others yearn for just a bit more. Drawing from the thousands of hours of real-life combat footage posted on the internet by US military personnel in Iraq, documentary filmmaker Deborah Scranton has
compiled the controversial film *The War Tapes* (2006). While Scranton's film
is an altogether more sophisticated offering than *Terrorists, Killers and Middle
East Wackos* (it would be difficult to be less sophisticated), neither film is
likely to do much for US–Arab relations. Sgt Steve Pink, Specialist Mike
Moriarty and Sgt Zack Bazzi shot the bulk of the video seen in *The War Tapes*
(Poole, 2006), and they would no doubt counter that Al-Qaeda and other
insurrectionist groups regularly use their own combat footage and edited execution images to drum up support for their cause. In any case, in a digital age
'winning hearts and minds' blurs into producing videos and scoring sound-
tracks – and war and its image collapse one into the other.

Amidst the contemporary mediascape, then, crime and violence become
cheap commodities, emptied of their embodied consequences, sold as seductions of entertainment and digital spectacle. These latest transformations in
mediated violence in turn reaffirm gender and class stereotypes, and highlight
a mean-spirited contemporary culture of marketed aggression and hyper-
violent machismo. Along the way they obliterate old distinctions between the
real and the image, between mediated cause and effect, becoming embedded
in the everyday cultures of youth and consumption. And so a troubling question: How might these tendencies develop in the future, as the technology of
entertainment becomes ever more sophisticated and pervasive?

'real war news, real war games': cultural criminology and 'real virtuality'

This is not a video game. This is real war.
General Norman Schwarzkopf, press conference,
First Gulf War (in De Long and Schuilenburg, 2006: 26)

At least one Marine seems ecstatic about being in a life-or-death gun fight. Nineteen-
year-old Corporal Harold James Trombley … has been waiting all day for permission to
fire his machine gun. … Now Trombley is curled over his weapon, firing away. …
Trombley is beside himself. 'I was just thinking one thing when we drove into that
ambush,' he enthuses. '*Grand Theft Auto: Vice City*. I felt like I was living it when I

seen the flames coming out of windows, the blown-up car in the street, guys crawling around shooting at us. It was fucking cool.'

(Wright, 2004: 6–7)

The phenomenon of unexpurgated war footage as internet entertainment illustrates an essential point for cultural criminologists: the way in which late-modern mediated violence contributes to the *reconstitution of everyday reality itself*. Given this, we must look beyond censorious concerns over the visceral violence of *The War Tapes* or *Bumfights*, and focus attention on the particular dynamics by which computer-mediated and internet-circulated communication explode the boundaries between the virtual and the real.

To do so we must first consider the internet and its function as a social prac-tice. Rather than viewing the internet simply as a digital tool, a piece of com-municative technology, we need to focus on the *experience of the internet* – how it functions in particular ways for particular purposes. Early theoretical work on the internet typically cast cyberspace in wholly celebratory terms. With its globalized labyrinth of information and entertainment, it was seen by many commentators as the perfect vehicle for self-construction and enhancement – a liberating, progressive space where individuals could celebrate difference and develop new 'online personas' and 'multiple virtual life projects', unen-cumbered by fixed class hierarchies and the demands of physical everyday reality (Rheingold, 1991, 1993; Turkle, 1997).

As internet analysis developed, though, many scholars began to doubt the idea of a separate or distinct 'online self', with Manuel Castells (1996) coining the classic notion of 'real virtuality' to highlight how our culture of 'embedded media' constantly impinges on physical reality. When filtered through the online social prisms of cyber communities, cyber networks and cyber (sub)cul-tures, the categories of the 'real' and the 'virtual' seem even more hybridized. As cultural criminologists, then, we're not interested in setting up rigid and ultimately false distinctions between virtual and real-world experience. Rather, as already seen in our other approaches to 'crime and the media', our line of analysis attempts to move beyond old formulas and old dualisms. As Kevin Robbins (1996: 16, 26) argues: 'Virtual reality and cyberspace are commonly imagined in terms of reaction against, or opposition to, the real world. ... Virtual reality is imagined as a nowhere-somewhere alternative to the dangerous conditions of contemporary social reality. ... The mythology of cyberspace is preferred over its sociology. ... It is time to re-locate virtual cul-ture in the real world. ... We must consider our state of suspension between these conditions.'

In this light we urge criminologists to undertake the study of this hybridized 'state of suspension'.[5] In a bid to encourage this process – and to continue our analysis of US military and insurgent violence as virtual entertainment – we offer yet another looping example of violence as commodified digital spectacle.

Media, Representation, and Meaning | 145

Our choice of subject matter – the latest innovations and developments in violent video games – allows us to revisit another theme as well: the fast-changing, dangerously creative world of digital gaming. Where better to consider the 'state of suspension' between the real and the virtual?

In *Mediapolis* (2006), Alex de Jong and Marc Schuilenburg investigate the 'military–entertainment complex', showing how the US Army has converted a host of video games, from early 1980s titles like *Battlezone* and *Army Battlezone* to more recent offerings like *Doom* (1993), *Medal of Honor* (1999), and *Counterstrike* (2001), into simulated combat conditioning exercises for infantry soldiers. That the US Army utilizes video games for training purposes is not especially surprising, given that the majority of young military personnel have been raised in environments where video gaming was commonplace (see Wright, 2004). More surprising perhaps – and certainly more criminologically important – is the extent to which the distinction between simulated, virtual training and real-life, on-the-ground soldiering is evaporating.

This conflation is the result of two interrelated processes. First, games industry innovations have facilitated enhanced re-creation of real-world environments. Marketed with the tagline 'Real War News, Real War Games', *Kuma War* (2004), for example, incorporates downloadable, up-to-date TV news footage from contemporary war zones. This allows online gamers 'to participate in the American hunt for members of Al Qaeda in the Shah-i-Kot Valley in Eastern Afghanistan', or to experience the 'bloody happenings at the centre of Fallujah' (De Jong and Schuilenburg, 2006: 21).

Second, the US Army itself has developed a series of temporally and spatially 'authentic' first-person-shooter games. Not content with simply converting existing video game platforms, in 2002 the US Army launched *America's Army: Operations* (followed in 2005 by *America's Army: The Rise of the Soldier*).[6] Costing over $6 million to develop, *America's Army* is now one of the top five online action games, with over 5.5 million registered users worldwide. Intended as a digital recruiting sergeant, *America's Army* doesn't just recreate basic military training, from weapons instruction to rudimentary battlefield medical procedures – it reproduces actual combat scenarios in graphic detail and, importantly, in real time. The primary goal here is to acculturate players to the tactics and nuances of combat – and so this is no free-fire fest. Indeed, one of the unwritten aims of *America's Army* is to encourage players to think more and fire less; trigger-happy gamers are discouraged. Participants are required to adhere to the same regulations that govern all Army personnel. Breaches of the rules see players banned from the site, while those who successfully pass tests and comply with regulations proceed to higher levels.[7]

Just one more shoot-'em-up war video game, albeit a particularly realistic one? Or an insidious international recruiting tool, designed to roll out military

Plate 5.1 Screenshot of 'Special Forces Extraction Alpha' from *America's Army*
Credit: De Long and Schuilenberg (2006), by permission

training and military ethos to a new generation of video gamers? Well, yes. And so another either/or dichotomy gone, as the illusory world of video games flows into the all too violently real world of contemporary warfare. This isn't the last loop in the spiral, either. Like Robbins, De Long and Schuilenburg (2006: 13) view developments in virtual space as echoes, maybe mirror images, of still other tendencies underway in everyday life. They see *America's Army*, *Kuma War*, and similar real/virtual hybrids like *The War Tapes* as manifestations of an increasing 'militarization of public space'.

> A military control net has been thrown across the city and the mesh is being drawn tighter and tighter, leading to an altered experience of one's own identity as well as the installation of a specific regime of rules and sanctions. Renowned war games such as *America's Army* and *Full Spectrum Warrior* represent these radical changes better than the last police report or academic manuscript. These games indicate how the militarization of life has become the most important input of a culture that is oriented towards security.(De Long and Schuilenburg, 2006: 13)

In virtual space as in 'real' life, though, every action has a reaction – and so another loop or two unwinds. While the US 'military – entertainment complex' goes about its business, in other parts of the world, huddled around glowing computer screens, small teams of games-savvy programmers use similar technology to pedal an altogether different ideological message. Even before *America's Army* was available as a download, Palestinian supporters were releasing their own online video games featuring digital recreations of actual combat scenes from the Israeli–Palestinian conflict. Their goals with games like *Under Ash* (Afkar Media, 2001), *Under Seige* (Afkar Media, 2004) and *Special Force* (Hezbollah, 2003) were twofold:[8] first to portray their own account of the struggle for Palestine, and second, to counter the worldwide hegemony of American-designed war games. In one such game – dedicated to Palestinian martyrs – players who utilize only (virtual) stones to take on Israeli soldiers are reminded to take the game out of its virtual environment and into the streets. 'Isn't this a lesson in the continual movement from the real to the virtual world and back?' ask De Long and Schuilenberg (2006: 67). 'The logic of the movement rests on the fact that each virtuality eventually becomes reality and that each reality sinks into a virtual world....'

Meanwhile, back in the USA, others are mounting their own digital challenge to American imperialism, both in its real-world form and as presented in 'War

Plate 5.2   Cover of *Under Siege* (Afkar Media, 2004)
Credit: Afkar Media

on Terror' video games like *Counterstrike*. Anne-Marie Schleiner's *Velvet-Strike* (2002) adopts the ethos of culture jammers – those who alter billboards or hack corporate websites – by subverting the very gameplay logic of *Counterstrike*. With *Velvet-Strike*, gamers can write subversive images and captions on the virtual surfaces of *Counterstrike*, thus infiltrating the militarized spaces of the virtual war on terror like so many street-wise political subversives. Yet once again, easy distinctions between the real and the virtual, the video console subversive and the street subversive, no longer hold. Shortly after *Velvet-Strike's* launch, game designer Anne-Marie Schleiner began to receive death threats – and while we've never met her, we're fairly certain that Schleiner would agree that death threats, whether arriving by written letter or emailed message, have a deleterious effect on one's sense of physical well-being!

Velvet-Strike leads us to other questions as well – questions essential to cultural criminology. Does a subversive video counter-move like *Velvet-Strike* constitute 'real' and meaningful resistance to imperialism, to political abuse, to pervasive violence? Or is it just another mediated ploy, the next loop in an endless spiral, coerced and corrupted easily enough by the machinery of the late modern mediascape.

crime into commodity, rebellion into money ... spirals into resistance

[M]ost political strategies are media strategies. The contest to determine news agendas is the first and last battle of the political campaign. (McRobbie and Thornton, 1995: 571)

Its thirty years since The Clash's Joe Strummer belted out the searing lyrics of 'White Man in Hammersmith Palais', venting his frustration at the anodyne state of the British punk and reggae scenes. Shocked at the way supposedly politically principled bands sold out to major recording labels, at the way in which musical non-conformity could become marketable commodity, Strummer succinctly described a process of 'turning rebellion into money'. Yet this period of the 1970s is seen by many as one of counter-cultural expression and artistic rebellion – it was, after all, less than a decade since the student revolts in London and Paris, the emergence of radical feminism, and the victories of the anti-Vietnam War movement. One can only imagine, then, what Strummer made of the music business by the time of his death in 2002. By that time Strummer's belovedly rebellious punk aesthetic had been appropriated by everyone from boy bands to gauche celebrity chefs and American automobile manufactures.

Minor Threat, for example, were a hardcore/punk band whose lead singer, Ian Mackaye, founded the label Dischord Records in the early 1980s. Dedicated to DIY politics, to mixing 'music and social movement', the band produced a 1984 album whose cover – a kid dressed in black, his shaved head resting on his folded arms – became an 'iconic symbol' of do-it-yourself cultural resistance. By 2005, though, Nike had produced a near-perfect 'Major Threat' imitation of the album cover, placing it on posters and websites to promote its Nike Skateboarding Tour. 'They stole it', said a representative of Dischord Records, when asked about the image. 'Nike represents just about the antithesis of what Dischord stands for and it makes me sick to my stomach to think that they are using this explicit imagery to fool kids into thinking that the general ethos of this label, and Minor Threat in particular, can somehow be linked to Nike's mission.'[9]

In one sense this contested image constitutes just another loop in the contemporary cultural flow – here flowing from Minor Threat's album cover to Nike's poster and website. Like Strummer, though, we see it as something more insidious: the hijacking of illicit meaning and counter-cultural protest for corporate ends. More broadly, it confirms for us a new media age, an age in which everything 'real' – real violence and warzone footage, street crime and street justice, political resistance and do-it-yourself community – comes eventually to be commodified, packaged, and sold within the economics of entertainment. As cultural criminologists, then, we take it as our job to find the political and economic contradictions unfolding amidst the loops and spirals of contemporary culture, to record the slippage between meaning and commodity, and to investigate the consequences for transgression, crime, and justice.

Consider as another example one of the most prevalent and visible forms of crime in contemporary Western societies: graffiti. Like punk music, hip hop graffiti has been around some thirty years now – and by now the spiralling twists and turns are almost too numerous to follow. Early on, graffiti writers appropriated mass media images and icons in developing a wildly stylized visual language that allowed them to 'hide in the light' (Hebdige, 1979) – that is, to hold public conversations and contests that remained nonetheless their private practice, largely impenetrable to public understanding. Still, photographers and documentary filmmakers noticed – and their photographs and films became style manuals that helped the spread of hip hop graffiti. Legal authorities noticed, too, and launched high-profile media and law enforcement campaigns designed to create an image of such graffiti as vandalism and criminal threat – all of which, ironically, accelerated graffiti's experiential seductions, pushed the graffiti underground from subculture to counter-culture, and helped construct hip hop graffiti over the next two decades as a global phenomenon.

Despite these aggressive anti-graffiti campaigns – and because of them – graffiti writers today continue to paint illegal graffiti worldwide; moreover, they now produce their own do-it-yourself magazines and books (sometimes promoting them through illegal graffiti 'billboards'), and even illicitly hang their unauthorized paintings in establishment galleries like the Louvre, the Museum of Modern Art, and the Tate (Snyder, 2006, 2009; S Jones, 2005: 20). Yet graffiti style has also gone mainstream; as graffiti has become the lingua franca of hip, artistic rebellion has indeed turned into big money. Corporations like Nike, McDonald's, and Sony now employ graffiti writers to paint corporate logos in city streets, while appropriating existing graffiti murals for CD covers and ad campaigns – suggesting of course that whatever cultural authenticity the law can't kill, the market can (Alvelos, 2004).

And the DNA of graffiti continues to spread like some mutating double helix, confounding art, crime, and commodity. Fashion designer Marc Ecko battles legal authorities to stage a public launch of *Getting Up: Contents Under Pressure* (2006, Atari)[10] – his Playstation game featuring famous graffiti writers – and later sells the film rights to MTV Films.[11] Meanwhile, original work by 'Generation Y' hero Banksy – a legendary graffiti artist who made his name by poking fun at legal authorities, hyper-materialism, and pompous art worlds – goes on sale in high-end galleries in Los Angeles and London, where it is quickly snapped up by the likes of Brad Pitt and Angelina Jolie. The Chrysler Corporation even creates its own self-graffitied billboards to promote its Plymouth Neon, so as to give the car an appealingly edgy 'personality' (Prigoff, 1995: 216). Likewise, canny advertisers embrace new marketing techniques like 'guerrilla marketing' ('ambient' and 'viral' promotions that use unconventional channels to disseminate product messages) and 'brandalism' (surreptitious media such as graffiti and illegal 'fly posters' to serve corporate ends). 'Most of the surfaces in the square are currently covered with stickers and flyposters advertising ... Travis, Elle Macpherson's lingerie company, and, ironically, George Monbiot's *Captive State*, a book which attacks brands' incursions into public spaces', Richard Benson (2001: 43) recently observed of London. 'You'll also find, tied to the railings, white ribbons with the name of a new East London art gallery written on them, and glued to the pavement, a hard-wearing ad for a website selling art. On the walls you'll see the name of several bands, in spray paint. From vandalism to brandalism.'

So it does indeed seem that 'real' crime and transgression are doomed these days to reappear as looping images of themselves – and worse, that moments of human creativity or political resistance are reduced soon enough to marketable commodities, to cheap parodies of their original intent. Maybe so – maybe today's pervasive media culture, powered by the insatiable momentum of the market, leaves no space for alternative meaning, edgy transgression, or political critique. Maybe attempting to resist this momentum is like erecting a little beach umbrella to ward off a mediated tsunami.

Plate 5.3 Defaced billboard, corner of Cambridge Heath Road and Whitechapel Road, East London, England

Credit: Keith Hayward (2002)

spiralling resistance

Or maybe not. Maybe it's just that new conditions require new strategies, new criminologies, another twist or two in the spiralling flow of meaning.

In fact, for contemporary activist and culture jamming groups such as the Billboard Liberation Front, the California Department of Corrections, and the Guerrilla Girls, the very pervasiveness of corporate culture is at the same time its vulnerability: the bigger the billboard, the more popular the website, the better known the image, the more sweeping can be the next subversive turn in the spiral of its public meaning. In their hands, a 'Most Powerful Luxury SUV on the Continent' billboard gets reworked so that it proclaims 'Most Wasteful Luxury SUV on the Continent'; a General Motors make-your-own-automobile-advert website gets hijacked and transformed into a critical forum on autos and oil (Lasn, 2000; Ritson, 2000). Likewise, when the White House turned the drug war into the war on terror, the progressive Drug Policy Alliance turned it back, launching a mediated counter-attack that parodied the White House's efforts and eventually led to the cancellation of the drugs-and-terrorism campaign (Brown, 2007). Anne-Marie Schleiner and *Velvet-Strike* aren't alone – they're part of a movement, and part of the spiral.

A half-century ago the Situationists – an oddball assemblage of artists, writers, and activists who were among the first to theorize the emerging world of mediated meaning – imagined just this sort of programme of subversive cultural diversion. If they could somehow 'seize the familiar and turn it into the other', if they could 'turn the words of [their] enemies back on themselves', the Situationists believed, they might be able to effect historic change, since after all, 'making meaning – or unmaking it – went hand in hand with making history' (Marcus, 1989: 178–9). Writing in 1956, watching as the swirling symbolism of mass culture began to overtake everyday experience, Guy Debord and Gil Wolman argued that under these conditions, 'any sign or word is susceptible to being converted into something else, even into its opposite.[12] So the Situationists developed the theory and practice of *detournement* – the theft of conventional meaning, the unauthorized appropriation of manufactured understanding – and went about undermining everyday order. Like today's culture jammers and activists, they diverted encoded scripts of obedience and consumption into invitations to innovation. Rewriting mass-produced cartoon panels, defiling sacred texts, plagiarizing popular plays, they engineered radical reversals of meaning, hard turns towards uncertainty and surprise amidst the saturating spiral of mass culture.

Fifty years on, the emerging mass culture confronted by the Situationists has become if anything all the more fluid and emergent, all the more saturated with mediated technologies and circulating meanings, its coded consequences coursing always through the situations of daily life – and yet, because of this very cultural availability, all the more susceptible 'to being converted into something else, even into its opposite'. And so, if in those early years the Situationists embraced as their programme and passion the subversive theft of mass meaning, the turning of dominant ideologies away from their own spiraling self-confirmations, cultural criminology embraces such subversion today as its programme and passion. Like culture jammers and billboard liberators, like the host of activists groups who today work to 'become the media' in the interest of progressive social change, cultural criminology's passion must be to investigate the flow of cultural meaning around issues of crime and justice – and its programme to insinuate itself into this flow, and so to turn it towards critique and change.

Of course none of this is to suggest that such a programme is a simple one. Under the slippery circumstances of late modernity, most any meaning can be stolen – but as the Plymouth Neon billboards and the Nike Major Threat campaign suggest, most any meaning can be stolen right back. Moreover, those who would maintain conventional meanings of crime and justice, or fight to recover them if somehow spirited away, have at their disposal sophisticated advertising campaigns, televised crime spectacles, weighty agency findings, and Uniform Crime Reports and Home Office Crime Statistics. Then again, cultural criminologists have quite intentionally developed in strategic counterpoint a certain sense of style, a facility for constructing little subversions and seductions, an eye for critique and insinuation, a flair for narrative and representation, a feel for 'newsmaking criminology' (Barak, 1994) – and increasingly, our own journals, books, websites, and conferences. A fair fight, this attempt by cultural criminology to infiltrate the late modern flow of meaning by way of intellectual seduction, to turn waves of corporate misinformation and wars on crime into something better? No, but a fight worth undertaking, and a fight that finds its logic of engagement within the very fluidity of contemporary culture.

This strategy of cultural insinuation and redirection can perhaps benefit broader progressive battles as well. The injustices of the police and the courts, the globalization of economic inequality, the endangering of human dignity within nation states and between them – all demand cultural criminology's critical attention, but also its cultural engagement. Fighting alongside labour strikers, immigrants, and the unemployed, the French sociologist Pierre Bourdieu has argued for the essential role of critical intellectuals in 'uncovering the specifically cultural and ideological dimensions' of repressive social conditions, since, as he says, progressive 'social movements are several symbolic revolutions behind their opponents, who use media consultants, public relations consultants and so on'. These opponents, Bourdieu adds, must be 'fought with intellectual and cultural weapons', and 'new forms of symbolic action' (Bourdieu, 1998: 52–4, 57). Revisiting his decades of engaged research with American street gangs, reaffirming the essential role of ethnic identity and culture, John Hagedorn likewise concludes that for gangs and others, 'culture in the information age is stronger than even industrial era subcultural theorists imagined, and different in nature' (Hagedorn, 2006: 141–51). Stronger and different indeed – a medium open to 'new forms of symbolic action', a medium vulnerable to insinuation and redirection.

To think critically about 'crime and the media', then – to move past simple measures of media content or media effects, and on to a sense of loops and spirals, of fluidity and saturation – is not only to understand the dynamics of crime and trangression in late modernity; it is to imagine new trajectories towards social justice. When crime policy is made in the media, when courts echo with media-made expectations, when police officers perform for their own cameras, criminologists must find ways to penetrate these dynamics if they're to humanize them. When crime collapses into commodity, war into entertainment, reality into virtuality, criminologists must find new forms of intellectual activism appropriate to these confounded circumstances.

Yet it's unlikely they'll succeed if they stick to the stale, sanitized sort of social scientific criminology that has dominated the last few decades. Instead, criminologists will need critiques that can converse with the culture at large, methods that can surf late modern flows of meaning, knowledge that can be dangerous to dominant understandings. The following chapter explores the methods by which such dangerous, fluid knowledge might be created. The book's final chapter ends with an attempt to insinuate such knowledge into the flow of meaning around crime and justice, and so to turn the spiral towards progressive understanding.

notes

1 Miss Moss's financial accounts certainly make interesting reading. Moss owns 100% of Skate Enterprises, a company established to manage her endorsements and image rights. Since the 'cocaine' incident Skate Enterprises' turnover doubled. 'The accounts are highly significant because the financial year they cover ended five months after the publication of the photographs. They suggest that even during the depths of her brief period of disgrace Moss was prospering' (Prynn 2007).

2 The policing of political protests likewise involves sophisticated photographic and video surveillance – and often, protestors and 'camcordistas' utilizing their own video cameras and micro-radio stations as avenues for performance and mediated self-defence (see Hoffman and Brown, 2008; and Ferrell, 2001/2).

3 The market's exploitation of rap music does not stop there. The porn industry is also keen to take advantage of hip hop's edgy youthful appeal. Cross-marketed simultaneous music and porn releases, co-hosted by major artists such as 50 Cent, Lil' John, and most notably Snoop Dogg, whose recent association with porn baron Larry Flint resulted in the biggest grossing porn movie ever, have greatly contributed to hardcore pornography's entry into the mainstream.

4 The commodification of crime in music is not confined to rap and hip hop. Crime has become a major theme in youth-oriented commercial music more generally, from the controversial Body Count album, 'Cop Killer', and the skate-punk group MDC (Millions of Dead Cops) to the sophisticated urban hip hop of the Fun Lovin' Criminals. However, perhaps the most explicit example is the recent video for the song '(it's Gonna Be A) Lovely Day' by clubbers' favourite Braccacio and Aisher: it depicts the theft and burning (or 'hotting' as it is known) of a stolen car.

5 Some interesting work is already underway, in particular on the way digital technology and cyberspace are reshaping the norms and practices of various subcultural groups. See Hier (2000) on hate groups; Jenkins (2001) on online paedophile rings; Greer on (2004) online 'grief communities' that emerge in the wake of high-profile crimes; Wilson and Atkinson (2005) on 'Rave' and 'Straightedge' subcultures; Zaitch and de Leeuw (2008) on the cyberpractices of football hooligan firms; and Anahita (2006) on 'virtual skinheads'.

6 *See also Full Spectrum Warrior* (THQ, 2004) and its sequel *Full Spectrum Warrior*: *Ten Hammers* (THQ, 2006); initially developed by the US Army as sophisticated combat simulators, these training aids were subsequently released to the general public as multi-format video games.

7 The use of military video game simulators has now extended to post-conflict rehabilitation. *Virtual Iraq* (2006) is a new game being used by US military clinics to help veterans re-experience the sounds and scenes that may have triggered painful memories of their tours of duty in Iraq. It is claimed that exposure to these simulated environments can help combat Post Traumatic Stress Disorder.

8 While *Special Force* and the Afkar Media games all hail from the same geographic region, they are very different both in terms of socio-political position and game play. While *Special Force* could be considered an Arabic reflection of *America's Army* or *Full Spectrum Warrior*, *Under Ash* and *Under Siege* are different in that they are based on real life stories of human suffering caused by the occupation.

9 Quotations from http:// threemindsorganic.com, 'Turning Rebellion Into Money', as visited November 2005.

10 See also Sony PSP's new video game *Free Running* (Core Design), based on the urban extreme sport of Parkour.

11 Interestingly, when the permit for the video games' in-the-street launch party is revoked by New York City officials concerned that the party will promote illegal graffiti, Ecko sues, and a District Court judge rules against the city, noting that 'by the same token, presumably, a street performance of *Hamlet* would be tantamount to encouraging revenge murder. … As for a street performance of *Oedipus Rex*, don't even think about it' (Vargas, 2006: C10).

12 Guy Debord and Guy J Wolman, 'A User's Guide to Detournement' (1956), at www.bopsecrets.org.

A selection of films and documentaries illustrative of some of the themes and ideas in this chapter

NETWORK, 1976, Dir. Sidney Lumet
A searing, multi-Oscar winning satire of mainstream media, *Network* tells the story of a fictional television network, Union Broadcasting System, and how it uses morally bankrupt methods to deal with its flagging ratings. 'I'm as mad as hell and I'm not going to take this anymore' screams Peter Finch's character shortly after threatening to kill himself live on air. However, rather than sack him from his job as UBS's news anchor, the network gives him his own show!

THE PERVERT'S GUIDE TO CINEMA (Parts 1–3), 2006, Dir. Sophie Fiennes
The entertaining philosopher Slavoj Zizek takes us on a visual journey through some of the most famous films in movie history – only this time we are asked to delve deep into the hidden language of cinema in a bid to reveal what movies actually tell us about our psychic selves. Skipping effortlessly from The Marx Brothers to Hitchcock to David Lynch, Zizek explains how fantasy, reality, sexuality, subjectivity, desire and materiality are all deeply embedded in the DNA of modern cinema. Screen any part of Zizek's trilogy and you'll never view movies in the same way again.

BUS 174, 2002, Dir. José Padhila
Described as 'the trajectory of a tragedy', *Bus 174* is a hard-hitting documentary about the hijacking of a bus in Rio de Janeiro on St Valentine's Day 2000. It tells two parallel stories. The first describes the hijacker's life of social deprivation in Rio's shanty towns and subsequent experiences inside Brazil's brutal prison system. The second is the story of the hijack itself, which was broadcast live on TV for over four hours. Taken together, the two stories illustrate why Brazil and other countries with similar social and economic problems are so violent (see www.bus174.com).

AILEEN WUORNOS: THE SELLING OF A SERIAL KILLER, 1992, Dir. Nick Broomfield
Veteran documentary maker Nick Broomfield's entertaining, if problematic, film about the media frenzy surrounding the serial killer Aileen Wuornos. In 1991, Wuornos confessed to the murders of seven men, each picked up on a Florida highway. From then until her execution in 2002 (see Broomfield's 2003 follow-up film *Aileen: Life and Death of a Serial Killer*) she found herself at the centre of a media maelstrom. The problem of course is that, despite good intentions, Broomfield has only added to the media furore surrounding Wuornos.

NATURAL BORN KILLERS, 1994, Dir. Oliver Stone

A heavy-handed and now somewhat dated satire about the way violent crimes are sensationalized and glamorized in the media. Perhaps even more interesting is the way the film itself became embroiled in a media loop when it was subsequently blamed for inspiring a series of copy-cat killing sprees. While not a great movie, *Natural Born Killers* is a veritable case study of the crime–media nexus.

dangerous knowledge

Mark Hamm (1998: 111) once described himself as 'a janitor for academic criminology', sweeping up and sorting through social discards – skinheads, terrorists, abusers, corrupters – other criminologists don't much care to encounter. Cultural criminology as a whole provides this same sort of janitorial service. For decades, orthodox criminology consigned various cultural artifacts to the intellectual dustbin, deeming them unworthy of serious scholarly analysis. Comic books and television programmes, football matches and graffiti walls, crime scene photographs and public memorials – all may be entertaining enough, the thinking went, but they certainly don't merit the same serious inquiry as do murder, robbery, and embezzlement. On the contrary, cultural criminologists came to understand these cultural phenomena as part of the process by which crime and crime control acquire collective meaning – and so they swept up criminology's intellectual discards, and in fact attempted to position them at the heart of criminological inquiry. Can the images and storylines in comic books tell us something about juvenile crime, or moral entrepreneurs, or popular notions of justice (Nyberg, 1998; Phillips and Stroble, 2006)? Do television programmes and newspaper headlines about crime help create public perceptions that underwrite misguided criminal justice policy, or other times provide a push for social justice (Cottle, 2005; Grimes, 2007)? Does the organized violence that sometimes accompanies football matches interweave with hegemonic masculinity, displaced class loyalty, and the symbolic violence of the sport itself? If so, the dustbin may hold as many answers as the textbook.

This sense of cultural criminology as a trashy counterpoint carries into methodology as well. The methods conventionally employed by orthodox criminologists may or may not tell us much about crime, but one thing is clear: they're carefully designed for neat execution and clean results. Sorting through governmental arrest statistics can be accomplished with barely a smudge to the hands or wrinkle to the suit – and when the sorting is done, results can be presented in sets of finely ruled tables. Likewise, victimization surveys can be constructed with precisely preset questions and answers, mailed to predetermined lists of respondents, and then compiled into carefully cross-tabulated data sets. So pervasive is this aesthetic of academic precision, in fact, that we've begun to suspect that the appeal of orthodox criminology – an academic orientation that generally disavows the validity of emotion and style in the investigation of human experience – is precisely its own aridly fastidious style, and the sanitary emotions such a style creates among those who long for certainty and assurance.

Cultural criminological research, on the other hand, tends to take place within an imprecise dynamic of method, style, and emotion, and so tends to reproduce in its results the messy uncertainty of people and their problems. Cultural criminologists are less likely to find themselves sorting statistics or mailing surveys, and more likely to get caught up in the dirty ambiguities of daily transgression, the dangerous details of criminal acts, even the swirling referentiality of symbolic communication. In such research, straight lines and neatly preset arrangements are a rarity; instead, tangents are taken and back alleys travelled, all while riding the staccato rhythms of criminality and control. As we'll see, these tangents in many cases lead cultural criminologists into the dark corners of social life, into trashy situations that others – politicians, justice system officials, even other criminologists – might not wish to have explored and illuminated. And as we'll also see, this sort of cultural criminological research regularly violates the time frames of academic criminology, flowing away from schedules and deadlines, enduring in some cases too long for efficient career advancement, in other cases sustaining itself not long enough for proper professional approval.

against criminological method

For some time now, 'Saturdays' of every kind – artistic, musical, and springtime 'Saturdays', etc. – are being invented. I remind you that there is only the 'Fascist Saturday'.

Achille Starace, Italian Fascist Party Secretary during
the Mussolini regime of the 1930s (in Sachs, 1987: 17)

In writing under the heading 'Against Criminological Method', we intentionally put our disavowal of mainstream criminological method in the company of two dangerous treatises on orthodoxy and its consequences: Paul

Feyerabend's (1975) *Against Method* and Stan Cohen's (1988) *Against Criminology*. In *Against Method*, Feyerabend demonstrates in some detail the manner in which methodological innovations in science have historically come wrapped in performance, persuasion, and intrigue – tricks of the trade necessary for gaining a bit of visibility and support, and for freeing intellectual innovation from the stifling orthodoxies of the time. Significantly, he also reveals the *post hoc* reifications by which these tricks are forgotten – that is, the reifications by which these dicey methodological advances are later defined as purely scientific, necessary ... even inevitable. In this way Feyerabend argues that the history of science resembles less a straight line towards greater and more objective scientific knowledge than it does a Fellini-esque carnival careening around the intellectual countryside, putting on little plays and seductions, occasionally falling apart and regrouping. And so for Feyerabend (1975: 23, emphasis in orginal) the lessons are: 'The only principle that does not inhibit progress is: *anything goes*' – and the only strategy for anyone serious about progressive knowledge is a refusal to take seriously the cannons of received wisdom.

Feyerabend's (1975: 118) passion for 'fruitful disorderliness' is equally evident in Cohen's *Against Criminology*. There Cohen carefully documents the importance of the intellectual uprisings against orthodox criminology during the 1960s and 1970s – and just as carefully documents the necessity of rising up against these uprisings to the extent that they settle in as a sort of alternative orthodoxy. Like Howard Becker (1963: 181), who never really intended for his interactionist criminology to become 'labelling theory', who then wandered away from it and into artworlds and other social milieu, Cohen is intellectually unwilling to toe the line, even one he helped draw. Instead, he understands the essential method of criminological inquiry to be not one technique or another, but the ongoing process of critique and incompletion. 'Lack of commitment to any master plan' in this way becomes an intellectual strength, or maybe a disciplinary necessity – and 'the unfinished' emerges as a practical strategy for negotiating the next moment, whether it be one of normal science or intellectual negation (1988: 109, 232).

Taken together Feyerabend and Cohen suggest a sort of anarchist understanding of method and knowledge; Feyerabend (1975: 17, 21) in fact explicitly offers an 'outline of an anarchist methodology', and argues that 'theoretical anarchism is more humanitarian and more likely to encourage progress than its law-and-order alternatives'. Said differently, both Feyerabend and Cohen invoke Dadaism as a reference point for their critiques. Looking back at the revolts against orthodox criminology in the 1960s, Cohen (1988: 11) sees them as perhaps closest to 'the products of radical art movements such as Dada and surrealism, anti-art created by artists'. Feyerabend (1975: 21) clarifies, noting that he might just as well call his work Dadaism, since

[a] Dadaist is utterly unimpressed by any serious enterprise and he smells a rat whenever people stop smiling and assume that attitude and those facial expressions which indicate that something important is about to be said. ... A Dadaist is prepared to initiate joyful experiments even in those domains where change and experimentation seem to be out of the question...

And so to clarify an anarchist or Dadaist critique as it might apply to a domain like today's orthodox criminology: the more seriously a criminological method takes itself – the further it positions itself above other approaches through invocations of 'objectivity' or 'science' – the more that method is suspect of impeding understanding rather than advancing it. Methods most accepted as the disciplinary core of criminology, then, must be those most aggressively challenged, cracked open, and made fun of (Ferrell, 1996: 191–2). Likewise, methodological neatness and intellectual closure suggest stasis and decay; trashy methods, methods ragged around the edges, methods not fully conceptualized or completed, suggest intellectual life and disciplinary vitality. The only way to move a discipline forward is through a healthy disrespect for the rules by which it defines itself – even for those rules by which it defines itself as moving forward. And if this is true of biology or art history, it is especially true of criminology. *The problems of crime and crime control are too serious to take criminology seriously.*[1]

Because of this we consider it our duty and our pleasure as criminologists to stand against criminology, in particular to stand against the intellectual arrogance and assumed acceptability of orthodox criminological method. But where to start? The methodological terrain of contemporary criminology is so barren, its conventional methods so inadequate for addressing the human pathos of crime and control, so wanting in any sense of intellectual elegance and innovation, that the discipline today seems a sort of methodological kakistocracy – an upside down world where the worst matters the most. Given this, perhaps the starting point shouldn't be the latest convenience-sampled survey of a professor's captive students, or the most recent unreadable and table-turgid issue of the US journal *Criminology*, but the historical process by which we got to this point. Perhaps we can begin to understand something of contemporary criminology's methodological bankruptcy by tracing, if only briefly, an earlier history of intellectual fraud and methodological misappropriation.

method past and present

Though one wouldn't know it from reading orthodox criminology journals today, many of contemporary criminology's foundational works emerged from idiosyncratic, impressionistic approaches that bore little resemblance to any sort of 'social scientific' method. When in the 1920s and 1930s Chicago School scholars conducted research – when Frederic Thrasher (1927) set out to document Chicago gang life and the 'ganglands' in which it unfolded, when Nels Anderson (1923) decided to explore the lives of the homeless – they did so largely according to their own sentiments and schedules. Thrasher (1927: xiii, 79), for example, notes that the research for his 571-page book, *The Gang*, 'occupied a period of about seven years', and in the book he not only presents in fine detail 'the thrilling street life of the gang', but includes his own *in situ* photos of gang rituals and juvenile gang life.

By the mid-twentieth century, though, this sort of engaged criminological field research had been usurped by a style of survey research that, as Patricia and Peter Adler (1998: xiii) note, 'has held sway within the discipline ever since'. This importation of serious and 'objective' methodologies like survey research into criminology was meant to position it as a science, or at least a social science, of crime; in culture and in consequence, the effect was similar to the introduction of scientific management methods into the office and factory a few decades before. For Frederick Taylor and other early 'managerial consultants' who advocated workplace scientific management, the stop-motion camera and the key stroke counter were utilized as forms of surveillance designed to divorce mental craft from manual labour, reducing the worker to an operator within the larger organization and routinizing the work process in the interest of profit and control (Braverman, 1974). For advocates of survey research, the alleged objectivity of sample procedures and preset question banks was designed similarly: to divorce from the research process the human particulars of both researchers and those they studied, with the intent of positioning the researcher as an operative within the larger professional organization of scientific criminology.

Of course, as already seen here and in Chapter 2, criminologists have more than once escaped this routinized, objectified criminology. During the 1950s and 1960s – decades that the Adlers (1998: xiii–xiv) label periods of 'Renaissance' and 'Abstract Expressionism' – the ascension of social scientific methodologies was challenged by an efflorescence of vivid subcultural ethnographies. Howard Becker's (1963) participatory studies of jazz musicians and marijuana users, Ned Polsky's (1967) insider take on pool halls, hipsters, and hustlers – these and other works wandered far from standards of random sampling and objective detachment, and often defiantly so. During this same period in Great Britain, equally unorthodox methods of engaged research were being used by Jock Young (1971), Stan Cohen (1972), and others. Sir Leon Radzinowicz recalls these moments of methodological abandon as something akin to the pranks of 'naughty schoolboys'; we've elsewhere characterized them more in terms of Feyerabend, or maybe Dada – as approaches that were 'hectic, irreverent, transgressive and, above all, fun' (Young, 2002).

Still, for all that, the serious business of survey research today continues to dominate criminology, and now with a full range of institutional underpinnings. Joe Feagin, Tony Orum, and Gideon Sjoberg (Feagin et al., 1991), for example, note that 'mainstream article sociology' – the efficient, routinized production of article-length research reports in sociology and criminology – has over time displaced the deeper intellectual, methodological, and temporal commitments of 'book sociology' as the measure of professional achievement. After all, like the answer sets produced by survey research, journals can be quantitatively ranked, with each scholar's articles therein counted as an arithmetic of professional stature – and survey research can itself generate such journal articles far more quickly and easily than Frederic Thrasher and his seven years of field research.

In the United States, Great Britain, and elsewhere, these shifts towards assembly-line research methods and objectivist measures of disciplinary productivity have been replicated in the universities themselves, with their increasing reliance on corporate management practices and a bureaucratic culture of actuarial control. For United States criminologists especially, this quantified academic machinery has increasingly been coupled, through criminal justice departments and Federal research grants, to a parallel state machinery of surveillance, imprisonment, and control – a state machinery that requires 'objective', quantifiable survey data for its operation and justification.

British criminologists in addition face the demands of the national Research Assessment Exercise (RAE), a regular evaluation of research productivity by which scholars, programmes, and universities are ranked. Like a Taylorist knowledge factory, the RAE puts a premium on regular and measurable production, with the effect of bullying scholars into research methodologies (and research projects) that can produce quick and efficient results (see relatedly, Walters, 2003; Hillyard et al., 2004). Echoing Feyerabend's feel for the stultifications of orthodoxy, Professor John Hyatt, director of Manchester Metropolitan University's Manchester Institute for Research and Innovation in Art and Design, notes another effect of the RAE:

> Imagination is the magnet that pulls knowledge forward, whereas knowledge is simply our best guess at the time. ... [A]rt has rather lost its confidence in the face of the Research Assessment Exercise. We're contorting ourselves to appease a pseudo-scientific process in order to get funding. ... [A]rt has over-embraced the scientific rationale and forgotten that only when you add imagination to knowledge do you reach understanding. We've come to a point where we have to assert a belief in our own methodology. (in Arnot, 2006)

Back in the United States, criminological researchers confront yet another organizational incentive for confining their work to survey research or office-chair speculation: the Institutional Review Board (IRB). Allegedly constituted to protect the 'human subjects' of academic research, IRBs are designed to conform to the requirements of the United States Department of Health and Human Services, staffed by a mix of university bureaucrats and professors, and charged with reviewing all academic research projects involving 'the participation of humans'. At a minimum, IRBs are sources of annoyance and delay for criminologists attempting to conduct research. But like the RAE, they are evidence as well of something more sinister: the degree to which criminological researchers are increasingly forced to forfeit scholarly independence in the interest of institutional oversight. Putting organizational risk management ahead of methodological independence, IRBs degrade the professional status of those they regulate. Even when administered with kindness and insight, even when genuinely concerned with 'human subjects' – as they sometimes are – Institutional Review Boards nonetheless embody the sort of corporate routinization that has come to define criminological inquiry.

Not surprisingly, the effects of this routinized surveillance on unconventional research methods are, to say the least, stifling. IRB guidelines peg the degree of board review to the perceived degree of risk that a research project carries for research subjects. In this context, the guidelines generally exempt from oversight methods that utilize 'existing data', that involve 'survey procedures', or that 'are conducted by or subject to the approval of department or agency heads' (TCU, 2007: 10, 11). They, on the other hand, reserve especially harsh consideration for proposed research that might put subjects 'at risk of criminal or civil liability', or for research involving 'vulnerable populations' (including prisoners) (TCU, 2007: 7, 10), and in any case they require elaborate procedures for gaining subjects' informed consent prior to research. As a result, those mailing surveys, mining existing governmental data sets, or otherwise engaging in organizationally approved research face few obstacles; those wishing to conduct independent field work with criminals or cops, to interview prisoners or young people, or to investigate organizational malfeasance, on the other hand, face endless impediments (Ross et al., 2000; Dentith et al., 2007). And so in consequence there develop some dirty disciplinary secrets, secrets that have been confessed to us in confidence time and again by frustrated doctoral students and junior faculty: knowing of the IRBs, dissertation advisers dissuade their students from field research, handing them old survey data sets for dissertation analysis instead. Junior faculty wishing to do field research learn better, too, learn that this method will earn them mostly bureaucratic constipation and career delay. 'Oh, I'd love to do the sort of research you do', they tell us, 'but I just *can't*.'

Thrasher and Anderson, Becker and Polsky couldn't either, not these days. As we've detailed elsewhere, many of criminology's most revered researchers interwove criminology and criminality in order to conduct studies now considered essential to the discipline, engaging by necessity in research that incorporated criminal conduct and 'dirty knowledge' (Ferrell, 1997). Today such research would simply not be possible by the standards of IRBs, and so to engage in it would position the researcher as an *academic* outlaw as well. Imagine if you will Howard Becker emailing his university IRB, requesting permission to play piano music and smoke marijuana with fellow jazz musicians, *in situ*. (In fact, Becker today subversively avoids any such emails by defining his research as 'conceptual art' [in Shea, 2000: 32] that falls outside the purview of the IRB.) Imagine Ned Polsky, told he must submit to the IRB a list of questions he plans to ask pool hall hustlers, and told as well that he is required to have them sign elaborate informed consent forms before he can ask. Imagine for that matter the response of an IRB to Patti Adler (1985) as she presents her plan for in-depth participatory research among active drug users and dealers. Why, if only we'd had the foresight to put IRBs (and RAEs) in place during the course of criminology's history … well, we really wouldn't *have* much of a criminological history.

disciplinary delusion and decay

And what sort of discipline results from this contemporary triumph of the bureaucrat and the survey statistician? What sort of discipline emerges when quantitative methodology becomes the preferred tool for satisfying the demands of professional surveillance and evaluation (Lawrence, 2007)? When methodology is defined by detachment and routinization – when it's unimaginable that the researcher might be one with the research setting, that informed consent forms and pre-approved questions might be unnecessary, not to mention impossible – what then does criminology become?

It becomes lifeless, stale, and inhuman. Just as the broader inhumanity of certain aspects of modernity resulted from the reduction of human subjects to rationalized categories of work, consumption, and control, the inhumanity of orthodox criminology results in large part from methodologies designed, quite explicitly, to reduce research subjects to carefully controlled categories of counting and cross-tabulation. Just as the stale redundancy of modern work stemmed from the Taylorist exhaustion of uncertainty and possibility, the thudding boredom of orthodox criminology stems from methodologies designed, again quite explicitly, to exclude ambiguity, surprise, and 'human error' from the process of criminological research. Coupled with a state control apparatus organized around similar ends, these methodologies bankrupt the promise of meaningful criminological scholarship, becoming instead the foundation for the sort of 'courthouse criminology' described by Ned Polsky (1967: 136) – the criminology of the 'technologist or moral engineer'.

In the same way that other of modernity's institutions – the public school and the reformatory, the fast-food outlet and the theme park – were designed to expunge craft and creativity from the practice of everyday life, the modern machinery of criminology functions to exhaust the idiosyncratic insights of grounded criminological inquiry. Just as the factory, the agency, and the marketplace were rationalized in the interest of efficiency and control, the contemporary enterprise of criminology has been so shaped towards professional efficiency that it dehumanizes both its practitioners and those it is designed to investigate or enlighten.

As a result, the great majority of mainstream criminological scholarship today can only be described as clean, safe ... and thoroughly unimaginative. Like other forms of circumscribed cultural expression, this intellectual drudgery results directly from the conditions of its production, from the methodological routinizations enforced against human beings in order to drain data sets and numeric summaries from their lives. For students in criminology classes and for readers of criminological journals, then, a shared disillusion, a disappointment – that the promise of the subject matter could be so thoroughly betrayed by the methods of its presentation. The vivid experiential agony of crime victimization transmogrified into abstract empiricism, the sensuality of the criminal event tabulated and footnoted – it would be a remarkable trick of methodological sanitation if only it weren't so damaging to the discipline.

Under the methodological regime of contemporary criminology, for example, the gendered tragedy and dangerous dynamics that animate women's attempts to escape domestic abuse become 'logistic odds ratios predicting help seeking and divorce or separation for female victims of spousal violence' (Dugan and Apel, 2005: 715), and all of this statistically derived from a victimization survey. The sneaky thrills and little moments of ritualized resistance that percolate through kids' delinquent careers are recoded as 'GLS and Tobit Random-Intercept Models Estimating Interactions Between Antisocial Propensity and Time-Varying Predictors of Delinquency' (Ousey and Wilcox, 2007: 332–3), with this recoding generating a set of survey-derived statistics so sweeping that it spans two journal pages. As noted in Daniel Nagin's 2006 Sutherland Address to the American Society of Criminology, the exploitative dynamics of sexual crime, the dark swirl of sexual transgression, indeed the very 'interaction ... between emotion and behavior', are investigated through a clinical experiment in which male undergraduates are randomly assigned to 'non-arousal' or 'arousal' conditions, with those assigned to the arousal condition then 'instructed to masturbate but not to the point of ejaculation while responding to a series of sex-related questions'. Nagin, Professor of Public Policy and Statistics at Carnegie Mellon University, speculates that the masturbators' responses may tell us something about their assessments of 'factors of long-standing interest to criminologists', and wonders also about the validity of criminological survey data derived from respondents who, unlike these student masturbators, are assumed to answer surveys 'in a "cool," non-aroused state' (Nagin, 2007: 265–6). We wonder about two things. First, what might Sutherland say about the uniform failure of this methodology to address key criminological issues of social interaction, social learning, and shared motivation? Second, assuming the erect undergraduates responded in writing to the 'sex-related questions' ... well, did the researchers select for ambidexterity?

This isn't criminology; this is madness, madness filling issue after issue of criminological journals that function primarily as warehouses of disciplinary delusion.

And of course there is method to the madness. 'Researchers' first deploy methods designed to deny any deep understanding of, not to mention immersion in, the lives of those who are their focus; in the delinquency study, for example, 9,488 school kids were targeted, and the fewer than 4,000 who eventually participated were allowed to choose only one of four simplistic, preset responses to statements like, 'I'm nervous or on edge' and 'My mother seems to understand me' (Ousey and Wilcox, 2007: 322–3, 351–3). Data from such surveys, little pencil marks on a response sheet or clicks on a computer screen, are then manipulated with overblown statistical packages, producing two-page tables, a distinct lack of explanatory analysis (Weisburd and Piquero, 2008), and outpourings of astoundingly obtuse intellectual gibberish. But like all good gibberish, of course, it's not really meant to make sense to those outside the delusion anyway; it's mostly for the entertainment of journal editors, tenure committees, and other keepers of the discipline. Twenty years ago, Stan Cohen (1988: 26) asked 'who can still take seriously' this sort of criminology, and argued that it should be 'relegated to the status of alchemy, astrology, and phrenology'. We would only add, twenty years hence, that this perhaps insults the astrologers.

A Deer in the Woods (A Survey Research Fable)

A criminologist wonders how it must feel to be a deer stalked by hunters. So the criminologist acquires a research grant, uses the grant money to hire a team of hunters, has the hunters stalk and shoot a deer, then has the deer's carcass processed into venison steaks and served to a random sample of restaurant patrons. Once the diners have finished, the criminologist presents them with a survey, the first question of which is, 'What does it feel like to be a deer stalked by hunters?' Answer options include 'very good', 'somewhat good', 'somewhat bad', and 'very bad'.

But maybe it's worse than generalized madness and delusion – maybe it's a particular form of *fundamentalist* delusion. The parallels between the fundamental, 'scientific' methods of orthodox criminology, and other of the world's fundamentalisms are, it must be said, striking: a resolute unwillingness to acknowledge internal absurdities. Certainty as to the innate correctness and superiority of the preferred approach. A culture of language and presentation whose incomprehensibility to outsiders matters little, since these others are in fact unqualified to understand it in the first place; in this sense incomprehensibility becomes even a point of internal pride. Denial of human agency, disavowal of ambiguity in meaning and interpretation. Most of all, claims to transcendental objectivity. And so, possessed by the spirit of social science, orthodox criminologists speak in a sort of fundamentalist glossolalia, a private prayer language of logistic odds ratios and intercept models, their tongues tied by their own ineptitude in appreciating other ways of seeing the world.

Significantly for criminology, this fundamentalism is more methodological than theoretical (see Kraska and Neuman, 2008). Discomforting as it may be to those who yearn for a unified theory of crime, most criminologists acknowledge, even embrace, the plethora of contemporary criminological theories, none of which reasonably claims determinate or comprehensive explanatory power. Method, though, is another matter. How much difference is there, after all, in the conventional claims of social scientific methodologists and Georg Lukacs' (1971: 1, emphasis in original) classic statement on Marxist orthodoxy? Orthodox Marxism, Lukacs argued, was not at all a matter of Marx's theses or his theory. Instead,

> Orthodox Marxism ... refers exclusively to *method*. It is the scientific conviction that dialectical materialism is the road to truth and that its methods can be developed, expanded and deepened only along the lines laid down by its founders. It is the conviction, moreover, that all attempts to surpass or 'improve' it have led and must lead to over-simplification, triviality and eclecticism.

Few criminologists today would share Lukacs' faith in foundational Marxism – but they might well share his faith in orthodox method, his sense of 'scientific conviction', his concern for the 'triviality and eclecticism' of other methodologies. Colonizing criminals, cops, school kids, and aroused undergraduates in the interest of scientific methodology, bringing the everyday world under the imperial power of sample design and data sets, contemporary criminology therefore attempts to colonize these other methodologies as well. In a recent issue of the journal *Criminology* otherwise suffused with quantitative research, for example, there appeared (at the back of the issue, mind you) a 'qualitative examination' of legal cynicism – a qualitative examination that incorporated six tables and a 'quantitative analysis' of the information gathered (Carr et al., 2007: 464).

For orthodox criminology, there may be the qualitative Saturday now and then, but ultimately there is only the quantitative Saturday. For orthodox criminology, the *method is the message*.

methodological culture and the emperor's new clothes

The *culture* of this methodological fundamentalism confirms its consequences for the discipline. We as cultural criminologists understand symbolic meaning and stylized communication to be the animating currents of human life, and so examine these cultural currents as they flow through crime and control. But if we recognize that style and representation shape the realities of those we study, then it seems only fair to consider how these same factors shape *our own* enterprise of criminology. If we claim the right to critically examine the cultural worlds of those we study, shouldn't we be willing to examine our own cultural world as well?

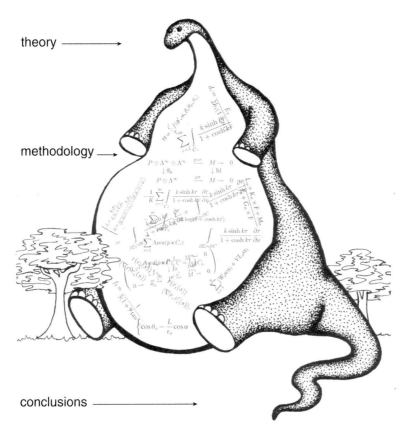

theory ⟶

methodology ⟶

conclusions ⟶

Plate 6.1 Various deformities emerge amidst the madness of orthodox criminology. The 'headless chicken of an argument' (J Young, 2004a: 26) is one. The Datasoraus is another – a creature with a very small theoretical brain, a huge methodological body, a Byzantine and intricate statistical gut, and a tiny, inconclusive tail wagging mindlessly from database to database

Credit: Drawing by Ellen Rose Wyatt (2007)

If so, then by the terms of its own cultural codes, the orthodox criminology of survey and experimentation seems a sadly failed project. This sort of criminology has certainly not become a 'science' in any conventional sense of analytic rigour or explanatory scope (DiCristina, 2006); a recent review of quantitative analysis in criminology, for example, finds that such research regularly leaves 'eighty or ninety percent of variance unexplained' (Weisburd and Piquero, 2008). Worse yet, the greater the effort in *making* criminology 'scientific', the more systematic has been the dehumanization of human subjects and the numeric abstraction of human experience. Confronting this failure, grasping for the illusion of scientific control, criminologists have turned to hyper-specialization and linguistic obfuscation, apparently on the aesthetic assumption that their work's got to be good looking if it's so hard to see. This sad pseudo-scientific trajectory has fostered a set of symbolic codes, a disciplinary culture, that embodies and perpetuates the problem: passive third-person writing, interruptive in-text referencing, big tables, long equations, and a general tyranny of the calculated number and the turgidly written word over the idea and the image. Note that all of these cultural codes emerge from the assumption, again, that the method is the message – that elegance and stylistic engagement are unnecessary, even inappropriate, when transmitting the objective results of scientific methodology from one researcher to another by way of the published page. Note also that the codes spawned by this assumption are distinctly arid, ugly, and inhuman, devoid of any cultural markers that would distinguish a criminological article from an actuarial report.

In this sense 'objective' or 'scientific' criminology has long operated more as anxious metaphor than accomplished reality. These cultural codes function as *symbolic performances* of scientific objectivity, as façades fronting the public presentation of criminology as a discipline. The passive voice in writing accomplishes a neat stylistic sleight of hand whereby the author's influence seems to disappear from the author's own text. Twenty-line tables and convoluted equations provide an assuring sense of precision and order, even for those uninterested in actually reading them. Pervasive in-text referencing offers the illusion of comprehensive disciplinary knowledge, and the image of progression towards scientific truth as each criminologist builds on the work of those before. Together, these coded communications assure criminologists, and their audiences, that methodological rigour continues to discipline the discipline of criminology; taken as a whole, they construct a persuasive *aesthetic of authority* (Ferrell, 1996) for the presentation of criminological knowledge.

Correlations Among All DV Scales: Each Vignette Separately

	(1)	(2)	(3)	(4)	(5)	(6)	(7)	(8)
(1)		0.17	0.17	0.07	0.25	0.02	0.45	0.25
(2)	0.11		0.28	0.42	−0.18	0.38	0.17	0.42
(3)	0.13	0.15		0.33	0.17	0.10	0.16	0.11
(4)	0.08	0.40	0.38		−0.04	0.38	0.12	0.31
(5)	0.42	−0.18	0.23	0.21		−0.10	0.28	−0.23
(6)	0.04	0.38	0.18	0.45	−0.10		0.21	0.31
(7)	0.41	0.17	0.13	0.14	0.21	0.28		0.51
(8)	0.20	0.44	0.12	0.32	0.28	0.38	0.32	

Note. *p < .05. **p < .01. Correlations above the diagonal are for Vignette 1 (n=135), those below the diagonal are for Vignette 2 (n=136).

Plate 6.2 The Aesthetics of Authority. This table is not only out of focus, it's made up. How would you know if others were made up? And what exactly does 'made up' mean in the current criminological climate?[2]

Credit: Table by Jeannine Gailey

But of course this is all collective performance, academic theatre, another of Feyerabend's little carnivals where a discipline displays and deceives itself. Rationality has no more displaced emotion and personal agenda in the practice of criminology than it has in the practice of crime. Many criminological research projects go forward under less than closely controlled conditions, despite the best efforts of IRBs and other bureaucratic overseers. The 'peer review' process by which criminologists review each other's research, while certainly helpful, is certainly *not* devoid of duplicity, individual predilection, and the occasional vendetta. And let's be honest: the statistical residues and objectivist protestations pulled up over criminologists' research hardly hide the pervasive obscenity of aggressive careerism, and the associated practice of methodological pimping to the highest bidder.

Yet, like other cultural constructions, these codes and performances create serious consequences, feeding back into the collective work that produces them. In the case of criminology, they set the tone for a particularly inappropriate approach to human life and human society. A disciplinary fondness for a style that is off-putting and inelegant helps perpetuate the false hierarchy of content over form, and helps render even the most seductive of subject matters sterile. This collection of off-putting cultural codes distances criminology from engaged public discourse, leaving it an intellectual side water with little hope of effectively confronting either the predations of criminals or the abuses of the criminal justice system (see Burawoy, 2005). Most of all, the culture of orthodox criminology completes what its methods begin: the dehumanization of those individuals and groups criminology allegedly seeks to understand.

'In the baseline model (model 1), no variables exert a significant effect on sexual coercion' (Piquero and Bouffard, 2007: 15); 'Results from level 2 of the HGLM demonstrated that seven of the eight life circumstances included in the model exhibited a statistically significant impact on likelihood of victimization...' (Armstrong and Griffin, 2007: 91); 'Recall that a key advantage of the tobit model is that it explicitly deals with the floor-value of the summative delinquency measure...' (Ousey and Wilcox, 2007: 340). Now what kind of way is that to talk about people? We doubt that those involved in sexual coercion appreciate being reduced to baseline models and (no) variable effects. It strikes us that disassembling victims into their component parts – sentiments, attitudes, life circumstances, all carved up like some intellectual butcher hard at a carcass – mostly makes them victims again. Whether delinquent youth or domestic violence victim or probation officer, it can't feel good to have words put in your mouth, to have your actions and the accounts you give of them translated into the jargon of those who claim to know you better than you know yourself. Abstract and obtuse, this sort of language is also revealing, illuminating a set of linguistic practices that systematically suck the life from those they describe.

Honestly, though, we don't mean to make this a personal attack on our colleagues, nor to single out for special criticism those we cite; in fact, the research we note was selected by simply opening recent issues of orthodox criminology journals and, sadly, picking most any article. Further, we're aware that, were our critique to be taken seriously, academic livelihoods would be lost, grant writing workshops evacuated, seminars in advanced statistics summarily cancelled. This is not our immediate interest either. Rather, as we've said elsewhere, 'What is of interest here is the awareness of thin ice, yet the ineluctable desire to keep on skating' (J Young, 2004a: 19). Or to put it differently: what interests us is how transparently non-existent are *the criminologist's new clothes*, how naked the fraud of objectivist criminology, save for everyone agreeing to agree that the clothes certainly do exist – and are damn fine clothes at that.[3]

As Feyerabend would suggest, this fraud may be a contemporary phenomenon, but it is a long time in the making. Some criminologists, for instance, might well object to our finding contemporary criminology's foundations in the Chicago School of the early twentieth century, arguing that the real roots of criminology, its scientific roots, can be traced to the nineteenth century and the pioneering positivist work of Cesare Lombroso. We would agree – and we would add that Lombroso was a performance artist, a cultural imperialist, and a scientific fraud. As Wayne Morrison demonstrates, 'positivist criminology was born amidst a dazzling and seductive spectacle' of collected skulls, catalogued tattoos, wall-mounted crime maps, and gelatinized human brains, with Lombroso's collections the most dazzling of all. Designed quite literally to *display* publicly the 'scientific' methods of the new criminology, these nineteenth-century exhibits and clinical collections were part of the process by which positivist criminology emerged as a 'cultural phenomenon' (Morrison, 2004b: 68). But these showcased methods of mapping and measurement no more constituted a 'science' of crime than do today's surveys and GPS crime maps; according to Lombroso's calculations, for example, Aboriginal art was commensurate with contemporary 'criminal art', and the historic tattoos of the Maori simply evidence of atavistic criminality. The methodological imperialism by which situated meaning is stolen in the name of science – by which survey methods reduce domestic violence to a data set, by which catalogues convert local culture into crime – operates now as it did then.[4]

As Feyerabend and Cohen would also suggest, stripping away the mythology of criminology's scientific beginnings, penetrating the cultural codes by which contemporary criminology presents itself as science, exposing the fraud of criminological fundamentalism – seeing, that is, through the criminologist's new clothes – provides just the sort of healthy disciplinary disrespect needed for intellectual progress. Freed from the collective delusion of scientific criminology, we awake to see that survey methods and statistical analysis forfeit whole areas of social and cultural life while inventing fictional social constructs out of their own methodological arrogance. Ignoring the situational and interactional dynamics of crime and crime control, missing entirely the mediated human meaning of crime and transgression, these methods imagine instead a world where data sets correlate with – indeed, somehow capture – the reality of crime and control. But of course survey methods and their resultant data sets do no such thing; they simply create that which they claim to capture.

Let's to be clear on this: there exist in the lived situations of crime and crime control *no such things* as 'logistic odds ratios predicting help seeking and divorce or separation for female victims of spousal violence', *no such things* as 'interactions between antisocial propensity and time-varying predictors of delinquency', *no such things* as 'results from level 2 of the HGLM'. Such phrases reference nothing more than the residues of methods that imagine such phenomena to exist, and in so doing call them into existence. These are the threads of the emperor's new clothes, and to believe that these loose threads can somehow be woven into an understanding of criminal motivation or personal trauma, and then generalized to 'public attitudes towards crime' or 'patterns of victimization', is to layer one imaginary garment over another. Hearing this sort of critique, concerned colleagues sometimes counter that we are asking them to give up all the facts they know: rates of vandalism in Boston, amounts of British domestic abuse, levels of public support for the death penalty. On the contrary: to the extent that such 'facts' derive from simplistic survey data collated and crammed through statistical grinders, then spit out and slathered with a thin sheen of science, we're asking them to give up what they *don't* know. Otherwise, we're afraid that their research, and ours, will remain mostly busy work in the service of a delusion, solving neither the problems of criminal victimization nor the abuses of state authority, and leaving us all little more than the intellectual caretakers of late modernity.

The National Youth Gang Survey

Since 1995 the US Department of Justice's Office of Juvenile Justice and Delinquency Prevention (OJJDP) has conducted a National Youth Gang Survey so as to 'facilitate analysis of changes and trends in the nature of youth gangs and their activities'. The 1996 survey, for example, found some 31,000 gangs with approximately 850,000 members – an important finding, since as OJJDP Administrator Shay Bilchik noted, 'sound data are essential to solving the problem of juvenile crime' (OJJDP, 1999: iii). By 2004, a decade's worth of yearly surveys allowed for the calculation of a ten-year average: 25,000 gangs with 750,000 members (National Youth Gang Center, 2007).

But big numbers aside, the emperor's new clothes are in this case notably threadbare. The OJJDP neither surveys nor otherwise studies any gangs or gang members – its surveys are mailed only to law enforcement agencies. At the agencies, by the OJJDP's own admission, those filling out the survey are asked to base their responses on 'records or personal knowledge', though it is 'impossible to determine which' – and most remarkably, 'no definition [is] presented regarding what constitutes a gang member or a gang incident,' since 'little agreement has been reached on what constitutes a gang, gang member, or gang incident...' (OJJDP, 1999: 7). Yet none of this precludes the production of aesthetically authoritative data; an early survey summary (OJJDP, 1999), for instance, includes 36 tables and 19 charts and figures, with further tables and formulae offered in Appendices A to L.

So, for governmental agencies and the criminologists who rely on them, 'sound data' apparently goes something like this:

'That which is not to be studied directly can nonetheless be surveyed definitively, based on the records, or perhaps the personal perceptions, of those whose job it is to eradicate that which they cannot define accurately'.

some methods of cultural criminology

Seeing through the orthodox criminologist's new clothes – shaking off the delusion of social scientific criminology – we're free to imagine fresh possibilities for engaging with the problems of crime and justice. Rejecting the supercilious self-importance of orthodox method, we're able to embrace methodological possibilities that are playful, dangerous, and unfinished. As before, the seriousness of the subject matter is such that we dare not take conventional criminology seriously, lest human tragedy get lost amidst a maze of cross-tabulations. Instead, it's our disciplinary duty to move beyond the stale certainty of orthodoxy, and towards approaches able to account for crime, transgression, and victimization as they are lived under contemporary circumstances.

As we have highlighted throughout this book, these are the circumstances of fluidity and reflexivity – an everyday world where meaning circulates and spirals, experience comes and goes, and images and emotions flow between individuals, situations, and global communities: a world of immigration, impermanence, and 'instant living' where transience trumps durability. In this world, *transgression* – the crossing of borders, the violation of taboos, the rupture of certainties – is the stuff of the mass marketer, the digital musician, the migrant worker ... and the criminal. In its very uncertainty, transgression becomes a shifting common ground for everyday experience.

Sent out into this world, the methods of orthodox criminology seem delusional indeed, and anachronistic. Set-question surveys and numeric summaries are residues of an earlier modernism, of rationalization and routinization. Such methods operate as a fixed-line knowledge factory, still churning out one widget of data at a time – and under new ownership of the IRB and the RAE, the factory's assembly line becomes all the more inflexible. These methods presume, indeed require, discrete categories, fixed populations and personalities, reliability, replicability – that is, all that liquid modernity denies. Consequently, they're ill-equipped to get inside the ephemeral images and emotions that animate everyday life, likewise ill-suited to surf the informational flows that shape it. Forty years ago, Martin Nicolaus (1969: 387) asked of sociology, 'What kind of science is this, which holds true only when men hold still?' Forty years later women and men, criminals and their images, are even less likely to hold still – and so the methods of orthodox sociology and criminology are even less likely to apply.

Instead, criminology must embrace methods that can catch the subtleties of transgressive situations while locating these situations in larger currents of meaning. It must imagine methods that can capture mediated law-and-order campaigns while also accounting for the variety of audiences such campaigns hit and miss. These methods – the methods of cultural criminology – must be attuned to crime as both a phenomenon emerging from local circumstances and a commodity marketed through global networks, must be sympathetic to contemporary identity as a source of existential stability and ongoing unease. At their best, such methods must mix instant living with long-term human commitment.

And if nothing else, these methods must be attuned to the image. Clearly, it's time to abandon the old social scientific hierarchy of content over form, and those methods that embody it by privileging the word over the image in the investigation of crime. A world in which images of crime and justice pervade everyday life, looping and spiralling through newscasts and conversations, spawning public fear and public policy – a world described in the previous chapter – is not a world that can be reduced to one of four survey answer options, or to dry prose and numbers. Understanding this world requires researching it on its own terms, on the terms of representational dynamics, symbolic discourse, and stylistic ambiguity. If our research results are to reflect this world, and to find currency in it, they themselves must become more stylish and more open to the image. A criminology of the contemporary world requires methods wired for image production, and for producing styles of communication more literary or artistic than 'scientific'. Today criminals, law makers, and law enforcement agencies all make their own media, creating websites, circulating images, and otherwise paying attention to the politics of communication. In studying them, we must do the same.

Much to ask of a discipline mired in methods that generally make for bad writing and ugly presentation (Ferrell, 2006b). But based on our experiences, we can promise certain benefits if the task is undertaken. The following methods demand more of researchers – but they also guarantee a good bit more intellectual adventure and experiential excitement than a survey form. Compared to orthodox criminological methods, these methods are all but certain to get researchers closer to crime and criminals – and closer to the audiences for crime, criminals, and criminology. And along the way, they're likely to get researchers closer to themselves, too.

Vignette: Who is Bozo Texino?

Plate 6.3   The Rambler and Colossus of Roads
Credit: Photos by Jeff Ferrell (1996)

For a century hobos, railyard workers, and unknown others have been writing a distinctive sort of line-drawing graffiti on the freight trains that criss-cross the American continent. Over a couple of years Jeff Ferrell (1998) wandered the American West, tracking and photographing this graffiti, and thinking about dislocated subcultures and symbolic conversations (Vail, 2001).

Bill Daniel did him one better – much better. Daniel spent over a decade hopping freight trains and living rough, all the while filming with a Super-8 camera or an old 16 mm Bolex. The result is Daniel's (2005) *Who Is Bozo Texino?*, a rolling, hypnotic, rail-clacking film that documents thousands of train graffiti images, and ultimately sets out to find Bozo Texino, The Rambler, Colossus of Roads, and other legendary train artists. Along the way Daniel finds bits of hobo conversation, too.

'I wonder where all these freedoms are these people talk about – I tell you I don't see them – you got all these rules and regulations', says one guy.

'I don't even believe in this', another hobo tells Daniel. 'They say this country was built on hard work. It was built on murder, mayhem, slavery, oppression, lies, stealing, and killing. You can't change it after it's started. Stay away from it, you're diminishing it by one.'

Think a survey could find those thoughts, or find Bozo Texino? A survey you couldn't mail to someone with no address, or call in to someone with no phone, or read to someone you couldn't find in the first place?

ethnography

Fairly or not, cultural criminology is often equated with ethnography, due largely to Jeff Ferrell's (1996, 2001/02, 2006a) book-length ethnographic studies, and to the collection *Ethnography at the Edge*, edited by Jeff Ferrell and

Mark Hamm (1998). In a critical review of cultural criminology, for example, Martin O'Brien (2005: 600) defines cultural criminology in part by its 'ethnographic imagination' and explores in detail its ethnographic methods; in another critical overview, Craig Webber (2007) investigates and critiques the interplay between cultural criminology and culturally-informed ethnography.

As practised by Ferrell and others, ethnography denotes long-term, in-depth participation with those under study; Ferrell's book on urban graffiti, for example, resulted from five years inside the graffiti undergrounds of Denver, Colorado, and other cities. Conducted in this way, ethnography does indeed seem a definitive method for cultural criminology, since as Paul Willis (1977: 3) says, it provides 'a sensitivity to meanings and values as well as an ability to represent and interpret symbolic articulations, practices and forms of cultural production'. Deeply immersed in the lives of criminals, crime victims, or cops, the criminologist can become part of the process by which meaning is made, witnessing the ways in which such people make sense of their experiences through symbolic codes and collective conversations. Sharing with them their situations and experiences, vulnerable to their tragedies and triumphs, the criminologist can likewise learn something of the emotions that course through their experiences of crime, victimization, and criminal justice.

For cultural criminologists, this goal of gaining deep cultural and emotional knowledge is embodied in the concept of *criminological verstehen* (Ferrell, 1997). As developed by the great sociologist Max Weber, the concept of *verstehen* denotes the subjective or appreciative understanding of others' actions and motivations – a deeply felt understanding essential for fully comprehending their lives. As Weber (1978: 4–5) argued, for research that 'concern[s] itself with the interpretive understanding of social action … empathic or appreciative accuracy is attained when, through sympathetic participation, we can adequately grasp the emotional context in which the action took place'. Here Weber, and cultural criminologists, stand orthodox criminology on its head. Rather than 'objectivity' guaranteeing accurate research results, it is in fact *emotional subjectivity* that ensures accuracy in research; without it, the researcher may observe an event or elicit information, but will have little sense of its meaning or consequences for those involved. This holds true, by the way, whether or not the researcher 'sympathizes' in a conventional sense with those being studied. In Ferrell's ethnographic work, for example, his submersion in the meaningful emotions of graffiti writers or homeless scroungers has allowed him to portray them in ways that counter their unjust demonization in the media and the criminal justice system. Mark Hamm (1997, 2002), on the other hand, has journeyed deep inside the dangerous emotional worlds of domestic terrorists with precisely the opposite intention and effect: dispelling stereotypes of them in the interest of better understanding and preventing their victimization of others. In either case, the conventional 'criminal category', as Philip Parnell (2003: 22) says, is 'a barrier worth pushing against through ethnographic practice…'.

In standing the objectivism of orthodox criminology on its head, this ethnographic approach also reclaims the criminological enterprise from methodologies dependent on official records, survey data, and numbers. Significantly, it is not simply that such methods aren't well equipped to take researchers inside situated emotions and meanings; it is that, by definition, they aren't *meant* to take researchers there. To engage in ethnography, to strive for criminological *verstehen*, is to humble oneself before those being studied, to seek and respect their understandings, and to take note of cultural nuance *because it matters*. To mail a survey or run a data set is to miss such nuance *by intention*, to believe that meaning can be deduced by the researcher and imparted to the subject matter. Engaging in ethnography, then, cultural criminologists focus their research on their subjects, but their critique on orthodox criminology. In the current disciplinary context ethnography exists as a subversion, a decision to affirm and explore the human agency of those we study, whether that agency produces crime, resistance, victimization, or injustice.

The disciplinary subversions of ethnographic research are temporal and existential as well. Ethnographic studies generally mix hours of tedium with explosions of surprise and moments of dangerous uncertainty. Such studies flow with the dynamics of situations, embracing the cultural meanings of others, and so carrying researchers beyond their own existential complacency and into uncomfortable ambiguities of crime and crime control. Within such studies progress is measured not by the efficient accumulation of data, but by the abandonment of professional efficiency to the rhythms of others' temporal worlds (Ferrell, 2006b; Barrett, 2007) – rhythms that by conventional standards may seem like so much dawdle and delay. Ultimately, this do-it-yourself method generates disciplinarily dangerous knowledge, spawning human engagement, oddball insight, and illicit meaning unimaginable – and unmanageable – within the sternly scheduled certainty of 'scientific' methods, IRBs, and RAEs.

At its extreme, ethnography suggests a process through which researchers learn to lose themselves inside a series of illicit situations – and by losing themselves, find the meanings and emotions that those situations carry. In this way ethnographic method comes to stand against 'methodology' itself, to the extent that methodology is conventionally conceptualized as a set of preordained procedures to be deployed as determinants of the research process. Good ethnography in contrast generally comes closer to following Feyerabend's injunction that 'anything goes', emerging as an alternative way of living for those willing to explore the uncertain nuances of transgression and control. The morality of ethnography is that of human engagement and situational decision, its politics more the do-it-yourself dynamics of anarchism than the governance of guidebooks and bureaucratic regulation.

Dangerous knowledge indeed.

And yet, despite cultural criminology's reputation, much of what today constitutes cultural criminology was not built from ethnographic research in a strict sense, and much of what it is to become will doubtless emerge from other approaches as well. Publication schedules and personal circumstances, RAEs and IRBs, little funding and low salaries all conspire to keep criminologists, cultural or otherwise, from deep, long-term ethnography (Adler and Adler, 1998; Webber, 2007). Put more positively, some cultural criminologists themselves prefer other research approaches, for reasons of subject matter or style. Cultural criminology, then, is not defined, and should not be defined, by the particular methods of conventional ethnography – but it can and should be defined by an *ethnographic sensibility*. However put into play, this ethnographic sensibility orients cultural criminology to particular practices: it opens research to the meaningful worlds of others, and seeks to understand the symbolic processes though which these worlds are made. It affirms the importance of emotional resonance, and embraces the nuance and texture of human culture. And it humbles the arrogant 'objectivity' of orthodox methodology to the fluid ambiguities of human agency.

Thought of in this way, 'ethnography' is not a method that excludes all but the most committed researchers, but an invitation to all researchers, all criminologists, to engage an attitude of attentiveness and respect. Thought of as a sensibility, ethnography can endure for months or for a moment, and can be brought to bear on social situations, mediated communications, or global processes.

instant ethnography

Traditionally, the quality of ethnography has been measured in part by its duration, on the assumption that the more time a researcher spent inside a group or situation, the more deeply could its cultural dynamics be understood. This can certainly be the case, and for a researcher studying a neighbourhood's crime prevention strategies, an urban youth gang's evolution, or a white-collar criminal's emergence from corporate culture, long-term research involvement may well be invaluable. The liquid instability of late modernity, though, means that crime can just as well come and go in an instant. A neighbourhood's long-term crime control strategy can collapse in a moment of haphazard violence; a youth gang's trajectory can change with one bad street brawl; embezzlement can emerge from ongoing corporate culture, or from one big loss at a Vegas craps table. As suggested in Chapter 4's excavation of everyday life, years of television viewing can spark fear of victimization, but so can a momentary misunderstanding – and crime control can be accomplished, sometimes, by little more than a gesture or a glance. With populations increasingly cut loose from stabilities of time and space through global immigration, short-term employment, and virtual communications, these little flashes of fear and transgression become all the more common.

But if crime can occur in an instant, can ethnography? Emerging work in cultural criminology and related fields suggests it can. Contrasting the tradition of tightly controlled, 'technique-driven' social science research with newer, postmodern notions of fluidity and ambiguity, Peter Manning (1995: 246) argues that this postmodern orientation can usefully reorient ethnography to the 'emergent, fragile, and reflexive character of modern life…'. Ethnographies of such fragile circumstances, Manning (1995: 249–51, emphasis in original) notes, would account for the 'fundamental perversity and *unpredictability* of human conduct' by weaving 'fragments and shards of events' into a new sort of 'ethnography of experience'. A veteran cultural ethnographer who has spent months and years in the field, Stephanie Kane (1998: 142–3) nonetheless finds similarly that moments of chaos and confusion, 'moments of extreme or unusual conditions', can themselves be interrogated as part of ethnographic work. Jarring the researcher loose from the traditional practice of ethnographic research, such moments are to be valued – maybe even engineered on occasion – for the phenomenological insights they can offer. 'Serendipity', Kane (2004: 317) says, 'can realign data', and so can reveal 'empirical patterns in novel ways'.

Theoretical work in cultural criminology helps us imagine instant ethnography as well. Just as Bauman (2000) has theorized the long currents of liquid modernity, cultural criminologists have theorized the situated dynamics by which liquid *moments* are lived illicitly. For Jack Katz (1988: 7, 216), the 'seductions of crime' are such that 'the causes of crime are constructed by the offenders themselves' in moments of criminal transgression, with these causes then operating as 'lures and pressures that they experience as independently moving them toward crime'. Understanding criminal dynamics, then, means documenting these situated constructions, and remaining ready to catch sight of them in 'exceptional circumstances' and moments of 'incongruent sensuality'. As conceptualized by Stephen Lyng (1990, 2005) and Jeff Ferrell (1996, 2005) – and as confirmed in the comments of countless outlaw motorcyclists, sky divers, and graffiti writers – experiences of 'edgework' and 'the adrenalin rush' are likewise characterized by a unity of skill and adventure that endures only until the parachute opens or the paint dries. Researching these experiences requires going 'inside the immediacy of crime' (Ferrell, 1997), inside an instant so fragile, so fleeting, that those involved consider it both ephemeral and ineffable. Katz (1988: 312) argues in this light that criminology's long-standing theoretical focus on 'background factors' rather than 'foreground' seductions has served to 'constitute the field back to front'. The same might be said of method. Perhaps conventional methods, even conventional ethnographies, have looked too long at the background and the beforehand, and not enough at the moments in which background factors explode into meaning and emotion (Ferrell, 1992; J Young, 2003).[5]

The ethnography of meaning's momentary construction, instant ethnography is also the ethnography of *performance*. Just as gender, ethnicity, and other markers

of identity are increasingly seen as situated accomplishments and public performances, Katz and others allow us to see crime, criminality, and criminal justice as
a series of contested performances undertaken in dangerous little everyday the-
atres. And so, just as ethnography provided Paul Willis with 'a sensitivity to meanings and values ... practices and forms of cultural production', 'performance
ethnography' today offers researchers like John Warren (2006: 318) a sensitivity
to 'cultural practices as living moments, enfleshed experiences, real people in real
places'. The late Dwight Conquergood (2002; *Heart Broken in Half: Chicago's
Street Gangs*, Siegel and Conquergood, 1990) conducted ethnography in precisely
this way, recording on paper and film the performative worlds of street gangs,
global refugees, and criminal justice practitioners, catching those moments in
which the meaning of their worlds came alive. Likewise, Robert Garot (2007a:
50) has documented the dynamics of the 'Where you from!?' street challenge,
showing that this bravura performance doesn't so much reflect gang membership
as it does *construct* it; gang identity, Garot argues, is not a 'fixed personal characteristic', but more 'a sensual response to a moment's vicissitudes'. Living as a
hardman or a badass (Katz, 1988), earning respect as a police officer, surviving as
a victim of assault – these are performances, too, performances meant to persuade
one audience or another. With its close attention to the choreography of everyday life, conventional ethnography can set the stage – but an ethnography of stage
presence is needed as well, a sense of those edgy, incandescent moments when the
performer and the performance make the dance of transgression what it is.

Instant Ethnography

Plate 6.4   BASE jumping off the New River Gorge Bridge, West Virginia, USA
Credit: Photo by Jeff Ferrell (1998)

Jeff Ferrell, Dragan Milovanovic, and Stephen Lyng (2001) conducted an instant ethnography of BASE jumpers – those who parachute from buildings and bridges. Here the ethnography is indeed instant, as the researchers record ephemeral experiences of BASE jumpers having only a few seconds to deploy their parachutes and negotiate a landing. Yet even here the loops and spirals seen in Chapter 5 appear, as BASE jumpers wear helmet-mounted video cameras, videotape jumps for later collective viewing and evaluation, and sell jump footage to mainstream media outlets in order to finance the next videotaped descent.

Elsewhere we've argued that moments of edgework and adrenalin embody a politics of illicit transgression, often carrying participants beyond the boundaries of law, work, and safety, if fleetingly, and into new realms of subversive possibility (Ferrell, 1996, 2005). Instant ethnography confirms such political possibility in the realm of method. Manning and Kane, you'll recall, talk of unpredictability and serendipity as spawning new understandings. John Warren (2006: 318), Norman Denzin (1997, 2003), Dwight Conquergood (1991) and others speak explicitly of performance ethnography as a form of political intervention, an act of transgressive insight based on 'seeing the constructed nature of our lives and then interrupting that seemingly stable process'. And in fact, the political potential of instant ethnography recalls a long intellectual history. The *epoché* of phenomenology, the breaching procedures of ethnomethodology, the *detournement* of the Situationists – all are intellectual practices suggesting that old understandings can be undermined in an instant, and new meaning made just as quickly. With instant ethnography we likewise engage the politics of transgressive possibility, and so embrace something of cultural criminology's progressive mandate. Whether committing a burglary, tackling a fleeing suspect, or conducting an illicit ethnography, what Henri Cartier-Bresson (1952) called a single 'decisive moment' can mean everything – and can change everything.

liquid ethnography

If instant ethnography catches up to the speed of late modernity, liquid ethnography finds a way to flow with its swirls of meaning, representation, and identity. *Liquid ethnography* suggests ethnography attuned to the dynamics of destabilized, transitory communities; ethnography immersed in the ongoing interplay of images; and ethnography comfortable with the shifting boundaries between research, research subjects, and cultural activism. For cultural criminologists, this methodological sensitivity to ambiguity and uncertainty offers a further benefit: the ability to engage with illicit communities on their own terms, and so to explore transgression as a source of dangerous knowledge and progressive possibility. Liquid ethnography in this way follows cultural criminology's trajectory away from the 'courthouse criminology' that Polsky rightly condemned, not only by moving criminological research outside the courthouse and the court records file, but by moving it outside the codified *definitions* of crime and transgression housed there.

We might hope that some of our own ethnographic work has anticipated this sort of liquid ethnography, as with Ferrell's (1996, 2006a: 1) appreciative and illegal ethnography of graffiti writers and their images, or the amorphous mix of 'field research and free form survival' that characterized his urban trash scrounging adventures. Whatever flows we may have found, though, other cultural criminologists are now riding the currents of late modernity further still. David Brotherton, Luis Barrios, and their associates have, for example, developed ethnographic approaches that are as nuanced in their cultural understandings as they are global in their scope (Brotherton and Barrios, 2004; Kontos et al., 2003). Immersing themselves in the cultural and political practices of the Almighty Latin King and Queen Nation and similar 'street gangs', they document the ways in which these groups in fact move beyond crime to intermingle political resistance, community empowerment, and religious practice in their emerging collective identities. Global forces also intersect in these identities; both the 'gangs' and their individual members embody the liquidity of immigration and mediated communication, and broadcast this polymorphous sensibility through global alliances that they construct (Brotherton, 2007). For gang members, criminal justice operatives, and ethnographers, the contested *image and self-image* of the 'gang' in this way constitute critical, intertwined issues. Consequently, while critiquing existing images and producing their own photographic records, these researchers also understand that the *politics* of the image must be investigated; as Richard Rodriguez (2003: 280) notes, the representation of gang life by gang members, cops, or ethnographers 'is never an innocent practice'.

Maggie O'Neill and her associates are likewise imagining new sorts of liquid research with prostitutes, immigrants, asylum seekers, and others pushed to the legal margins of the global economy. Utilizing a form of 'participatory action research' that explicitly engages researchers and researched communities in collaborative projects for progressive change, O'Neill pushes further still beyond orthodox methods by incorporating art, photography, and performance in this collaborative process. Echoing the politics of the performance ethnographers, O'Neill (2004: 220) argues that this sort of 'performative praxis' can 'explore and represent the complexity of lived reality, transgressing conventional or traditional ways of presenting research data'. When staged in public settings, this performative research does indeed flow into other realms, moving criminology into popular debate, and providing marginalized communities the opportunity to counter mediated demonization with their own dignified images. A research strategy perfectly attuned to the permutations of liquid modernity, this approach collaborates with even the most transitory and contingent communities in creating meaning and identity, developing the *verstehen* of shared emotional knowledge, and achieving a grounded, holistic sense of social justice (O'Neill, 2001; O'Neill et al., 2004; O'Neill et al., 2007).

More liquid ethnography is emerging in cultural criminology, of course – Greg Snyder's (2006, 2009) visually charged work that traces, and participates in, the trajectory of urban graffiti from illicit public painting to underground global media, for example – and we trust that by the time you read this, more will have emerged still. Appropriately enough, we don't know where liquid ethnographies of culture and crime will spill over next: across national borders alongside political refugees, against the atrocities of one war or another, or with some contingent community fighting to free itself from enforced misrepresentation. As Stephanie Kane (2003: 293) says, it's 'a great global bricolage of deceit, revenge, and pathology' that today constitutes 'crime's ideological power', and somewhere amidst the shifting deformities of that great global remix, the next wave of liquid ethnography will break.

visual criminology

A decade ago Peter Manning (1999) suggested that contemporary surveillance, transgression, and control can't be understood without a sharp sense of the visual, and an awareness of the many screens on which visual information is circulated and displayed. A decade later, the screens have morphed and multiplied, the flow of visual information has accelerated, and Manning's point is all the more important. The everyday experience of late modernity may or may not be suffused with crime, but it is certainly suffused with images, and with images of crime. Television offers an avalanche of crime imagery, from local news reports to prime-time crime dramas. On the movie screen, clouded images of crime, enforcement (Brown, 2007), and imprisonment (Fiddler, 2007) are layered into the latest release. Images of transgression, victimization, and vigilante justice punctuate the internet, popping up on computer screens and cell phone displays. Criminals videotape their crimes, protesters photograph their protests, police shoot far more images than they do people, security agents scrutinize the image-making of criminals and protestors – and a million surveillance monitors keep pace (Biber, 2007; Parks, 2007). All the while, the liquidity of these images leaks them from one medium to another, with downloads, cross-postings, and video clips cutting illicit images loose from their origins, freeing them to circulate from screen to street to cell phone, freeing them to become part of the collective consciousness by which we make sense of crime and control. How, today, can there be a viable criminology that is not also a visual criminology?

Some might argue that a visual criminology has already emerged. After all, phrases like 'images of' and 'media constructions of' are now common, and commonly accepted, prefixes to conventional criminological categories such as domestic violence or policing, and even orthodox criminology's own books and journals today include analyses of representation, even photographic illustrations. Yet this disciplinary drift into the realm of the image hardly constitutes an adequate visual criminology; unless coupled to a concomitant methodological reorientation, it's likely to create more confusion than clarity. Simply importing images into a discipline defined by words and numbers is in fact likely to *retard* the development of a visual criminology, since it will leave in place the ugly notion that written or numeric analysis can somehow penetrate the obfuscation, conquer the opaqueness, of the image. Images relegated to the status of illustration likewise simply reinforce this tyranny of the word and the number, and as seen in Chapter 4's critique of juvenile delinquency textbook covers, generally hide more than they reveal.

Put bluntly, the tradition of social scientific criminology is no foundation on which to build a late modern visual criminology. But there are other foundations. We can usefully turn to the long tradition of documentary photography, to Walker Evans, whose photographs were 'not illustrative [but] coequal, mutually dependent, and fully collaborative' with the text, or to W Eugene Smith, who described his approach as 'photographic penetration deriving from study and awareness and participation' (Agee and Evans, 1960: xiv–xv; Miller, 1997: 150). We can recall the early work of the Birmingham School and the National Deviancy Conference, whose members drew on critical theorists, literary writers, and image makers to develop what Tony Jefferson (1976: 86) called a '"grammar"' for decoding cultural symbols, a grammar

Plate 6.5   Graffiti? Or corporate advertising? Graffiti palimpsest, including tags, advertisements, and political message, London, England
Credit: Heitor Alvelos (1999)

that could 'discern the hidden messages inscribed in code on the glossy surfaces of style' (Hebdige, 1979: 18). We can look around and beyond criminology today, to visual research methods and visual sociology (Harper, 2001; Greek, 2003; A Young, 2004; Stanczak, 2007), or to the new generation of street gang scholars already noted, whose deep understanding of visual politics substantiates the primacy of photography in their work. And we can certainly look to the work of those who have developed the very sort of visual grammar that Jefferson embraced: Camilo José Vergara (1995), for example, who shot 9,000 images of urban space over eighteen years and developed from them thematic 'pictorial networks' of social change, or Heitor Alvelos (2004), who through an intricate, long-term photographic study of urban graffiti was able to reveal subtly shifting patterns in the production of illicit urban meaning.

If all of this work suggests a foundation on which to build a visual criminology, it implies also an important tension with which to animate it: the tension between precise visual attentiveness and politically-charged critical analysis. At times cultural criminologists embrace this tension by engaging in a close, contextualized analysis of existing images in hopes of drawing insights into larger issues of justice and injustice. Wayne Morrison (2004b: 341), for example, 'uses as data for cultural criminology an album of photographs taken by German soldiers and policemen involved in the Holocaust' in order to understand links between 'genocidal tourism' and crime. Through a detailed deconstruction of torture photographs taken at Iraq's Abu Grhaib prison, Mark Hamm (2007) likewise documents patterns of physical abuse that transcend the actions of individual US soldiers and trace to the highest levels of the US political system. In these and other cases, important critiques of the largest sorts of crimes – transnational torture, human rights abuses, genocide – develop not only from a visual criminology, but from detailed attention to the smallest particulars of images and their production.

Others concerned with crime and justice build this tension into their *own* photography, producing images attentive both to little moments of human pathos and to larger patterns of social harm. In this, Cartier-Bresson's notion of the 'decisive moment' can usefully be recalled. One of the great documentary photographers, Cartier-Bresson conceptualized the decisive moment as 'the simultaneous recognition, in a fraction of a second, of the significance of an event as well as a precise organization of forms which give that event its proper expression' (in Miller, 1997: 102). With the well-timed click of the shutter, then, a moment of *instant visual ethnography* – and an image whose particular subject matter and composition say something significant about the world the image represents. At just the moment a homeless woman crosses in front of a 'No Loitering' sign, a decisive image of law and social exclusion; at just the moment an intoxicated husband turns angrily to his wife, a decisive image of domestic violence and its antecedents. Here of course the tension

Plate 6.6 A decisive moment

Credit: Cecile Van de Voorde (2007)

between the visual moment and the larger lesson is particularly fragile, particularly fleeting, and the skills of the visual criminologist most rigorously tested. Even in a world suffused with such decisive moments, most will elude us – yet those caught will create criminological insights few other methods can match.

At its best, then, visual criminology becomes an essential method in cultural criminology's attempt to account for meaning, situation, and representation, and to confront the harms of injustice and inequality (Ferrell, 2006b; Van de Voorde, 2007; Hayward and Presdee, 2008). Exemplars abound, though unsurprisingly, outside the box of orthodox criminology: photographer Taryn Simon and her shocking images of the wrongly convicted, photographed at the scenes of the crimes they didn't commit, sometimes accompanied by those who falsely accused them (Courtney and Lyng, 2007); documentary filmmakers and cultural criminologists David Redmon and Ashley Sabin, their films on Mardi Gras and post-Katrina New Orleans intercutting do-it-yourself hope with damning indictments of global injustice; activist artists like Seth Tobocman (1999) and Peter Kuper (Lovell, 2006), whose condemnatory images of capital punishment and interpersonal violence are graphic indeed. As visual sociologist Emmanuel David (2007: 251) says, work of this sort functions as a form of 'visual resistance', not only to the powerful and their officially promulgated imagery, but to 'the milieu of social researchers who choose not to look at the world'.

In this regard we'd suggest above all the work of W Eugene Smith. Smith was there at the birth of modern jazz in the 1950s, catching on film the furious creativity of Charles Mingus and Thelonious Monk. He was there in Pittsburgh in the 1950s – there too long, in fact, sent on assignment for a couple of weeks, defiantly staying to study and photograph for a couple of years. And he was there at Minamata in the early 1970s. A Japanese fishing village, Minamata had seen its citizens poisoned and killed, its children grossly deformed, by the Chiso Corporation's pervasive dumping of toxic mercury, and Smith went to their aid. Existing for three years on a diet of 'home-grown vegetables, rice and whiskey', beaten almost blind by company thugs, Smith produced a series of searing photographs that became an early visual criminology, dare we say a cultural criminology, of corporate crime.

'Each time I pressed the shutter', he said, 'it was a shouted condemnation' (Hubbard, 1994; Miller, 1997: 140, 156; Smith, 1998; Ferrell, 2001/2).[6]

ethnographic content analysis

Exploring in Chapter 5 the looping dynamics of contemporary media, we noted that conventional content analysis – the method of measuring static content categories within media texts – was ill-equipped to account for the fluid uncertainty of late modern media. Multiple audiences, shifting meanings, samples and mashups, media consumers doubling as media producers – none of the forces that drive the contemporary interplay between media, crime, and criminal justice can be captured in quantitative summaries of textual word frequency or source type. Yet much of criminology's recent movement into the analysis of crime and the media has relied on precisely this methodological framework – and with predictably constipated results. Certainly content analysis can function as a useful tool for suggesting patterns of presentation; utilized as a free-standing method of inquiry, though, it can't catch the fluid, *cultural* dynamics of crime and the media.

Numeric summaries of discrete textual categories miss the larger aesthetic within which a text takes shape, and ignore the structural frames that shape a text's flow of meaning. The methodological myth of objectivity that traditionally accompanies content analysis reproduces the old notion that we can free content from its hiding place behind the façade of stylized presentation; in this way, it likewise denies the sensual and aesthetic experiences by which texts come to have meaning for their audiences. Moreover, content analysis is regularly utilized with the intent of proving the degree of divergence between the 'real' nature of a crime issue and a 'biased' media representation of it. Missing the essentially symbolic construction of crime, justice, and social issues, this approach also misses the multiplicity of audiences, audience interpretations, and public debates that will continue to confound the real and the representational as an issue runs its course.

Confronting these problems, David Altheide (1987: 68; 1996) has developed the method of *ethnographic content analysis*, an approach that situates textual analysis within 'the communication of meaning', and conceptualizes such analysis as a process of ongoing intellectual give and take. Rejecting the myth of content analysis as objective textual measurement, he instead acknowledges the importance of deep involvement with the text, such that the researcher is able to develop a thickly descriptive account of the text in all its complexities of 'information exchange, format, rhythm, and style'. Rather than seeing the text as a unitary entity to be analyzed, he likewise understands the text and its meanings to be a cultural process, and so embraces emergent concepts and categories that develop from the interplay of text and researcher, or text and text. Here once again we see the value of conceptualizing ethnography not as a single method of field research, but as a methodological sensibility: a sensitivity to subtleties of meaning, an openness to the orientations of others – even if those others are textual in nature. We also see a style of content analysis appropriate to a criminology of late modernism – one that retains the power of such analysis to identify textual patterns while recognizing the fluid dynamics of inter-textuality and inter-subjectivity within which such patterns take shape.

Utilizing this approach as a method of cultural criminological analysis, Jennifer Grimes (2007) has untangled the complex process by which the 'three strikes and you're out' policy emerged as part of punitive criminal justice politics in the United States. As she shows, existing criminal justice policies were ramped up and reinvented as 'three strikes' approaches amidst the hysteria of a high-profile murder case, with various mass media outlets providing both emotional cues for the hysteria and a set of imagined remedies for it. Overriding individual reservations – even on the part of the murder victim's father and grandfather – this mutually reinforcing interplay of crime, criminal justice policy, and public perception flowed from one media source to another, from one state legislature to another, as 'three strikes' came to define the mediated debate over crime and punishment – and continued to do so off and on for a decade. By employing ethnographic content analysis, Grimes (2007: 97) goes deep inside 'the intersection of symbolism created within the mass media, and collective behavior which results in cultural change'; said differently, she investigates moral panic as a cultural process, and so traces the life history of a panic and its consequences (see also Chancer, 2005). Charles Acland (1995:

19) argues that 'the appraisal of a cultural phenomenon involves following traces of cultural forms, activities, and histories…'. Ethnographic content analysis offers a tool for just such cultural tracking.

Towards a Cultural Victimology

Victimology – the scholarly concern for crime victims and victimization – often reduces crime victims to sets of aggregate victimization data, or worse, takes them hostage to a mean-spirited politics of retributive justice. In light of the methods discussed in this chapter, we might imagine a different sort of *cultural victimology* – a victimology attuned to human agency, symbolic display, and shared emotion. Such a victimology would consider performances of

Plate 6.7   Roadside shrine, New Mexico, USA
Credit: Jeff Ferrell (2005)

victimization and enactments of grief through which the meaning of victimization is constructed. It would explore the symbolic environments created by victims, their families, and their friends as they come to terms with their experiences. And it would trace the path of personal pain as it moves through the mass media and the criminal justice system, and so re-emerges as a collective accomplishment.

In this task, as W Eugene Smith showed, methods of visual criminology would be essential for exposing the often hidden victims of corporate and governmental crime. Visual methods could also record the many displays of emotion and remembrance that emerge around victimization: roadside shrines (Ferrell, 2004b), 9/11 shrines and tattoos (A. Young, 2007), graffiti 'rest in pieces', commemorative T-shirts, MySpace communities of grief (Grear, 2004) – even the body's own scar tissue. Instant ethnographies could go inside those decisive moments when a robbery goes bad, when a woman finally flees ongoing domestic abuse, or when grief unexpectedly overwhelms an earnest effort to forget; long-term ethnographies might explore a family's slow process of recuperation from victimization, or the parallel course of trial, appeals, and imprisonment

for the perpetrator. Here liquid ethnography would also be of help, watching for the ambiguous reconstruction of personal victimization as a criminal justice category or media phenomenon; through ethnographic content analysis, we might well find a high-profile victim made eventually into a mediated *cause célèbre*, or transformed yet again into social policy. Most importantly perhaps, a sense of *verstehen* would attune our research to the human agency of those victimized – might even aid in some small way as they work to regain human dignity – and would remind us to look for signs of resistance and survival amidst the emotional scar tissue of misfortune (Mawby and Walklate, 1994). This approach might even suggest a sort of historical victimology, as with labour organizer Joe Hill, murdered by firing squad in 1915, and offering to his fellow workers a rousing benediction:
'Don't mourn – organize'.[7]

dangerous knowledge

Cultural criminology has come to be known, at least in part, for what some consider its sensational subject matter: skinheads and domestic terrorists, underground graffiti writers, skydivers and BASE jumpers, outlaw motorcycle racers, prostitutes, drug users, dumpster divers, street buskers, and urban radicals. Critics of cultural criminology fear that this sensationalism, this 'adrenaline-pumping, here-and-now quality of cultural criminology' (Webber, 2007: 154), constitutes a sort of cheap intellectual trick. By picking amidst the cultural detritus for oddities and titillations, they say, cultural criminology draws attention to itself. By then dressing up this degraded subject matter in stylish language and presentation – by offering 'a gilded invitation to readers to revel pruriently and voyeuristically in the exotica of ... deviant doings' (O'Brien, 2005: 610) – cultural criminology manages to generate easy public interest and fraudulent intellectual excitement.

Such criticisms, we would argue, mistake subject matter for method. Sparks of dangerous sensuality may sometimes fly from bikers or street buskers, or from their flinty clashes with the authorities – but as such groups and situations become the subject matter of criminology, those sparks are snuffed out, or fanned into flame, by *method*. As we demonstrated in the first half of this chapter, even the most sensational of subject matters can be reduced to tedious abstraction with the proper methodology. Think about it: the orthodox criminology we explored earlier had as its subject matter some truly sensational issues – sexual assault, escape from domestic abuse, anti-social juvenile crime – and yet the *criminology* of these issues, as produced by survey research and clinical trial, couldn't have been less engaging. And with those same methods, the alleged sensationalism of cultural criminology could quite easily be extinguished: skydivers drained of adrenaline, dumpster divers imbued with measurable motivation, terrorists brought to heal by tobit models and time-varying predictors. The contemporary enterprise of orthodox criminology, as played out in its own journals and conferences, confirms it: nothing kills good criminology like bad method.

Whatever intellectual vigour cultural criminology may offer, then, comes mostly from its *methodological engagement* with its subjects of study. In actuality, attentive ethnography, sharp-eyed visual criminology, and crisp cultural analysis don't require BASE jumpers or drug users for intellectual excitement; as cultural criminologists have already shown, such methods can find vivid insight and critique in historical photos, old motel rooms, new legal regulations … even in boredom itself (Hamm, 1998, 2004; Ferrell, 2004a; Morrison, 2004a). From such situations – from any such everyday situation – these methods can generate genuinely dangerous knowledge as well (see Miller and Tewkesbury, 2000). Critics like Steve Hall and Simon Winlow (2007) contend that this focus on motorcycles and motel rooms prevents cultural criminology from addressing deeper structures of injustice, and so from posing any real political danger to the powers that be. On the contrary, cultural criminology is designed to be dangerous, and to draw that danger directly from everyday situations. As we noted in Chapters 1 and 4, structures of inequality and injustice permeate the situations of everyday life and everyday crime – it is precisely their presence there that gives them such great power. Cultural criminology's goal is to expose that presence to those who might not notice it, thereby helping ourselves and others to understand and confront the everyday reality of injustice – with the *tools* for accomplishing this liberatory communication to be found in methods of attentive observation and compassionate analysis. Exposing injustice, unpacking ideologies of crime and victimization, giving voice to those unheard and unnamed, such methods can make for some decidedly dangerous knowledge.

And for cultural criminology that's just the question: How best can we endanger existing arrangements of predatory crime, punitive criminal justice, and pervasive late modern exclusion? The stale methods of orthodox criminology offer neither the analytic insight nor the invitational edge necessary for constructing a collective counter-assault; similarly unhelpful and unappealing is the disavowal of human meaning in the interest of calculated abstraction. Methods of inquiry attuned to the swirling cultural dynamics of late modernity, open to the human construction of collective meaning, attuned to both the harm and the hope of transgression – now those methods, on the other hand, promise real problems for those invested in the *status quo*.

Because what good is knowledge, really, if it's not a danger to those who would deny it?

notes

1 An anarchist critique of knowledge need not result in the sort of extreme relativism that leaves one perspective epistemologically indistinguishable from another. Even when absolute knowledge claims are rejected – or, more accurately in the case of

Feyerabend and Cohen, deconstructed – decisions can still be made and preferences expressed. As we hope to demonstrate later in this chapter, it is the *grounds* for these preferences and decisions that are different – no longer the alleged epistemic certainty of 'truth' or 'scientific method', but rather the provisional persuasion offered by stylistic elegance, human affinity, and social awareness.

2 Our thanks to Trey Williams, pioneer of the intentionally out-of-focus table.

3 To paraphrase Sinead O'Conner's (1990) *The Emperor's New Clothes*: through their own articles they will be exposed.

4 Speaking of frauds and performers, what of Robert K Merton? Merton was certainly *not* an intellectual fraud, but he was certainly not a 'social scientist' either, more a magician, an inventor of his own identity, and an aesthetician of theory (Cullen and Messner, 2007).

5 From this view, even long-term ethnography can be seen as an elongated moment, a temporal slice of something more – with the question for ethnographers, then: how big the slice, how long the moment?

6 The journal *Crime, Media, Culture* now provides a venue for publishing photographic work and other forms of visual criminology.

7 See, similarly, the final passage of John Steinbeck's (1972 [1936]) *In Dubious Battle*, and Mythen (2007) for a different sense of 'cultural victimology'.

A selection of films and documentaries illustrative of some of the themes and ideas in this chapter

THE TRAP: WHAT HAPPENED TO OUR DREAM OF FREEDOM, 2007 (3 parts), Dir. Adam Curtis
A brilliant three-part documentary series that shows how reliance upon simplistic statistical models of human behaviour combined with an exaggerated belief in human selfishness has created a 'cage' for Western humans. Essential viewing for anybody who wants to understand the neo-liberal world of performance indicators, league tables, quotas constituted from dubious statistics, and ever more controlling systems of social management.

HEART BROKEN IN HALF: CHICAGO'S STREET GANGS, 1990, Producers Taggart Siegel and Dwight Conquergood
An intimate documentary that goes behind the headlines to confront the human reality and complexity of street gangs in urban America. Based on Dwight Conquergood's ground-breaking ethnographic research, and drawing on personal interviews, *Heart Broken in Half* debunks stereotypes and reveals the reality of gang life. 'Here is an intricate web of symbols and passions, territory and brotherhood, honour and, all too often, death.'

BRAZIL, 1985, Dir. Terry Gilliam
One man takes on an administrative state obsessed with terrorism and technology in Terry Gilliam's retro-future fantasy. Part surreal fantasy, part profound sci-fi satire on totalitarian bureaucracy, *Brazil* makes for interesting viewing in a post-Patriot Act world.

WHO IS BOZO TEXINO?, 2005, Dir. Bill Daniel
Like *Recycled Life* and *Kamp Katrina* (see earlier film links), *Who is Bozo Texino?* takes us inside the sort of off-the-radar world that would never appear in a social scientific survey. Bill Daniel's film is a rolling, rail-clacking account of one man's search for a legendary and elusive freight train graffiti artist.

THE YES MEN, 2005, Dirs Chris Smith, Dan Ollman and Sarah Price
Political activism for the *Jackass* generation. A documentary that charts the various 'performance protests' of the co-founders of the *Yes Men* organization as they set about impersonating political leaders and corporate figures in a bid to publicly humiliate them. Not a great piece of filmmaking, but a useful 'how to' manual for those interested in performance as protest. Get involved yourself at www.theyesmen.org.

KITCHEN STORIES, 2003, Dir. Bent Hammer
Based on a truly boring 1950s documentary about Swedish time-and-motion studies of housewives, *Kitchen Stories* is a comedy that highlights the problems that can emerge when one attempts to scientifically observe human behaviour.

cultural criminology:
an innovation

...I am terrified of cops who stare at kids with fear in their eyes
instead of protection...
I am terrified of a news system that keeps us
locked in terror
I am terrified of guns and nervous hands
and humiliated spirits
I am terrified of a music industry with no conscience
I am terrified of military recruiters who see poor youth as potential property
I am terrified of white black and Latino kids who diss Arab kids with the power
of their words
I am too terrified to worry about **terrorism**

Baruch 'Baba' Israel (www.openthoughtmusic.com)

cultural criminology: the politics of meaning

The issue of meaning makes a question mark of orthodox criminology and
criminal justice – and cultural criminology is intended to facilitate just such
punctuation. As scholars and as citizens, our lives are littered with 'facts' about
crime, from crime statistics to fear-of-crime percentages and gang member
head counts. Knowing something of meaning and representation, though, we
can see these 'facts' for what they are: myopic snapshots of a moving world,
more deserving of critical interrogation than unthinking acceptance.
Reconsidered through the lens of cultural criminology, crime statistics appear
mostly as political accomplishments – embodiments of police discretion and

governmental agenda, certainly – but just as certainly not representations of crime's lived reality. The percentage of the population reported to be 'somewhat afraid' of crime is shown to be a double duplicity, a fiction of conceptualization and of method, as survey researchers imagine the shifting contours of collective fear to be a measurable category of individual emotion, and then imagine they can capture this category with little answer sets. An always shifting and ambiguous entity even within gang life itself, 'the number of gang members' currently residing in Birmingham or Boston, as announced by criminal justice agencies or the mass media, is seen to be mostly a projection of prejudiced perception and racial anxiety.

Re-encoded in this way, the valences of orthodox criminology and criminal justice are reversed. The taken-for-granted authority of policing agencies and government-funded researchers is questioned. The assumed hierarchy of credibility that situates agency reports and media accounts at the forefront of our understanding of crime is inverted. Instead, the experience and everyday reality of crime for those involved in it come to the front – and the issue of representation is not far behind.

> *The rate of domestic violence declined in the last year by 34 per cent?* We hope so – but whose numbers are these? In what way might they reflect women's fear of reporting domestic violence, or police officers' disinclination to code it, or perhaps new laws narrowing the legal definition of domestic violence?

> *Three out of five UK citizens say that they are afraid of crime?* To whom do they say it, and in what way? Are they afraid of crime, or afraid of what the media presents as crime? And what does 'afraid of crime' mean for their lives, for the choices they make when no researcher or reporter is present?

> *Gang membership is on the increase in large urban areas?* Who decides when a young person is 'in' or 'out' of a gang? How can such a fluid identity be counted with any certainty? How and why is the media reporting this 'fact'? And most importantly, is there governmental grant money riding on this asserted increase, or a political career?

In counterpoint to orthodox assertions about crime, cultural criminology unashamedly offers more questions than it does answers – or maybe it provides some new answers by questioning the old ones.

Notice also that the politics of cultural criminology is no after-the-fact overlay; it's inherent in the approach itself. To concern oneself with the collective human construction of meaning is to undermine those who claim authoritative knowledge of crime, and to confront those who make meaning disappear inside mazes of numbers and jargon. Likewise, to understand the power of representation is to appreciate the loops and spirals by which image and experience intertwine – and to realize that those who claim otherwise, who claim to present the un-mediated truth about crime, are mostly marketing delusion, diversion, or ideology. Cultural criminology is in this sense innately subversive; by paying attention to meaning and representation, it undermines the authority of politicians, police commissioners, and orthodox criminologists, looking instead to discover perspectives less noticed or less understood.

In the complex, contested and ambiguous late modern world seen throughout this book, this subversion of epistemic authority seems all the more necessary and appropriate. In a world animated by morphing identities and increasing human migration, in a world awash in new meanings and new media, stern truth claims about 'crime' or 'criminal justice' seem downright ludicrous – a sad attempt to measure precisely how many criminals can be incarcerated on the point of some punitive pin. As we suggested in the previous chapter, such claims seem dangerous as well, suggesting a longing for surety at any cost, a fondness for an epistemic orderliness that can somehow staunch the flow of late modern uncertainty. When politicians launch 'zero tolerance' drug campaigns or promise to simply 'eliminate' anti-social behaviour, when criminologists present statistical summaries as self-evident factual statements, their reports reveal a reactionary recoil against the world they inhabit, an echo of dinosaurs dying hard. Now is no time not to notice these reductionist absurdities, and their effects.

About those effects let us be clear. Social worlds saturated with surveillance technologies today drain freedoms of movement and identity from the practice of everyday life. American anti-gang injunctions and British ASBOs add their repressive weight, further criminalizing the minutia of personal movement and public presence. In the USA., Britain, France, and elsewhere, expanding police states continue to pass themselves off as democratic systems of criminal justice; elsewhere, fundamentalist 'justice' systems continue to demean and destroy the lives of girls, women, and non-believers. Reactionary American criminal justice policies such as determinant sentencing and 'life in prison without parole' disenfranchise millions while stretching institutionalized hopelessness over a slow accumulation of decades. For the thousands of Americans now serving such sentences for crimes committed before their eighteenth birthdays, an additional existential ache: the more life you have left, the longer your sentence. Meanwhile, from Mexico to Malaysia, international trade laws and local legal corruption protect a global economy that destroys other young lives, and their lived environments as well.

We can do better than this. We can create a world in which late modern fluidities of people and meaning are cause for polymorphous celebration, sparks for cultural invention, not reasons for official reaction. We can create a world in which the ambiguities of late modernity usefully call into question rigid categories of race and medieval forms of religion, rather than calling forth their vengeful return (J Young, 2007). We can imagine something better for millions of the world's citizens than predatory victimization amidst environmental degradation, or for others, deadening work intercut with imprisonment. To do so, though, we must have a criminology that is effective, persuasive, and unafraid. If orthodox criminologists and criminal justice practitioners insist on certainty and essentialism, insist on reducing people to quantifiable categories and their cultures to dangerous abstractions, then we must have a criminology that can leverage up the very intellectual foundations of their work. If late modern political orders find it increasingly effective to 'govern through crime' (Simon, 2007) – that is, to recast social issues as crime issues, to define crime and victimization as the essential dynamic of social life, and so to govern through fear and exclusion – then we must have a criminology that can confront this political transformation, and define social life in other, more progressive terms.

cultural criminology: performance and persuasion

In this sense cultural criminology is designed to be a form of performance and persuasion appropriate to this progressive political imperative.

Among cultural criminology's central insights is the notion that all those engaged with crime at the same time engage in symbolic performance. Perpetrators of crime display their dominance to their victims, and subtle signs of insider status to their compatriots. Individually and collectively, victims of crime perform their role, showing appropriate markers of victimhood and distress. The courtroom in which perpetrator and victim come together is in turn a mélange of interlocking, sometimes aggressively antagonistic, performances on the part of prosecutors, defence attorneys, and judges. On a larger stage, lawmakers and criminal justice system operatives engage in endless public performance, from press conferences to displays of everyday policing authority. As argued in the previous chapter, even orthodox criminology operates as a staged performance of professionalism, objectivity, and moral righteousness, though generally not a very appealing one.

Thought of in terms of political strategy the lesson is clear: if we understand all human communication as symbolic performance, then our obligation is to choose the performance most appropriate to the situation and most persuasive to the audience – and in a late modern world of swirling ideas and incendiary images, we would argue, rarely will that performance be a turgidly written sentence or a summary table. Instead, we must find ways to tune the performance of criminology to its circumstances, to the jazzed cacophony of the contemporary world. Put differently, put in terms of another of cultural criminology's foundational notions: style matters. Style is the fluid in which meaning floats, the essential medium for collective communication, the connecting tissue between individual and society – and so criminology must pay close attention to styles that best connect and communicate With this in mind, we've quite intentionally tried to design this book as an exercise in persuasive performance and aesthetic engagement, with vignettes, photographs, and narrative structures all meant to reinforce stylistically what our words communicate intellectually.

And with this final chapter, we're just getting started. The dangerous circumstances we face today – circumstances mixing the poison of punishment and exclusion into the already toxic waters of late capitalism – demand all we can muster in response.

diptychs, triptychs, and *detournement*

A little magic might be a good place to begin.

Increasingly, a visual image exists as a sort of public performance, and often a very persuasive one at that. But put that already powerful single image in conversation with another image, and magic happens: the persuasive power is amplified, not additively but exponentially, as each image now alters and accelerates the meaning of the other. Juxtaposed, the images become something more, creating a new context for making sense of each image, and of the world they represent. Nothing has changed, neither image altered, but through a sort of epistemic sleight of hand, much has changed. To use an example from a recent issue of the journal *Crime, Media, Culture*, a photo of a prison kitchen worker assembling dozens of sandwiches tells you something about the routine of prison life. A photo of an ex-prisoner examining a wall of employment centre job postings tells you something about the slim possibilities of post-prison life. But seeing these images side by side, seeing that the sandwiches and the job postings both exist as a series of little white squares – indistinguishable, unappealing, lined up according to somebody else's rules – begins to tell you something more, something about the sad continuities between prison life and life on the outside, maybe even something about mass culture, bureaucratic incarceration, and alienation (Aitchison and Greer, 2007: 208).

Photographers and artists call this sort of image juxtaposition a diptych, or if three images are involved, a triptych. And if the magic works by putting prison sandwiches next to post-prison job postings, imagine how much analytic magic there can be in other juxtaposed images. The office cubicle put next to the prison cell. The cop's uniform presented beside the gang member's uniform. The billboard beside the graffiti-covered wall. The politician's campaign photo crowding the mug shot made upon later arrest. Significantly, such juxtapositions not only forge new insights from a combination of old images; they often serve to *steal away* official meanings, reversing the assumed authenticity of the police officer's uniform or the politician's campaign photo through recontextualization, forcing everyday understanding into a sort of auto-critique whereby a single truth is shown to be a double lie.

All of which brings us back to a concept seen throughout this book: *detournement*. As practised by Situationists and others, *detournement* signifies a theft of meaning, a turning of everyday understanding back on itself so as to undermine that very understanding. This reversal of meaning is indeed meant to be political magic, a magic that can convert the suffocating sameness of orthodox culture into its undoing – since everyone is familiar with the codes of day-to-day living, the logic goes, everyone will understand a critique based in the perversion of those same formulaic codes.

Plate 7.1 Prisoners at work

Credit: © Andy Aitchison (2007), by permission

Here's an example, a little advert for dumpster diving that Ferrell thought up while living as an urban scrounger, a *detournement* of a popular credit card advertising campaign in the US:

> *Scrounged shirt: zero dollars.*
>
> *Scrounged pants: zero dollars.*
>
> *Scrounged boots: zero dollars.*
>
> *Telling your corporate masters to piss off: priceless.*
>
> *(The best things in life are free; for everything else there's Master Dumpster.)*

Like the diptych, *detournement* is designed to make new meaning, even create critique and analysis, from simple recontextualization. In both cases the criminologist doesn't retreat into academic abstraction, but instead mines late modernity's own saturations of image and information for alternative understanding. In this regard we'd suggest that the following vignette contains, along with a visual triptych and a detourned quotation, a good bit of cultural criminology.

Now Hiring

1. *I can hire one half the working class to kill the other half*

Plate 7.2   Credit: www.iww.org

In February 1886, railroad workers went on strike against the Texas and Pacific Railroad, part of the US rail system controlled by financier, railroad magnate, and 'robber baron' Jay Gould. During such strikes wealthy capitalists and the corporations they controlled regularly hired thugs and gunmen to battle striking workers – thus Gould's infamously confident comment at the time that 'I can hire one half the working class to kill the other half'. Often these company thugs were in turn deputized by local legal authorities working on the side of the companies. The violence then committed by these 'deputy sheriffs' against strikers was protected by the authority of law – and the strikers who stood up to deputized thugs faced charges of assault on a law officer. By April of that year, in fact, the railroad strike had been lost, as strikers were unable 'to hold out any longer against hunger, mass arrests, [and] unprovoked attacks by police, sheriffs, troops, and vigilantes....' (Foner, 1975: 86)

2. *I can hire one half the working class to guard the other half.*

Plate 7.3   Credit: © Andy Aitchison (2007), by permission

A hundred years later, the United States prison population passed two million, having tripled in just the fifteen years from 1980 to 1995 as a result of the 'war on drugs', mandatory sentencing guidelines, and other aggressively punitive policies. With millions of mostly working-class and ethnic minority prisoners to be guarded, a new growth industry developed in the United States: the building of public and private prisons, and the employment of working-class men and women as prison guards. So pervasive and profitable was this prison boom that new 'prison robber barons' like Corrections Corporation of America and CiviGenics now came to replace the old barons like Jay Gould – and in small cities and rural areas, the building of a prison came to offer about the only hope for new jobs and economic development. A 'prison–industrial complex' – a highly profitable, self-confirming con game run by politicians, prison lobbyists, and private contractors – had emerged (Schlosser, 1998; Carceral, 2006). Once Jay Gould could hire half the working class to kill the other; now the vast American gulag of public and private prisons was hiring one half the working class to guard the other. Meanwhile, Mexican prison officials continued profiting from the surreptitious sale of prisoner-made furniture, and Chinese officials continued 'harvesting' the organs of executed prisoners to supply China's lucrative organ transplant industry.

3. I can hire one half the working class to indebt and intoxicate the other half.

Plate 7.4   Credit: Robin Jones

With the new century, the prison–industrial complex continues, and so does the shift in the developed world from an economy of industrial production to an economy of retail sales and personal services. In the United States, Great Britain, and elsewhere, this economy employs millions of people in low-wage, low-skilled retail jobs, where they hustle and cajole others much like themselves into buying the latest consumer products. Requiring a Third World gulag of dangerous factories, underaged workers, and cheaply made imports, the economy also requires First World consumers willing to carry staggering debt in order to have the best and latest. Today, half the working class sells, the other half buys ... and then they switch places.

And after a hard day of work and shopping, they get drunk. As seen in Chapter 4, a British 'nighttime economy' of corporate mega-pubs now employs millions of service workers, and spawns criminal violence at every turn. As a result, police and hospital emergency room workers now notice new waves of alcoholism, drunk driving and 'drug driving', fatal wrecks, and disfiguring bar brawls. Television programmers notice too; programmes like *Booze Britain 2* now broadcast this effusion of 'violence, vomit, vandalism, and obscene behaviour' (Hayward and Hobbs, 2007: 438). Indebted and intoxicated, the working class staggers on.

Wonder who's hiring next?

manifestos

A manifesto is a marvelous thing – a pointed declaration of purpose and intent, a statement of how things are and how they should be, a call to analysis and action. A good manifesto is more a series of intellectual hammer blows than a carefully reasoned argument, more political rap than intellectual mood music. A good manifesto blows open the box that is conventional understanding, creating a sort of 'temporary autonomous zone' (Bey, 2003) in which to think, imagine, and critique. As such, the manifesto would seem a useful form for criminological analysis – except of course that the manifesto is antithetical to orthodox criminology. By design it offers no citations, no footnotes, no article-length discussion, no 'proof'. It offers – demands – only a re-evaluation of present arrangements.

All the more reason for a manifesto. And as you read it, consider a couple of questions: What if you only had space to leave a hundred words on a hacked criminal justice website? What if you only had fifteen minutes to speak at a criminology conference, and wanted to blow open the box? What would you say?

cultural criminology: for a criminology of the twenty-first century

1. Mainstream criminology is an abject failure. Many criminologists, having spent their working lives futilely trying to explain the inexorable rise in crime rates, now face explaining the opposite: a crime drop in many industrial countries. If they never quite got adjusted to the high modernity of the post-World War II period, they're certainly unprepared for late modernity.
2. Criminology is unprepared in part because it is today dominated by positivism and by rational choice theory, itself a form of market positivism. With the first lens all one can see is determinism and misery, with the second

only pallid choice and the mundane. We need instead a criminology which can grasp the phenomenology of everyday life: the experiences of joy, humiliation, anger, and desperation, the seductions of transgression and vindictiveness, the myriad forms of resistance and the repressive nature of acquiescence. We need a criminology of energy and tension, not one of listlessness and inertia.

3. A new genre has emerged in the leading criminology journals. Articles begin with insubstantial theoretical overviews, follow with extensive discussions of methodology, proceed to obligatory statistical analyses, and end with brief and inconclusive results. The theory is desiccated and devalued; the research is poor sociology or indeed anti-sociology, as econometrics abounds and natural scientific methods are emulated; and the thinness of the argument hides behind the sophistication of the statistics. The abstracted empiricism of which C Wright Mills warned us is here; journals which once melded sophisticated theory with deep social research now include little of either, as scholars are replaced by statistical functionaries. We must reclaim criminology for sociology, for ideas, for engagement, for critique.

In the 1960s criminology and the sociology of deviance were at the very centre of sociological and political debate. There were good reasons for this: their focus on situations where norms form and break, natural milieu of pluralism and contested value; their critique of power and stigmatization, and the social construction of statistics. A revanchist positivism now seeks to ignore all of this. We must reconnect with our traditions in the Chicago School, in social constructionism and subcultural theories, and in the National Deviancy Conference and the Birmingham Centre for Contemporary Cultural Studies. We must go back to go forward, critically developing this tradition in the context of late modernity.

4. Late modernity brings with it a qualitative change in the conditions of life – a world of ontological anxiety and economic insecurity, of vindictiveness and humiliation, of othering and counter-othering, where moral panics abound, rates of imprisonment soar despite drops in crime, and 'anti-social behaviour' expands as tolerance declines. Here mediated images loop and spiral through everyday life, the generalized other becomes the generalized elsewhere, hyperpluralism animates the great cities, place and culture part ways, and cultural globalization begets transnational identification. Cultural criminology seeks to understand this world where culture shakes loose of its structural moorings, where identity becomes constant reinvention – yet it seeks to do so within the gross material inequalities and hegemonies of power within late modernity.

5. The crisis of late modernity results in large part from the predations of global capitalism. Societies in the West and elsewhere are increasingly constituted around consumerism and marketed individualism, around commodified celebrity and neophelia. Cultural criminology must find ways to intervene, to challenge and combat the casino capitalism that increasingly characterizes late modernity.

6. The way forward is to investigate both crime and crime control as cultural processes, processes where meaning is constructed and displayed, processes

suffused with contestation, inequality, and uncertainty. With crime and crime control now the primary symbolic terrain on which conflicts over morality, economy, and identity are fought, we cannot account for the politics and emotions of crime – indeed, we cannot account for the contemporary politics of social order and social change – without analyzing the contested cultural dynamics of crime and crime control. If by 'real' we mean those dimensions of social life that produce consequences and alter lives, then the image of crime and the symbolic meaning of crime control are now as real as the commission of crime and the practice of policing; in fact they are largely and increasingly indistinguishable. Media, meaning, commodity, style, symbolism, emotion – all now constitute the appropriate and necessary subject matter of criminology. Without them there can be no criminology … that matters.

true fiction

The last few decades have seen a radical blurring of fiction and non-fiction, with new appreciations of ethnography as story-telling, narrative as mélange, and fictional work as carrier of essential insight. Orthodox criminology, on the other hand, seems not to have noticed; still committed to the 'objective' non-fiction of social science, still confined within the stifling narrative structure of the conventional journal article, it toddles on towards a truth long since lost.

A more useful approach might be to acknowledge today's porous boundaries between fiction and non-fiction, and then to imagine ways of conducting criminological analysis, and remaining honest and open about our work, within such circumstances. As we hope to have demonstrated in Chapter 4, one possibility is 'true fiction' – various non-fictional accounts woven into a larger, fictionalized narrative. Here the criminologist combines traditional practices of careful documentation and analysis with the skills of story-telling in an effort to engage the reader with issues at hand. At its best, we would argue, true fiction can also function as sophisticated criminological theory and critique – but can do so in such a way that the usual abstractions of theory are absent, replaced instead by the texture of everyday experience. In the context of late modern fluidity, true fiction also catches something of the loops and spirals that confound fact and fiction in the first place – and as we suggested in Chapter 5, can perhaps push these loops and spirals in more progressive directions.

True fiction: pretty girls make graves

'Pretty girls make graves'.

Jack Kerouac planted that line in his 1958 book *The Dharma Bums*, an extended rumination on loneliness, sex, friendship, and existential wandering. Kerouac didn't

---

just include the line; he put it in quotation marks, writing that 'pretty girls make graves' was a mantra he invoked whenever he found himself confronting sexual temptation. For a while, Kerouac had embraced a sort of Zen celibacy, on the notion that lust produces sex, sex produces birth, birth produces existence – and so evolves the existential suffering of the universe. 'Pretty girls make graves' served as his shield, his reminder, to keep himself celibate in order to reduce his own suffering and that of the world – especially during his time lost in Mexico City, lost to the tragic junkie charms of Tristessa, a woman for whom he wrote the book *Tristessa*.

Then again that was half a century ago, and *The Dharma Bums* is generally thought to be a less significant book than Kerouac's *On The Road* (1957), so why bother remembering that Kerouac said 'pretty girls make graves'? One reason would be that so many others have. Twenty-six years after *The Dharma Bums* was published, the legendary British band The Smiths came out with the song 'Pretty Girls Make Graves'. As written and sung by lead singer Morrissey, the song was unmistakably an echo of Kerouac and his lament, with a pretty girl urging Morrissey to 'give in to lust, give up to lust.' Morrissey doesn't give in, though – he wants to, but it's just not in him. 'I'm not the man you think I am', he tells her. 'Nature played this trick on me.'

A quarter-century after Kerouac, nothing and everything had changed. For Morrissey, the suffering wasn't unrequited lust, it was no lust at all – not for pretty girls, anyway. After all, to be gay in a social world where sexuality and desire are defined by pretty girls is to suffer a sense of ongoing existential sadness, a sense that you can never be the man the world thinks you should be. Then again, despite his desires for pretty girls, Kerouac probably had some understanding of this as well. After all, he did hang out with Allen Ginsberg and other Beat writers whose subversive celebrations of gay sexuality were tinged with a good bit of their own sexual suffering. Ginsberg (1955), you might remember, didn't just howl against the blank conformity of middle-class, mid-century America; he howled for his own illicit sexuality, raging against a world of locked-down straight-laced sex.

If all that's getting a bit deep, a bit too nostalgic for a by-gone Beat age, then consider this: these days you can download The Smith's 'Pretty Girls Make Graves' as a ring tone for your mobile phone, or download the Smashing Pumpkins' Kerouac-inspired song 'Tristessa' on to your computer. And consider this, too: Seattle, Washington, the birthplace of bands like Nirvana and Pearl Jam, recently gave birth to another band, a band by the name of ... Pretty Girls Make Graves. The band's lead singer, Andrea Zollo, recalls that, long before Pretty Girls Make Graves, she got her start as part of the local Riot Grrl scene. 'I was absolutely inspired by Riot Grrl bands', she remembers, 'because there were so many women playing music.' She hopes that more women will start their own bands today, since 'we have to change the ratio of women to men in music!' And she recounts the origins of the band's name. 'One day [we] were listening to records and when we flipped through The Smiths' first album, we started talking about what a great song title it was, and we agreed it would be a great band name.'

Andrea Zollo's recollections aren't to be found in the liner notes of the Pretty Girls Make Graves' album, *The New Romance*, by the way. They're part of an interview she did with the women at *SuicideGirls.com* in 2006, and posted at their website. The website has other interviews, critical news postings – and photos of Suicide Girls in various states of undress. A pay website, it's been described as 'a punk rock Vogue ... with artful nude photos', and a source of 'post-modern pinup girls for the alternative nation'. 'The great thing about *SuicideGirls* is that they completely tear down that Pamela Anderson image', says Dave Grohl, once drummer for Nirvana and now leader of the Foo Fighters, in a 2006 posting on the website. 'They're beautiful ladies with crazy tattoos, piercings, and dreadlocks.' Looks like pretty girls don't just make graves; they make bands and websites, too, and maybe along the way play with the very notion of 'pretty' itself, by turns resisting and reproducing it, mixing and cutting it with moments of information, pleasure, and empowerment.

You have to wonder what ol' Jack Kerouac would think were he still around, surfing the web and stumbling on to *SuicideGirls.com*. Would he be bothered that Andrea Zollo seems to have lost track of the original reference amidst the spiral of popular culture, discovering 'pretty girls make graves' in The Smiths' album instead of *The Dharma Bums*? Or would he just be turned on by the nude photos of the suicide girls – and so be forced to confront the meaning of his old mantra in another way? Put simply: if pretty girls can make graves, can images of pretty girls make graves, too? Pinups and pornography must have some effect on those who view them – they keep *SuicideGirls.com* and a thousand other pay porn websites going. Whether or not such images make graves, it seems they do – for a price – make for little worlds of privatized desire played out in the glow of the computer screen. They do on some level make the women who pose for them into empty representations, postmodern commodities even, to be bought and sold. Perhaps, by pervasively objectifying women and their sexuality, such images somehow do eventually make for real sexual violence against women – make graves, even.

So maybe pretty girls make graves – or maybe, more accurately, men make graves for them. Long before Kerouac wrote The *Dharma Bums*, fans of various popular music genres would've certainly been diggin' such graves. Fans of British ballads or bluegrass would've listened to popular songs like 'Pretty Polly' or 'The Knoxville Girl', where jealous men stab women, beat them to death, throw them into open graves because 'you can never be my wife'. Blues aficionados would've heard countless variations on the old blues line 'if I can't have your love, baby, there won't be nothin' left behind', or more chillingly Sonny Boy Williamson's Delta blues classic, 'Your Funeral and My Trial'. Kids crazy for rock 'n' roll would've sung along with The Beatles song 'Run for Your Life', and its lyrical warning to the singer's 'little girl' that he'd rather see her dead than with someone else.

Notice that the grave's getting deeper, the dynamic more dangerous. Jealous men are digging graves for pretty girls, girls they can't quite control, girls whose 'roving eyes' disqualify them from marriage ... or from life itself. For the crime of being a pretty girl, the death penalty.

Now one might argue that these sorts of lyric are sometimes more male fantasies of power than they are real threats to women and girls; Stephanie Kane (1998), for example, notes that the often violently vulgar stories and 'toasts' that men recite about pimps and prostitutes incorporate this sort of complex lyrical bravado. Even so, it's certainly interesting how common these moments are in the culture at large, now pervading the lyrical narratives of hip hop and other mediated music forms as well. And if we know that mediated messages have at least *some* effect on those who consume them, that in fact subscribers gladly *pay* for the effects that the Suicide Girls have on them – well, then, isn't it at least worth considering what effect these accumulated stories of pretty girls and graves have on us, seeping out of our songs and stories and into our collective sensibility? 'I do wonder about the circulation of these images of prostitutes', Kane (1998: 142) says. 'The way they are encoded in artistic forms like toasts and pornographic photographs, how they are authored, and how they reproduce a circumscribed set of racial conventions that organize the circuit of money and pleasure that is sex work....'

Pornographic photographs do indeed offer us some evidence of how cultural images intersect with violence and desire; so do photographs of men making graves for pretty girls. The book *New York Noir* (Hannigan, 1999), for example, gathers old crime scene photographs from the archives of the *New York Daily News* newspaper – and among those old photographs are some images of women, men, and violence as brutally direct as any Delta blues lyric. One shows a handcuffed man, with the caption 'killed her with a deer rifle after she left him ... because of his interest in another woman'. In another, entitled 'Sweetheart Shot', a young woman slumps against an automobile door, dead at the hands of a 'sweetheart' who then killed himself. A third, 'A Marriage Ends', shows two bodies piled together on the sidewalk; the caption explains that he 'shot his estranged wife as she left home ... and then turned the gun on himself. Their 4-year-old son watched from the window as his mother was shot.'

And if there's photographic evidence that all of this about pretty girls and graves is more than literature or lyrical boasting, there's also good evidence that such tragedies continue today. In their study of homicide/suicides – the great majority involving men killing girlfriends or spouses, especially at the point of estrangement or divorce, and then killing themselves – Neil Websdale and Alex Alvarez (1998) report details of contemporary interpersonal violence every bit as grisly as those old photographs. As importantly, they show that newspaper reporting focuses tightly on just these grisly details – but not on the patterns of male-on-female violence within which such details take on more significant meaning. As a result, unlike other media reports on violent crime, reports on male-on-female murder/suicides tend not to present the male perpetrators as dangerous folk devils. Likewise, such reports seldom note the accumulation of murder/suicide cases, and so underplay the prevalence of domestic violence and of lethal male violence against women. As Websdale and Alvarez (1998: 139) conclude, the reports 'suffer from what we call 'internal myopia' because they fail to look at and report social structural patterns evident in their own patterns of reporting crime.' The tragedy of men making graves for women and for themselves is doubled, first by the dual violence itself, and again by a public inability to see the ongoing threat that such violence poses. What popular music haltingly recalls, the newspaper systematically forgets.

As it turns out, cultural forms of all sorts – novels, popular songs old and new, newspaper reports, websites, band names – play with the notion that 'pretty girls make graves', encoding the notion in our consciousness, documenting it, celebrating it, turning it back on itself as irony or tragedy. In all of this we see not simple equations of cause and effect but an ongoing conversation among cultural forms, a complex and spiralling interconnection between literature, music, photography, murder, and suicide. And in that light we might consider one more complexity of pretty girls making graves: the tragedy of anorexia and bulimia. It's not just that the band Schoolyard Heroes sometimes shares the stage with Pretty Girls Make Graves, playing songs like 'Battlestar Anorexia'. It's that anorexia and bulimia are social problems, cultural problems, echoes of a culture obsessed with a reed-thin standard of beauty and a circumscribed sense of what makes for 'pretty'. On the stage and off, it does indeed seem that in this way also, pretty girls make graves – not pretty girls as people, but pretty girls as a marketing strategy, a fashion construction, a commodified sense of identity sold like so much self-medication. After all, as W I Thomas said long ago, unreal standards have real consequences; at worst, they create a different sort of suicide girl, a slow suicide by means of deteriorating self-image.

Long ago someone also said, 'Men make their own history, but they do not make it just as they please; they do not make it under circumstances chosen by themselves, but under circumstances directly encountered, given, and transmitted from the past. The tradition of all the dead generations weighs like a nightmare on the brain of the living' (Marx, 1959: 320).

We say: pretty girls make graves, but they don't make them just as they please. They don't make them under circumstances chosen by themselves, but under existing circumstances transmitted from the past by way of Jack Kerouac and Pretty Polly, Sonny Boy Williamson and Andrea Zollo. The culture of men killing women, the consequences of commoditized beauty, weigh like a nightmare on the lives of the living.

Or something like that. But in any case, as Kerouac (1992 [1960]: 96) wrote in closing Tristessa: 'This part is my part of the movie, let's hear yours.'

cultural criminology: an invitation

We mean it: let's hear yours.

Critics of cultural criminology have questioned whether it can be considered a fully unified theory, or instead a 'collection of individuals sharing some issues in common' (Webber, 2007: 140). It's probably somewhere in between, though as we've said elsewhere, we're comfortable enough thinking of it as a 'loose federation of outlaw intellectual critiques' (Ferrell, 2007: 99) organized around issues of meaning, representation, and power. Whatever the case, there's one great advantage to this 'looser' sense of cultural criminology: it keeps cultural criminology open and invitational. From the first we've conceptualized cultural criminology as a free intellectual space from which to launch critiques of orthodox criminology and criminal justice, and in which to develop humane alternatives. We invite you into that space.

This isn't just some sappy book ending by the way; it's more like another manifesto. If as cultural criminologists we take the notion of *verstehen* seriously – the notion that we must find emotional affiliation with the various moments of crime and crime control in order to understand them – then we know that we need more, and more diverse, participants in this project. A diversity of backgrounds and identities among cultural criminologists isn't a nicety; it's a *methodological imperative* for investigating the complex, hyperplural circumstances of late modern transgression. Women and men, gay and straight, artists and authors, street activists and scholars – the more thoroughly cultural criminology embodies the polymorphic fluidity of contemporary Western society, the better it can comprehend and critique the many meanings of crime within it.

We invite especially the outsiders. As we noted in an earlier chapter, decades of 'war on crime' have spawned generations of prisoners, some of whom have turned their imprisonment on its head by developing a searing 'convict criminology' of state injustice. As we've recorded throughout the book, new generations now face ASBOs and civil gang injunctions, harsh anti-graffiti ordinances, clampdown immigration policies and racial profiling, zero tolerance statutes and anti-drug propaganda in schools, mandatory transfers to adult court, and other campaigns that push the pain of injustice right into the heart of their everyday lives. We urge those of you caught in these campaigns to join us, and to bring the pain and anger with you – not as a reason for violence or retribution, but as a fire from which to forge activism and critique. Sunonda Samaddar (2007) has said that 'hip-hop seems to be a cumulative layering of a cathartic pain rather than a formation of an organized political expression'. As with Baba Israel's poem that began this final chapter, we urge you to turn that pain into politics, to create your own cultural criminology, to join us in writing the next manifesto.

There is after all so much to be done. We need to understand better the cultures of the prison, the police, and the courtroom, need to know more about the semiotic codes of corporate crime. We need a cultural criminology that can investigate Africa's 'football slavery', Columbia's violent young *sicarios* assassins, Mexico's *narcocorridos* folk singers and their killers, France's restrictions on 'real world' internet violence, British police officers and their helmet-mounted cameras. Amidst the global dynamics of late modernity we need to know more about internet broadcasts of border surveillance video, about music as an instrument of torture and war, about the US soldiers and media outlets like Al-Zawraa TV that make combat footage into music videos. If we want to confront and change this world, we'll need to know more about the multi-mediated dynamics of street protest and police response, about alternative media as new forms of political organization, about the world politics of travel and cross-border transgression.

And of course that's no comprehensive list – just some ideas for outsider intellectual critique.

So let's hear yours.

filmography

Aileen Wuornos: The Selling of a Serial Killer (1992)	Dir. Nick Broomfield
Aileen: Life and Death of a Serial Killer (2003)	Dir. Nick Broomfield
All the President's Men (1976)	Dir. Alan J Pakula
Alphaville (1965)	Dir. Jean-Luc Godard
The Battle of Algiers (1966)	Dir. Gillo Pontecorvo
Berkeley in the Sixties (1990)	Dir. Mark Kitchell
Brazil (1985)	Dir. Terry Gilliam
Brick (2006)	Dir. Rian Johnson
Bus 174 (2002)	Dir. José Padhila
A Clockwork Orange (1971)	Dir. Stanley Kubrick
The Corporation (2003)	Dirs Jenifer Abbott and Mark Achbar
Crash (2004)	Dir. Paul Haggis
The Deer Hunter (1978)	Dir. Michael Cimeno
Deep Throat (1972)	Dir. Gerard Damiano

Dogville (2003)	Dir. Lars von Trier
Dankey Without a Tail (1997)	Dir. Sergio Bloch
Easy Rider (1969)	Dir. Dennis Hopper
Falling Down (1993)	Dir. Joel Schumacher
Fatal Attraction (1987)	Dir. Adrian Lyne
Fight Club (1999)	Dir. David Fincher
Goodfellas (1990)	Dir. Martin Scorsese
Heart Broken in Half: Chicago's Street Gangs (1990)	Producers Taggart Siegel and Dwight Conquergood
Kamp Katrina (2007)	Dirs David Redmon and Ashley Sabin
A Kind of Loving (1962)	Dir. John Schlesinger
Kitchen Stories (2003)	Dir. Bent Hammer
Look Back in Anger (1959)	Dir. Tony Richardson
The Loneliness of the Long Distance Runner (1962)	Dir. Tony Richardson
Mad Max (1979)	Dir. George Miller
Mad Max II: The Road Warrior (1982)	Dir. George Miller
Mardi Gras: Made in China (2005)	Dir. David Redmon
Minority Report (2002)	Dir. Steven Spielberg
Natural Born Killers (1994)	Dir. Oliver Stone
Network (1976)	Dir. Sidney Lumet
No End in Sight (2007)	Dir. Charles H Ferguson
One Flew Over the Cuckoo's Nest (1975)	Dir. Milos Forman
The Pervert's Guide to Cinema (2006)	Dir. Sophie Fiennes
The Politics of Nightmares (series, 3 parts)	Dir. Adam Curtis
Quadrophenia (1979)	Dir. Franc Roddam
A Rebel Without a Cause (1955)	Dir. Nicholas Ray
Recycled Life (2006)	Dir. Leslie Iwerks
Spare Parts (2003)	Dir. Damjan Kozole
A Taste of Honey (1961)	Dir. Tony Richardson

This is England (2006)	Dir. Shane Meadows
Traffic (2001)	Dir. Steven Soderbergh
Trainspotting (1996)	Dir. Danny Boyle
The Trap: What Happened to Our Dream of Freedom (2007)	Dir. Adam Curtis
The War on Democracy: A Film by John Pilger (2007)	Dirs Christopher Martin and John Pilger
The War Tapes (2006)	Dir. Deborah Scranton
When the Levees Broke (2006)	Dir. Spike Lee
Who is Bozo Texino? (2005)	Dir. Bill Daniel
The Wire (series, 5 parts) (2002–2008)	Creator: David Simon
The Yes Men (2005)	Dirs Chris Smith, Dan Ollman and Sarah Price

Bibliography

Abend, L (2006) 'Paying to be kidnapped', *The New York Times* (15 January), p. V2

Acland, C (1995) *Youth, Murder, Spectacle*. Boulder, CO: Westview Press

Adbusters (2005) 'Why we steal: an interview with Yomango', *Adbusters: The Magazine* 62, @ http://adbusters.org

Adler, P (1985) *Wheeling and Dealing*. New York: Columbia University Press

Adler, P and Adler, P (1998) 'Foreword', in J Ferrell and M Hamm (eds), *Ethnography at the Edge*. Boston: Northeastern University Press

Agee, M (2006a) 'Teen fight DVDs lead to 4 arrests', *Ft. Worth Star-Telegram* (11 May), pp. 1A, 17A

Agee, M (2006b) 'Street-fight DVDs still for sale, despite arrests', *Ft. Worth Star-Telegram* (31 May), p. 8B

Agee, J and Evans, W (1960) *Let Us Now Praise Famous Men*. New York: Ballantine

Aitchison, A and Greer, C (2007) 'Prisoners at work', *Crime, Media, Culture* 3(2): 207–14

Altheide, D (1987) 'Ethnographic content analysis', *Qualitative Sociology* 10(1): 65–77

Altheide, D (1996) *Qualitative Media Analysis*. Thousand Oaks, CA: Sage

Alvelos, H (2004) 'The desert of imagination in the city of signs', in J Ferrell et al. (eds), *Cultural Criminology Unleashed*. London: GlassHouse

Alvelos, H. (2005) 'The Glamour of Grime', *Crime, Media, Culture* 1(2): 215–224

Amster, R (2004) *Street People and the Contested Realms of Public Space*. New York: LFB

Anahita, S (2006) 'Blogging the border: virtual skinheads, hypermasculinity, and heteronormativity', *Journal of Political and Military Sociology*, 34(1): 143–164

Anderson, E (1999) *Code of the Street*. New York: W W Norton and Co

Anderson, N (1923) *The Hobo*. Chicago: University of Chicago Press

Anderson, S and Howard, G (eds) (1998) *Interrogating Popular Culture*. Guilderland, NY: Harrow and Heston

Angelou, M (1969) *I Know Why the Caged Bird Sings*. New York: Bantam

Appadurai, A (1996) *Modernity at Large*. Minneapolis: University of Minnesota Press

Armstrong, G and Griffin, M (2007) 'The effect of local life circumstances on victimization of drug-involved women', *Justice* Quarterly 24(1): 80–104

Arnot, C (2006) 'John Hyatt: Punk Professor' *The Guardian* (UK) (11 April), @ education.guardian.co.uk

Associated Press (2005) 'Convoy: 11 Mad Max fans are arrested', *Ft. Worth Star-Telegram* (19 April), p. 8B

Austin, J, Marino, B, Carroll, L, McCall, P and Richards, S (2001) 'The use of incarceration in the United States', *Critical Criminology* 10(1): 17–24

Ayala, E-M and Agee, M (2006) 'Gang is behind street-fight DVDs, police say', *Ft. Worth Star-Telegram* (12 May), p. 1A, 23A

Bailey, F and Hale, D (eds) (1998) *Popular Culture, Crime and Justice*. Belmont, CA: Wadsworth

Bakhtin, M (1984) *Rabelais and this World*. Bloomington: Indiana University Press

Bandura, A (1973) *Aggression*. Englewood Cliffs, NJ: Prentice-Hall

Bandura, A (1977) *Social Learning Theory*. New York: General Learning Press

Bandura, A, Ross, D and Ross, S (1961) 'Transmission of aggression through imitation of aggressive models', *Journal of Abnormal and Social Psychology* 63: 575–82

Bandura, A, Ross, D and Ross, S (1963) 'Imitation of film-mediated aggressive models', *Journal of Abnormal and Social Psychology* 66: 3–11

Banks, M (2005) 'Spaces of (in)security: media and fear of crime in a local context', *Crime, Media, Culture* 1(2): 169–87

Banksy (2005) *Wall and Piece*. London: Century

Barak, G (1994) *Media, Process and the Social Construction of Crime*. New York: Garland

Barak, G (ed.)(1996) *Representing O.J.* Guilderland, NY: Harrow and Heston

Barbalet, J (1998) *Emotion, Social Theory and Social Structure*. Cambridge: Cambridge University Press

Barrett, C (2007) A Place Apart: Responding to Youth Charged as Adults in a Specialized New York Criminal Court (unpublished PhD thesis, CUNY Graduate Center)

Bartollas, C (2000) *Juvenile Delinquency* (5th edition). Boston: Pearson

Bartollas, C (2006) *Juvenile Delinquency* (7th edition). Boston: Pearson

Bauder, D. (2007) 'If you see Chris Hansen, it's trouble', *Ft. Worth Star Telegram*/Associated Press (1 April), p. 2B.

Baudrillard, J (1981) *For a Critique of the Political Economy of the Sign*. St Louis: Telos

Baudrillard, J (1983) *Simulations*. New York: Semiotext(e)

Baudrillard, J (1985) 'The ecstasy of communication', in H Foster (ed.), *Postmodern Culture*. London: Pluto

Baudrillard, J (1996) *The System of Objects*. London: Verso

Bauman, Z (1999) *Culture as Praxis*. London: Sage

Bauman, Z (2000) *Liquid Modernity*. Cambridge: Polity Press

Bauman, Z (2005) 'Living and occasionally dying in an urban world' in S Graham (ed.), *Cities, War and Terrorism*. Oxford: Blackwell

BBC News (2004) '"Manhunt" game flying off the shelves', bbc.co.uk (4 August)

Beck, U (1992) *Risk Society*. London: Sage

Becker, G (1968) 'Crime and punishment: an economic approach', *Journal of Political Economy* 76: 169–217

Becker, H (1963) *Outsiders*. New York: Free Press.

Becker, H (1965) 'Deviance and deviates', in D Boroff (ed.), *The State of the Nation*. Englewood Cliff, NJ: Prentice-Hall, reprinted in H S Becker (1971) *Sociological Work*. London: Allen Lane

Becker, H (2005) 'Introduction', *Outsiders*, (Danish edition). Copenhagen: Hans Reitzel

Bendelow, G and Williams, S (1998) *Emotions in Social Life*. London: Routledge

Bennett, H and Ferrell, J (1987) 'Music videos and epistemic socialization', *Youth and Society* 18(4): 344–62

Benson, R (2001) 'It's a stick-up: tags, graffiti, fly-posters – it's an anti-establishment underworld, right?' *The London Evening Standard Magazine* (12 October), p. 43

Berger, P (1972) *Ways of Seeing*. Harmondsworth: Pelican

Berman, M (1982) *All That Is Solid Melts Into Air*. London: Verso

Bey, H (2003) *T.A.Z.: The Temporary Autonomous Zone*. New York: Autonomedia

Biber, K (2007) *Captive Images: Race, Crime, Photography*. London: Routledge

Bloch, S (1997) *Donkey without a Tail* (documentary film). New York: Filmmakers Library

Boekhout van Solinge, T (2008) 'Eco–crime: the tropical timber trade', in D Siegel and H Nelen (eds), *Organized Crime*. Dordrecht: Springer

Bourdieu, P (1998) *Acts of Resistance*. New York: New Press

Bourgois, P (1995) *In Search of Respect*. Cambridge: Cambridge University Press

Bovenkerk, F, Siegel, D and Zaitch, D (2003) 'Organized crime and ethnic reputation manipulation', *Crime, Law and Social Change* 39: 23–38

Bovenkerk, F and Yesilgoz, Y (2004) 'Crime, ethnicity, and the multicultural administration of justice', in J Ferrell et al. (eds), *Cultural Criminology Unleashed*. London: GlassHouse

Boyd, D (2005a) '"Ambush" for TV backfires for husband', *Ft. Worth Star-Telegram* (12 May), pp. 1B, 8B

Boyd, D (2005b) 'Reality TV Show "revictimized" wife, expert says', *Ft. Worth Star-Telegram* (14 May), p. 4B

Brake, M (1980) *The Sociology of Youth Culture*. London: Routledge & Kegan Paul

Brake, M (1985) *Comparative Youth Culture*. London: Routledge & Kegan Paul

Branch, A and Boyd, D (2005) 'Officer suspended for 90 days over affair in park', *Ft. Worth Star–Telegram* (23 September), p. 3B

Braverman, H (1974) *Labor and Monopoly Capital*. New York: Monthly Review

Bridges, S (2006) 'Retailer Target branches out into police work', *The Washington Post* (29 January) @ www.washingtonpost.com, p. A1

Brotherton, D (2007) 'Proceedings from the transnational street/organisation seminar', *Crime, Media, Culture* 3(3): 372–81

Brotherton, D and Barrios, L (2004) *The Almighty Latin King and Queen Nation*. New York: Columbia University Press

Brown, M (2007) 'Mapping discursive closings in the war on drugs', *Crime, Media, Culture* 3(1): 11–29

Burawoy, M (2005) 'The critical turn to public sociology', *Critical Sociology* 31(3): 313–26

Burfeind, J and Bartusch, D (2006) *Juvenile Delinquency*. New York: Jones and Bartlett

Burke, K, Fox, A and Martinez, J (2007) 'Hobo madness hits Madison Ave', *New York Daily News* (18 January), @ www.nydailynews.com

Burns, R and Katovich, M (2006) 'Melodramatic and consentient images in introductory criminal justice textbooks', *Journal of Criminal Justice* 34: 101–14

Burroughs, W (1959) *Naked Lunch*, Paris: Olympia

Bushnell, J (1990) *Moscow Graffiti*. Boston: Unwin Hyman

Butler, J (1999) *Gender Trouble*. New York: Routledge

Bynum, J and Thompson, W (1996) *Juvenile Delinquency: A Sociological Approach*. Boston: Allyn and Bacon

Bynum, J and Thompson, W (2007) *Juvenile Delinquency: A Sociological Approach* (7th edition). Boston: Pearson

Campbell, C (1989) *The Romantic Ethic and the Spirit of Modern Consumerism.* London: Blackwell

Camus, A (1961) *Resistance, Rebellion and Death* (trans. J.O'Brien). New York: Random House

Carceral, K (2006) *Prison, Inc.* New York: New York University Press

Carr, P, Napolitano, L and Keating, J (2007) '"We never call the cops and here is why": a qualitative examination of legal cynicism in three Philadelphia neighborhoods', *Criminology* 45(2): 445–80

Carter, C and Weaver, C K (2003) *Violence and the Media.* Buckingham: Open University Press

Cartier–Bresson, H (1952) *The Decisive Moment.* New York: Simon & Schuster

Cavender, G and Deutsch, S (2007) 'CSI and moral authority: the police and science', *Crime, Media, Culture* 3(1): 67–81

Castells, M (1996) *The Information Age* (Vol. 1). Oxford: Blackwells

Cerulo, K (1998) *Deciphering Violence.* New York: Routledge

Chan, W and Rigakos, G S (2002) 'Risk, crime and gender', *The British Journal of Criminology* 42: 743–61

Chancer, L (2005) *High-Profile Crimes.* Chicago: Chicago University Press

Cheatwood, D (1998) 'Prison movies: films about adult, male, civilian prisons: 1929–1995', in F Bailey and D Hale (eds), *Popular Culture, Crime and Justice.* Belmont, CA: Wadsworth

Chermak, S (1995) *Victims in the News.* Boulder, CO: Westview Press

Chermak, S (1998) 'Police, courts and corrections in the media', in F Bailey and D Hale (eds), *Popular Culture, Crime and Justice.* Belmont, CA: Wadsworth

Chermak, S, Bailey, F and Brown, M (2003) *Media Images of September 11th.* Newport, CT: Praeger

Chomsky, N (1989) *Necessary Illusions.* London: Pluto

Chomsky, N and Herman, E (1994) *Manufacturing Consent.* London: Vintage

Clark, D (2004) 'The raw and the rotten: Punk cuisine', *Ethnology* 43(1): 19–31

Clarke, J, Hall, S, Jefferson, T and Roberts, B (1976) 'Subcultures, cultures and class', in S Hall and T Jefferson (eds), *Resistance through Ritual.* London: Harper Collins

Clear, T (2007) *Imprisoning Communities.* Oxford: Oxford University Press

Clemner, D (1940) *The Prison Community.* New York: Holt, Rinehart, Winston

Cloward, R and Ohlin, L (1960) *Delinquency and Opportunity: A Theory of Delinquent Gangs.* New York: Free Press

Cohen, A (1955) *Delinquent Boys: The Culture of the Gang.* New York: Free Press

Cohen, P (1972) 'Subcultural conflict and working class community', CCCS *Working Papers* 2: 5–53

Cohen, P (1997) *Rethinking the Youth Question.* Basingstoke: Macmillan

Cohen, S (1972/2002a) *Folk Devils and Moral Panics* (3rd edition, 2002a). London: MacGibbon and Kee

Cohen, S (1979) 'The punitive city: notes on the dispersal of social control', *Contemporary Crises* 3: 339–63

Cohen, S (1980) 'Symbols of Trouble', Introduction to the 2nd edition of *Folk Devils and Moral Panics.* Oxford: Martin Robertson

Cohen, S (1981) 'Footprints in the sand', in M Fitzgerald, G McLennan and J Pawson (eds), *Crime and Society.* London: Routledge & Kegan Paul

Cohen, S (1988) *Against Criminology.* Oxford: Transaction

Cohen, S (2002b) *States of Denial.* Cambridge: Polity Press

Cohen, S and Taylor, L (1976) *Psychological Survival*. Harmondsworth: Penguin

Cohen, S and Young, J (1973) *The Manufacture of News*. Beverley Hills, CA: Sage

Connell, R (1995) *Masculinities*. Cambridge: Polity Press

Conquergood, D (1991) 'Rethinking ethnography: towards a critical cultural politics', *Communications Monographs* 58: 179–94

Conquergood, D (2002) 'Lethal theatre: performance, punishment, and the death penalty', *Theatre Journal* 54(3): 339–67

Cornish, D and Clarke, R (1986) *The Reasoning Criminal*. New York: Springer-Verlag

Cornish, D and Clarke, R (2006) 'The rational choice perspective', in S Henry and M Lanier (eds), *The Essential Criminology Reader*. Boulder, CO: Westview Press

CorpWatch Report (2007) *Goodbye Houston: An Alternative Annual Report on Halliburton*, @ www.corpwatch.org

Cottle, S (2005) 'Mediatized public crisis and civil society renewal', *Crime, Media, Culture* 1(1): 49–71

Courtney, D and Lyng, S (2007) 'Taryn Simons and The Innocence Project', *Crime, Media, Culture* 3(2): 175–91

Cullen, F and Messner, S (2007) 'The making of criminology revisited: an oral history of Merton's anomie paradigm', *Theoretical Criminology* 11(1): 5–37

Cunneen, C and Stubbs, J (2004) 'Cultural criminology and engagement with race, gender and post-colonial identities', in J Ferrell et al. (eds), *Cultural Criminology Unleashed*. London: GlassHouse

David, E (2007) 'Signs of resistance: marking public space through a renewed cultural activism', in G Stancak (ed.), *Visual Research Methods*. Los Angeles: Sage

Davis, M (1990) *City of Quartz*. London: Verso

de Beauvoir, S (1958) *The Memoirs of a Dutiful Daughter*. Paris: Gallimard

De Certeau, M (1984) *The Practice of Everyday Life*. Berkeley, CA: University of California Press

De Haan, W and Vos, J (2003) 'A crying shame: the over-rationalized conception of man in the rational choice perspective', *Theoretical Criminology* 7(1): 29–54

De Jong, A and Schuilenburg, M (2006) *Mediapolis*. Rotterdam: 010 Publishers

Dentith, A, Measor, L and O'Malley, M (2007) 'Stirring dangerous waters: forbidden topics and other dilemmas of research with young people', paper presented at the American Educational Research Association Conference, April, Chicago, USA

Denzin, N (1997) *Interpretative Ethnography*. Thousand Oaks, CA: Sage

Denzin, N (2003) *Performance Ethnography*. Thousand Oaks, CA: Sage

DiCristina, B (2006) 'The epistemology of theory testing in criminology', in B Arrigo and C Williams (eds), *Philosophy, Crime and Criminology*. Urbana, IL: University of Illinois Press

Dick, P K (1968) *Do Androids Dream of Electric Sheep?* New York: Ballantine Books

Ditton, J (1979) *Contrology*. Basingstoke: Macmillan

Dobash, R and Dobash, P (1992) *Rethinking Violence Against Women*. London: Sage

Downes, D (1966) *The Delinquent Solution*. London: Routledge & Kegan Paul

Downes, D and Rock, P ([1988] 2007) *Understanding Deviance*. Oxford: Oxford University Press

Dribben, M (2006) '"CSI" effect has jurors expecting more evidence', *Ft. Worth Star-Telegram* (2 March), p. 4E

Dugan, L and Apel, R (2005) 'The differential risk of retaliation by relational distance: a more general model of violent victimization', *Criminology* 43(3): 697–726

Durkheim, E (1964) *The Rules of Sociological Method*. New York: Free Press

Durkheim, E (1965) *Essays in Sociology and Philosophy*. Edited by K Wolff. New York: Harper & Row

Dylan, B (2004) *Chronicles (Vol. 1)*. New York: Simon & Schuster

Edemariam, A (2005) 'I steal, therefore I am...', *Guardian Weekly* (9–15 September), p. 20

Ekblom, P (2007) 'Enriching the Offender' in G Farrell, K Bowers, S Johnson and M Townsley (eds), *Imagination for Crime Prevention: Essays in Honour of Ken Pease*. Cullompton: Willan

Ericson, R (1995) *Crime and the Media*. Aldershot: Dartmouth

Exum, M L (2002) 'The application and robustness of the rational choice perspective in the study of intoxicated and angry intentions to aggress', *Criminology* 40(4): 933–66

Farrell, G and Pease, K (2001) *Repeat Victimization* (Crime Prevention Studies, Vol. 12). Monsey, NJ: Criminal Justice Press

Feagin, J, Orum, A and Sjoberg, G (1991) *A Case for the Case Study*. Chapel Hill: North Carolina University Press

Featherstone, M (1991) *Consumer Culture and Postmodernity*. London: Sage

Felson, M (1998) *Crime and Everyday Life*. Thousand Oaks, CA: Pine Forge Press

Fenwick, M and Hayward, K (2000) 'Youth crime, excitement and consumer culture: the reconstruction of aetiology in contemporary theoretical criminology', in J Pickford (ed.), *Youth Justice*. London: Cavendish

Ferrell, J (1992) 'Making sense of crime: review essay on Jack Katz's *Seductions of Crime*', *Social Justice* 19(2): 110–23

Ferrell, J (1995) 'Style matters', in J Ferrell and C Sanders (eds), *Cultural Criminology*. Boston: Northeastern University Press

Ferrell, J (1996) *Crimes of Style*. Boston: Northeastern University Press

Ferrell, J (1997) 'Criminological *Verstehen*: inside the immediacy of crime', *Justice Quarterly* 14(1): 3–23

Ferrell, J (1998) 'Freight train graffiti: subculture, crime, dislocation', *Justice Quarterly* 15(4): 587–608

Ferrell, J (1999) 'Cultural criminology', *Annual Review of Sociology* 25: 395–418

Ferrell, J (2001/2) *Tearing Down the Streets*. New York: St Martins Press/Palgrave

Ferrell, J (2004a) 'Boredom, crime, and criminology', *Theoretical Criminology* 8(3): 287–302

Ferrell, J (2004b) 'Speed kills', in J Ferrell et al (eds), *Cultural Criminology Unleashed*. London: GlassHouse

Ferrell, J (2005) 'The only possible adventure: edgework and anarchy', in S Lyng (ed.), *Edgework*. New York: Routledge

Ferrell, J (2006a) *Empire of Scrounge*. New York: New York University Press

Ferrell, J (2006b) 'The aesthetics of cultural criminology', in B Arrigo and C Williams (eds), *Philosophy, Crime, and Criminology*. Urbana, IL: University of Illinois Press

Ferrell, J (2007) 'For a ruthless cultural criticism of everything existing', *Crime, Media, Culture* 3(1): 91–100

Ferrell, J, Greer, C and Jewkes, Y (2005) 'Hip Hop graffiti, Mexican murals, and the War on Terror', *Crime, Media, Culture* 1(1): 5–9

Ferrell, J and Hamm, M (eds) (1998) *Ethnography at the Edge*. Boston: Northeastern University Press

Ferrel, J, Hayward, K, Morrisan, W and Presdee M (eds) (2004) *Cultural Criminology Unleashed*. London: Glass House

Ferrell, J, Milovanovic, D and Lyng, S (2001) 'Edgework, media practices, and the elongation of meaning', *Theoretical Criminology* 5(2): 177–202

Feyerabend, P (1975) *Against Method*. London: Verso

Fiddler, M (2007) 'Projecting the prison', *Crime, Media, Culture* 3(2): 192–206

Fishman, M and Cavender, G (1998) *Entertaining Crime*. New York: Aldine de Gruyter

Fitzgerald, M (1977) *Prisoners in Revolt*. Harmondsworth: Penguin

Foner, P (1975) *History of the Labor Movement in the United States* (Vol. II). New York: International Publishers

Foucault, M (1977) *Discipline and Punish: The Birth of the Prison*. London: Penguin (first published in French 1975)

Franko-Aas, K (2006) '"The body does not lie": identity, risk and trust in technoculture', *Crime, Media, Culture* 2(2): 143–58

Friedan, B (1963) *The Feminine Mystique*. Harmondsworth: Penguin

Fromm, E *The Sane Society*. New York: Holt, Rinehart and Winston

Furedi, F (2007) *Invitation to Terror*. London: Continuum

Gadd, D and Jefferson, T (2007) *Psychosocial Criminology*. London: Sage

Gailey, J (2007) 'The Pro-Ana culture as edgework', paper presented at the American Society of Criminology Annual Meeting, November, Atlanta

Gans, H (1980) *Deciding What's News*. London: Constable

Garfinkel, H (1956) 'Conditions of successful degradation ceremonies', *American Journal of Sociology* 61: 420–4

Garfinkel, H (1967) *Studies in Ethnomethodology*. Englewood Cliffs, NJ: Prentice-Hall

Garland, D (1997) '"Governmentality" and the problem of crime: Foucault, criminology and sociology', *Theoretical Criminology* 1(2): 173–214

Garland, D (2001) *The Culture of Control*. Oxford: Oxford University Press

Garot, R (2007a) '"Where You From!": gang identity as performance', *Journal of Contemporary Ethnography* 36(1): 50–84

Garot, R (2007b) 'Classroom resistance as edgework', paper presented at the On the Edge: Transgression and the Dangerous Other Conference, New York

Gauntlett, D (1998) 'Ten things wrong with the effects model', in R Dickson et al. (eds), *Approaches to Audiences*. London: Edward Arnold

Gerbner, G and Gross, L (1976) 'Living with television: the violence profile', *Journal of Communication* 26(1): 173–99

Gibbs, J (1968) 'Crime, punishment and deterrence', *Southwestern Social Science Quarterly* 48: 515–30

Giddens, A (1984) *The Constitution of Society*. Cambridge: Polity Press

Giddens, A (1990) *The Consequences of Modernity*. Cambridge: Polity Press

Gillette, F (2006) 'Is it life imitating art-or is it journalism?', *CJR Daily* (2 August), @ www.cjrdaily.org

Ginsberg, A (1955) *Howl and Other Poems*. San Francisco: City Lights

Goffman, E (1959) *The Presentation of Self in Everyday Life*. Garden City, NY: Doubleday

Goffman, E (1961) *Asylums*. New York: Doubleday

Goffman, E (1979) *Gender Advertisements*. New York: Harper & Row

Gottfredson, M and Hirschi, T (1990) *Positive Criminology*. London: Sage

Graczyk, M (2005) 'Killer whose attorneys blamed rap lyrics is executed', *Ft. Worth Star-Telegram* (7 October), p. 5B

Grassian, S. and Friedman, N. (1986) 'Effects of sensory deprivation in psychiatric seclusion and solitary confinement', *International Journal of Law and Psychiatry*, 8, pp. 49–65.

Green, P and Ward, T (2004) *State Crime*. London: Pluto

Greenwell, M (2006) 'Dumpster divers scavenge for groceries', *Houston Chronicle* (20 August), p. G8

Greek, C. (2003) 'Visual Criminologies: Using photography as a research tool in criminal justice settings'. Paper presented at the meetings of the Academy of Criminal Justice Sciences, March, Boston, MA

Greer, C (2004) 'Crime, media and community: grief and virtual engagement in late modernity', in J Ferrell et al. (eds), *Cultural Criminology Unleashed*. London: GlassHouse

Greer, C (2005) 'Crime and the media', in C Hale et al. (eds), *Criminology*. Oxford: Oxford University Press

Greer, C (ed) (2008) *Crime and Media: A Reader*. London: Routledge

Grimes, J (2007) Crime, Media, and Public Policy (unpublished PhD thesis, Arizona State University)

Hagedorn, J (2006) 'Gangs as social actors', in S Henry and M Lanier (eds), *The Essential Criminology Reader*. Boulder, CO: Westview Press

Hall, S, Critcher, C, Jefferson, T, Clarke, J and Roberts, B (eds) (1978) *Policing the Crisis*. London: Macmillan

Hall, S and Jefferson, T (eds) (1976) *Resistance through Ritual*. London: HarperCollins

Hall, S. and Winlow, S (2005) 'Anti-nirvana: Crime, culture and instrumentalism in the age of insecurity', *Crime, Media, Culture*, 1(1), 31–48

Hall, S and Winlow, S (2007) 'Cultural criminology and primitive accumulation', *Crime, Media, Culture* 3(1): 82–90

Halsey, M and Young, A (2006) '"Our desires are ungovernable": writing graffiti in urban space', *Theoretical Criminology* 10(3): 275–306

Hamm, N (1995) *American Skinheads: The Criminology and Control of Hate Crime*. Westport, CT: Greenwood Press

Hamm, M (1997) *Apocalypse in Oklahoma*. Boston: Northeastern University Press

Hamm, M (1998) 'The ethnography of terror', in J Ferrell and M Hamm (eds), *Ethnography at the Edge*. Boston: Northeastern University Press

Hamm, M (2002) *In Bad Company*. Boston: Northeastern University Press

Hamm, M (2004) 'The USA Patriot Act and the politics of fear', in J Ferrell et al. (eds), *Cultural Criminology Unleashed*. London: GlassHouse

Hamm, M (2007) 'High crimes and misdemeanours: George W Bush and the sins of Abu Ghraib', *Crime, Media, Culture* 3(3): 259–84

Hamm, M S and Ferrell, J. (1994) 'Rap, cops and Crime' *ACJS Today*, 13, pp.1, 3 and 29.

Hannigan, W (1999) *New York Noir*. New York: Rizzoli

Harper, D (2001) *Changing Works: Visions of a Lost Agriculture*. Chicago: University of Chicago Press

Harrington, M (1962) *The Other America*. New York: Macmillan

Harvey, D (1990) *The Condition of Postmodernity*. Cambridge, MA: Blackwell

Harvey, D (2006) 'Neoliberalism as creative destruction', *ANNALS, AAPPSS* 610: 21–44

Hayden, T (2004) *Street Wars*. New York: New Press

Hayward, K (2001) Crime, Consumerism and the Urban Experience (unpublished PhD thesis, University of East London)

Hayward, K (2003) 'Consumer culture and crime in late modernity', in C Sumner (ed.) *The Blackwell Conpanion to Criminology*. Oxford: Blackwell

Hayward, K (2004) *City Limits: Crime, Consumer Culture and the Urban Experience*. London: GlassHouse

Hayward, K (2007) 'Situational crime prevention and its discontents: rational choice theory versus the "culture of now"', *Social Policy and Administration* 41(3): 232–50

Hayward, K and Hobbs, D (2007) 'Beyond the binge in Booze Britain: market-led liminalization and the spectacle of binge drinking', *British Journal of Sociology* 58(3): 437–56

Hayward, K and Presdee, M (eds) (2008) *Framing Crime*. London: Routledge

Hayward, K and Yar, M (2006) 'The "Chav" phenomenon: consumption, media and the construction of a new underclass', *Crime, Media, Culture* 2(1): 9–28

Hayward, K and Young, J (2004) 'Cultural criminology: some notes on the script', *Theoretical Criminology* 8(3): 259–73

Hayward, K and Young, J (2007) 'Cultural criminology', in M Maguire, R Morgan and R Reiner (eds), *The Oxford Handbook of Criminology* (4th edition). Oxford: Oxford University Press

Healy, P (2007) 'Hikes pay homage to path taken by illegal immigrants', *Ft. Worth Star-Telegram* (4 February), p. 5H

Hebdige, D (1979) *Subculture: The Meaning of Style*. London: Methuen

Hebdige, D (1988) *Hiding in the Light*. London: Comedia

Heller, J (1961) *Catch-22*. New York: Simon and Schuster

Hier, S (2000) 'The contemporary structure of Canadian racial supremacism: networks, strategies and new technologies', *Canadian Journal of Sociology* 25: 471–94

Hillyard, P, Sim, J, Tombs, S and Whyte, D (2004) 'Leaving a 'stain upon the silence': contemporary criminology and the politics of dissent', The British *Journal of Criminology* 44(3): 369–90

Hirschi, T (1969) *Causes of Delinquency*. Berkeley: University of California Press

Hobbs, D (2007) 'East Ending: dissociation, de-industrialization and David Downes', in T Newburn and P Rock (eds), *Politics of Crime Control*. Oxford: Clarendon Press

Hobbs, D, Winlow, S, Hadfield P and Lister, S (2005) 'Violent Hypocrisy: Post Industrialism and the Night-time Economy', *European* Journal of Criminology 2(2): 161–8

Hobsbawn, E (1994) *The Age of Extremes*. London: Michael Joseph

Hochschild, A (2003) *The Managed Heart*. Berkeley: University of California Press

Hoffman, A (1971) *Steal This Book*. New York: Grove

Hoffman, B and Brown, M (2008) 'Staging an execution: the media at McVeigh', in K Hayward, and M Presdee (eds), *Framing Crime: Cultural Criminology and the Image*. London: Routledge

Howe, A (2003) 'Managing men's violence in the criminological arena', in C Sumner (ed.), *The Blackwell Companion to Criminology*. Oxford: Blackwell

Hubbard, J (1994) *Shooting Back from the Reservation: A Photographic View of Life by Native American Youth*. New York: New Press

Huntington, S (1993) 'The Clash of Civilizations', *Foreign Affairs* 71(3): 22–49

Iwerks, L (2006) *Recycled Life* (documentary film). Place: An Iwerks/Glad Production

Jacobs, J (1961) *The Death and Life of Great American Cities*. New York: Random House

Jackson, R (2005) *Writing the War on Terror*. Manchester: Manchester University Press

Jameson, F (1991) *Postmodernism or the Cultural Logic of Late Capitalism*. London: Verso

Jamieson, R (1999) 'Genocide and the social production of immorality', *Theoretical Criminology* 3(2): 131–46

Jarvis, B (2007) 'Monsters Inc: serial killers and consumer culture', *Crime, Media, Culture* 3(3): 326–44

Jefferson, T (1976) 'Cultural responses of the Teds', in S Hall and T Jefferson (eds), *Resistance through Rituals*. London: Hutchinson

Jenkins, P (1999) 'Fighting terrorism as if women mattered', in J Ferrell and N Websdale (eds), *Making Trouble*. New York: Aldine de Gruytes

Jenkins, P (2001) *Beyond Tolerance*. New York: New York University Press

Jensen, G and Rojek, D (1992) *Delinquency and Youth Crime*. Chicago: Waveland

Jewkes, Y (2004) *Media and Crime*. London: Sage

Jhally, S. (1987) *The Codes of Advertising: Fetishism and the Political Economy of Meaning in Consumer Socity*. New York: Routledge

Jones, N (2006a) 'City commission to target youth violence', *Ft. Worth Star-Telegram* (16 May), p. 5B

Jones, N (2006b) '4 indicted in connection with DVDs', *Ft. Worth Star-Telegram* (2 August), p. 10B

Jones, R (2000) 'Digital rule: punishment, control and technology', *Punishment and Society* 2(1): 5–22

Jones, S (2005) 'Artful Dodger goes to the wall', *Guardian Weekly* (19–25 August), p. 20

Jones, R (2005) 'Surveillance', in C Hale, et al (eds), *Criminology*. Oxford: Oxford University Press

Kane, S (1998) 'Reversing the ethnographic gaze', in J Ferrell and M Hamm (eds), *Ethnography at the Edge*. Boston: Northeastern University Press

Kane, S (2003) 'Epilogue', in P Parnell and S Kane (eds), *Crime's Power*. New York: Palgrave Macmillan

Kane, S (2004) 'The unconventional methods of cultural criminology', *Theoretical Criminology* 8(3): 303–21

Katz, J (1988) *Seductions of Crime*. New York: Basic Books

Katz, J (1999) *How Emotions Work*. Chicago: University of Chicago Press

Katz, J (2002a) 'Start here: social ontology and research strategy', *Theoretical Criminology* 6(3): 255–78

Katz, J (2002b) 'Response to commentators', *Theoretical Criminology*, 6(3): 375–80

Kemper, T D (1990) *Research Agendas in the Sociology of Emotions*. New York: New York State University Press

Kerouac, J (1957) *On the Road*. New York: New American Library

Kerouac, J (1958) *The Dharma Bums*. New York: New American Library

Kerouac, J (1992 [1960]) *Tristessa*. New York: Penguin

Kidd-Hewitt, D, and Osborne, R (1995) *Crime and the Media*. London: Pluto

Kilbourne, J. (1999) *Deadly Persuasions*. New York: Free Press

Kimes, M (2006) 'Garbage Pail Kids' *The New Journal* (October), pp. 11–17

Kontos, L, Brotherton, D and Barrios, L (2003) *Gangs and Society*. New York: Columbia University Press

Kraska, P and Neuman, W (2008) *Criminal Justice and Criminology Research Methods*. Boston: Pearson

Krawesky, A (2006) 'Motorist vs. courier', *City Noise (Toronto)*, @ www.citynoise.org

Kruglanski, A (2006) 'Precarity explained to kids: a medley', *Journal of Aesthetics and Protest* 4, @ www.journalofaestheticsandprotest.org

Kubrin, C E (2005) 'Gangstas, thugs and hustlas: identity and the Code of the Street in rap music', *Social Problems* 52(3): 360–78

Lasn, K (2000) *Culture Jam*. New York: Harper Collins

Lawrence, P (2007) 'The mismeasurement of science', *Current Biology* 17(15): 583–5

Lee, J (2006) *Talk Back*. New York: Mark Batty

Lemert, E (1967) *Human Deviance, Social Problems and Social Control*. Englewood Cliffs, NJ: Prentice-Hall

Levy, A (2007) 'Chasing Dash Snow', *New York Magazine* (15 January), @ nymag.com

Lewis, J (2005) *Language Wars: The Role of the Media and Culture in Global Terror*. Ann Arbor, MI: Pluto Press

Lilly, J R, Cullen, F and Ball, R (1989) *Criminological Theory*. Thousand Oaks, CA: Sage

Lindgren, S (2005) 'Social constructionism and criminology', *Journal of Scandinavian Studies in Criminology and Crime Prevention* 6: 4–22

Livingstone, S (1996) 'On the continuing problems of media effects', in J Curran and M Guervitch (eds), *Mass Media and Society*. London: Edward Arnold

Lois, J (2001) 'Peaks and valleys: the gendered emotional culture of edgework', *Gender & Society* 15(3): 381–406

Lois, J (2005) 'Gender and emotion management in the stages of edgework', in S Lyng (ed.), *Edgework*. New York: Routledge

Lombroso, C (2006 [1876]) *The Criminal Man*. Trans M Gibson and N Rafter. Durham, NC: Duke University Press

Lovell, J (2006) 'This is not a comic book', *Crime, Media, Culture* 2(1): 75–83

Lowry, D, Nio, T and Leitner, D (2003) 'Setting the public fear agenda: a longitudinal analysis of network TV crime reporting, public perceptions of crime and FBI crime statistics', *Journal of Communications* 53(1): 61–73

Lukacs, G (1971) *History and Class Consciousness*. Cambridge, MA: MIT Press

Lupton, D and Tulloch, J (1999) 'Theorizing fear of crime: beyond the rational/irrational opposition', *British Journal of Sociology* 50(3): 507–23

Lury, C (1996) *Consumer Culture*. Cambridge: Polity Press

Lyng, S (1990) 'Edgework', *American Journal of Sociology* 95(4): 851–86

Lyng, S (1991) 'Edgework revisited: a reply to Miller', *American Journal of Sociology* 96: 1534–9

Lyng, S (ed.) (2005) *Edgework*. New York: Routledge

Lyng, S and Bracey, M (1995) 'Squaring the one percent: Biker style and the selling of cultural resistance', in J Ferrell and C Sanders (eds), *Cultural Criminology*. Boston: Northeastern University Press

Lyotard, J-F (1984) *The Postmodern Condition: A Report on Knowledge*. Manchester: Manchester University Press (first published in French 1979)

McCarthy, M (2006) 'Illegal, violent teen fight clubs face police crackdown', *USA Today* (1 August), @ USATODAY.com

McLeod, J (1995) *Ain't No Makin' It*. Boulder, CO: Westview Press

McRobbie, A (1994) *Postmoderism and Popular Culture*. London: Routledge

McRobbie, A and Thornton, S (1995) 'Rethinking "moral panic" for multi-mediated social worlds', *British Journal of Sociology* 46(4): 245–59

McVicar, J (1979) *McVicar*. London: Arrow

Macek, S (2006) *Urban Nightmares*. Minneapolis: University of Minnesota Press

Macpherson, C (1977) *The Life and Times of Liberal Democracy*. Oxford: Oxford University Press

Maffesoli, M (1996) *The Time of the Tribes*. London: Sage

Maffesoli, M (2004) 'Everyday tragedy and creation', *Cultural Studies*, 18 2:3, 201–210

Maguire, M, Morgan, R and Reiner, R (eds) (1994) *The Oxford Handbook of Criminology* (1st edition). Oxford: Oxford University Press

Maguire, M, Morgan, R and Reiner, R (eds) (2000) *The Oxford Handbook of Criminology* (3rd edition). Oxford: Oxford University Press

Maher, C and Adamy, J (2006) 'Do hot coffee and "wobblies" go together?', *The Wall Street Journal* (21 March), pp. B1, B6

Mann, S, Nolan, J and Wellman, B (2003) 'Sousveillance: inventing and using wearable computing devices for data collection in surveillance environments', *Surveillance and Society* 1(3): 331–55

Mannheim, H (1948) *Juvenile Delinquency in an English Middletown*. London: Routledge & Kegan Paul

Manning, P (1995) 'The challenge of postmodernism', in J Van Maanen (ed.), *Representation in Ethnography*. Thousand Oaks, CA: Sage

Manning, P (1998) 'Media loops', in F Bailey and D Hale (eds), *Popular Culture, Crime and Justice*. Belmont, CA: Wadsworth

Manning, P (1999) 'Reflections: the visual as a mode of social control', in J Ferrell and N Websdale (eds), *Making Trouble*. New York: Aldine de Gruyter

Marcus, G (1989) *Lipstick Traces*. Cambridge, MA: Harvard University Press

Martin, P (2004) 'Culture, subculture and social organization', in A Bennettt and K Khahn Harris (eds), *After Subculture*. Basingstoke: Palgrave

Marx, G (1995) 'New telecommunications technologies require new manners', *Cybernews* 1(1), @ www.lex-electronica.org

Marx, K (1959) 'The Eighteenth Brumaire of Louis Bonaparte', in L Feuer (ed.), *Marx and Engels*. Garden City, NY: Anchor

Matza, D (1969) *Becoming Deviant*. Englewood Cliffs, NJ: Prentice-Hall

Matza, D and Sykes, G (1961) 'Juvenile delinquency and subterranean values', *American Sociological Review* 26: 712–19

Mawby, R and Walklate, S (1994) *Critical Victimology*. London: Sage

Matza, D (1964) *Delinquency and Drift*. New York: John Wiley and Sons

Mayhew, M (2006) 'Some like it swat', *Ft. Worth Star-Telegram* (4 January), pp. 1F, 7F

Measham, F and Brain, K (2005) '"Binge" drinking: British alcohol policy and the new culture of intoxication', *Crime, Media, Culture* 1(3): 262–83

Mehan, H and Wood, H (1975) *The Reality of Ethnomethodology*. New York: Wiley

Merlean-Ponty, M (1962) *Phenomenology of Perception* (trans. Colin Smith). London: Routledge and Kegan Paul

Merton, R K (1938) 'Social structure and anomie', *American Sociological Review* 3: 672–82

Miles, S (1998) *Consumerism as a Way of Life*. London: Sage

Miller, D (2001) 'Poking holes in the theory of "Broken Windows"', *The Chronicle of Higher Education* 47(22) (9 February), pp. A14–A16

Miller, E M (1991) 'Assessing the risk of inattention to class, race/ethnicity and gender: comment on Lyng', *American Journal of Sociology* 96: 1530–4

Miller, J (1995) 'Struggles over the symbolic: gang style and the meanings of social control', in J Ferrell and C Sanders (eds), *Cultural Criminology*. Boston: Northeastern University Press

Miller, J (2001) *One of the Guys*. Oxford: Oxford University Press

Miller, J M and Tewkesbury, R (2000) *Extreme Methods*. London: Allyn and Bacon

Miller, R (1997) *Magnum*. New York: Grove Press

Miller, W (1958) 'Lower class culture as a generating milieu of gang delinquency', *Journal of Social Issues* 14: 5–19

Mills, C W (1940) 'Situated actions and vocabularies of motives', *American Sociological Review* 5(6): 904–13

Mills, C W (1956) *The Power Elite*. Oxford: Oxford University Press

Mills, C W (1959) *The Sociological Imagination*. Oxford: Oxford University Press

Mitchell, M (2006) 'Teen describes attack that led police to fight videos', *Ft. Worth Star-Telegram* (12 May), p. 23A

Mooney, J (2000) *Gender, Violence and the Social Order*. Basingstoke: Macmillan

Mooney, J (2007) 'Shadow values, shadow figures, real violence', *Critical Criminology* 15(2): 59–70

Mopas, M (2007) 'Examining the 'CSI effect' through an ANT lens', *Crime, Media, Culture* 3(1): 110–17

Morris, T (1957) *The Criminal Area: A Study in Social Ecology*. London: Routledge & Kegan Paul

Morris, T and Morris, P (1963) *Pentonville*. London: Routledge & Kegan Paul

Morrison, W (1995) *Theoretical Criminology*. London: Cavendish

Morrison, W (2004a) '"Reflections with memories": everyday photography capturing genocide', *Theoretical Criminology* 8(3): 341–58

Morrison, W (2004b) 'Lombroso and the birth of criminological positivism: scientific mastery or cultural artifice?', in J Ferrell et al. (eds), *Cultural Criminology Unleashed*. London: GlassHouse

Morrison, W (2006) *Criminology, Civilization and the New World Order*. London: GlassHouse

Mythen, G (2007) 'Cultural victimology', in S Walklate (ed.), *Handbook on Victims and Victimology*. Cullompton: Willan Publishing

Nagin, D (2007) 'Moving choice to center stage in criminological research and theory: the American Society of Criminology 2006 Sutherland Address', *Criminology* 45(2): 259–72

National Youth Gang Center (2007) *National Youth Gang Survey Analysis*. Retrieved 24 September 2007 from http://www.iir.com/nygc/nygsa/

Nicolaus, M (1969) 'The professional organization of sociology: a view from below', *Antioch Review* (Fall): 375–87

Nightingale, C (1993) *On the Edge*. New York: Basic Books

Nyberg, A (1998) 'Comic books and juvenile delinquency: a historical perspective', in F Bailey and D Hale (eds), *Popular Culture, Crime, and Justice*. Belmont, CA: Wadsworth

O'Brien, M (2005) 'What is *cultural* about cultural criminology?', *British Journal of Criminology* 45: 599–612

O'Brien, M (2006) 'Not Keane on prawn sandwiches: criminal impoverishments of consumer culture', paper presented at the Second International Conference on Cultural Criminology, May, London

O'Brien, M (2008) *A Crisis of Waste?* New York: Routledge

O'Conner, S (1990) *The Emperor's New Clothes*. New York: Golden

O'Malley, P and Mugford, S (1994) 'Crime, excitement and modernity', in G Barak (ed.), *Varieties of Criminology*. Westport, CT: Praeger

O'Neill, M (2001) *Prostitution and Feminism*. Cambridge: Polity Press

O'Neill, M (2004) 'Crime, culture and visual methodologies: ethno-mimesis as performative praxis', in J Ferrell et al. (eds), *Cultural Criminology Unleashed*. London: GlassHouse

O'Neill, M, Campbell, R, Hubbard, P, Pitcher, J and Scoular, J (2008) 'Living with the Other: street sex work, contingent communities and degrees of tolerance', *Crime, Media, Culture* 4(1): 73–93

O'Neill, M, Woods, P and Webster, M (2004) 'New arrivals: participatory action research, imagined communities and "visions" of social justice', *Social Justice* 32(1): 75–89

Office of Juvenile Justice and Delinquency Prevention (1999) *1996 National Youth Gang Survey*. Washington, DC: US Department of Justice

Ousey, G and Wilcox, P (2007) 'The interaction of antisocial propensity and life-course varying predictors of delinquent behavior: differences by method or estimation and implications for theory', *Criminology* 45(2): 313–54

Paik, H and Comstock, G (1994) 'The effects of television violence on antisocial behaviour', *Communications Research* 21(4): 516–46

Palahniuk, C (2000) *Choke*. London: Vintage

Parks, L (2007) 'Points of departure: the culture of US airport screening', *Journal of Visual Culture* 6(2): 183–200

Parnell, P (2003) 'Introduction: crime's power', in P Parnell and S Kane (eds), *Crime's Power*. New York: Palgrave MacMillan

Patterson, C (2006) *Resistance*. New York: Seven Stories Press

Pearson, G (1978) 'Goths and Vandals: crime in history', *Contemporary Crises* 2(2): 119–40

Pease, K (2006) 'Rational choice theory', in E McLaughlin and J Muncie (eds), *The Sage Dictionary of Criminology*. London: Sage

Phillips, N and Stroble, S (2006) 'Cultural criminology and Kryptonite: apocalyptic and retributive constructions and crime and justice in comic books', *Crime Media Culture* 2(3): 304–31

Phillips, S (1999) *Wallbangin'*. Chicago: University of Chicago Press

Piquero, A and Bouffard, J (2007) 'Something old, something new: a preliminary investigation of Hirschi's redefined self–control', *Justice Quarterly* 24(1): 1–27

Polsky, N (1967) *Hustlers, Beats and Others*. New York: Anchor

Poole, O (2006) 'Pentagon declares war on internet combat videos', *The Daily Telegraph* (26 July), p. 13

Potter, G and Kappeler, V (1998) *Constructing Crime*. Prospect Heights, IL: Waveland

Powell, B (2006) 'Many wade into Toronto brawl online', *Toronto Star* (31 January), A8

Presdee, M (2000) *Cultural Criminology and the Carnival of Crime*. London: Routledge

Presdee, M (2005) 'Volume crime and everyday life', in C Hale et al. (eds), *Criminology*. Oxford: Oxford University Press

Prigoff, J (1995) 'Graffiti: social deviance or art form?', in D Newman (ed.), *Sociology*. Thousand Oaks, CA: Pine Forge

Pryce, K (1979) *Endless Pressure*. Harmondsworth: Penguin

Prynn, J (2007) 'Moss doubles her money after, "Cocane Kate" Scandal', *London Evening Standard*, 12 June

Pynchon, T (1966) *The Crying of Lot 49*. New York: J B Lippincott

Raban, J (1974) *Soft City*. London: Hamilton

Radford, J, Friedberg, M and Harne, L (eds) (2000) *Women, Violence and Strategies for Action*. Buckingham: Open University Press

Rajah, V (2007) 'Resistance as edgework in violent intimate relationships of drug-involved women', *British Journal of Criminology* 47: 196–213

Rapaport, R (2007) 'Dying and living in "COPS" America', *San Francisco Chronicle* (7 January)

Regoli, R and Hewitt, J (2006) *Delinquency in Society*. Boston: McGraw-Hill

Reiner, R (2002) 'Media made criminality: the representations of crime in the mass media', in M Maguire, R Morgan and R Reiner (eds), *The Oxford Handbook of Criminology*. Oxford: Oxford University Press

Reinerman, C and Duskin, C (1999) 'Dominant ideology and drugs in the media', in J Ferrell and N Websdale (eds), *Making Trouble*. New York: Aldine de Gruyter

Retort Collective (2004) 'Afflicted powers: the state, the spectacle and September 11', *New Left Review* (27 May/5–21 June): 5–21

Rheingold, H (1991) *Virtual Reality*. London: Secker & Warburg

Rheingold, H (1993) *Virtual Community*. Reading, MA: Addison-Wesley

Richards, S and Ross, J (2001) 'Introducing the New School of Convict Criminology', *Social Justice* 28(1): 177–90

Ritson, M (2000) 'Consumer proactivity', in J Pavitt (ed.), *Brand.New*. London: V&A Publications

Roane, K (2005) 'The CSI effect', *US News and World Report* (25 April), p. 48

Robbins, K. (1996) 'Cyberspace and the world we live in', in J Dovey (ed.), *Fractual Dreams*. London: Lawrence and Wishart

Rodriguez, R T (2003) 'On the subject of gang photography', in L Kontos, D Brotherton and L Barrios (eds), *Gangs and Society*. New York: Columbia University Press

Ross, J, Ferrell, J, Presdee, M and Matthews, R (2000) 'IRBs and state crime: a reply to Dr. Niemonen', *Humanity and Society* 24(2): 210–12

Rossol, J (2001) 'The medicalization of deviance as an interactive achievement: the construction of compulsive gambling', *Symbolic Interaction* 24(3): 315–41

Rowbotham, S (1973) *Hidden from History*. London: Pluto

Ruggiero, V (2005) 'Review: *City Limits: Crime, Consumer Culture and the Urban Experience*', *Theoretical Criminology* 9(4): 497–9

Sachs, H (1987) *Music in Fascist Italy*. New York: WW Norton

Said, E (2005) *Orientalism*. New York: Vintage (First published 1978)

St John, W (2006) 'Market for Zombies?', *The New York Times* (26 March), pp. 1, 13

Samaddar, S (2007) 'Multiculturalism versus the Hip-Hop Nation', paper presented at the conference 'On the Edge: Transgression and the Dangerous Other', August, New York

Sanchez-Tranquilino, M (1995) 'Space, power and youth culture', in B Bright and L Bakewell (eds), *Looking High and Low*. Tucson: University of Arizona Press

Sanders, C and Lyon, E (1995) 'Repetitive retribution: media images and the cultural construction of criminal justice', in J Ferrell and C Sanders (eds), *Cultural Criminology*. Boston: Northeastern University Press

Scahill, J (2007) *Blackwater*. New York: Serpent's Tail Publishing

Scheff, T (1990) *Microsociology*. Chicago: Chicago University Press

Schelsky, H (1957) 'Ise die Dauerreflektion Institutionalisierbar?', *Zeitschrift für Evangelische Ethik* 1: 153–74

Schofield, K (2004) 'Collisions of culture and crime: commodification of child sexual abuse', in J Ferrell et al. (eds), *Cultural Criminology Unleashed*. London: GlassHouse

Schlosser, E (1998) 'The prison-industrial complex', *The Atlantic Monthly* 282: 51–77

Schmalleger, F and Bartollas, C (2008) *Juvenile Delinquency*. Boston: Pearson

Sellin, T (1938) *Culture, Conflict and Crime*. New York: Social Science Research Council

Shea, C (2000) 'Don't talk to the humans: the crackdown on social science research', *Lingua Franca* (September): 27–34

Signorielli, N and Morgan, M (eds) (1990) *Cultivation Analysis*. Newbury Park, CA: Sage

Simon, J (2007) *Governing Through Crime*. Oxford: Oxford University Press

Smith, W E (1998) *W. Eugene Smith: Photographs 1934–1975*. Edited by Gilles Mora and John T Hill. New York: Harry Abrams Publishers

Snyder, G (2006) 'Graffiti media and the perpetuation of an illegal subculture', *Crime, Media, Culture* 2(1): 93–101

Snyder, G (2007) 'Crime space vs. cool space', paper presented at American Sociological Association Conference, August, New York

Snyder, G (2009) *Graffiti Lives*. New York: New York University Press

Soueif, A (2003) 'Genet's Palestinian Revolution', *The Nation* (24 February), 25–9

Stanczak, G (2007) *Visual Research Methods*. Los Angeles: Sage

Stanko, E (1997) 'Conceptualizing women's risk assessment as a "technology of the soul"', *Theoretical Criminology* 1(4): 479–99

Star, D (2001) *Beneath the Paving Stones*. Edinburgh: AK Press

Starkey, G (2006) *Balance and Bias in Journalism*. Basingstoke: Palgrave

Steinbeck, J (1972 [1936]) *In Dubious Battle*. New York: Viking

Struckhoff, D (2006) *Annual Editions: Juvenile Delinquency and Justice*. New York: McGraw-Hill

Sykes, G (1958) *The Society of Captives*. Princeton NJ: Princeton University Press

Sykes, G and Matza, D (1957) 'Techniques of neutralization: a theory of deviance', *American Sociological Review* 22: 664–70

Tari, M and Vanni, I (2005) 'On the life and deeds of San Precario, Patron Saint of Precarious Workers and Lives', *Fibre Culture* 5, @ http://journal.fibreculture.org

Taylor, I, Walton, P and Young, J (1973) *The New Criminology*. London: Routledge & Kegan Paul

Taylor, I Walton, P and Young, J (1975) *Critical Criminology*. London: Routledge and Kegan Paul

Taylor, L (1971) *Deviance and Society*. London: Michael Joseph

TCU (2007) *Faculty Handbook*. Ft Worth, TX: Texas Christian University

Thompson, H S (1971) *Fear and Loathing in Las Vegas*. New York: Popular Library

Thrasher, F (1927) *The Gang*. Chicago: University of Chicago Press

Tobocman, S (1999) *You Don't Have to Fuck People over to Survive*. New York: Soft Skull

Trend, D (2007) *The Myth of Media Violence*. Oxford: Blackwell

Tunnell, K (1992) *Choosing Crime*. Chicago: Nelson-Hall

Turkle, S (1997) *Life on the Screen: Identity in the Age of the Internet*. London: Phoenix

Turner, B (2007) 'The enclave society: towards a sociology of immobility', *European Journal of Social Theory* 10(2): 287–303

Ulrich, E (2006) 'Gun makers focus on what women want', *Medill News Service* (24 May), @ cbs2chicago.com

Vail, D A (2001) 'Researching from afar: distance, ethnography, and testing the edge', *Journal of Contemporary Ethnography* 30(6): 704–25

Valier, C (2000) 'Looking daggers: a psychoanalytical reading of the scene of punishment', *Punishment and Society* 2(4): 379–94

Valier, C and Lippens, R (2005) 'Moving images, ethics and justice', *Punishment and Society* 6(3): 319–33

Van de Voorde, C (2007) 'Visual ethnography', paper presented at the American Sociological Association, August, New York

Van Hoorebeeck, B (1997) 'Prospects of reconstructing aetiology', *Theoretical Criminology*, 1(4): 501–18

Vargas, J (2006) 'Urban scrawl', *The Washington Post* (13 February), p. C10

Veblen, T (1953 [1899]) *The Theory of the Leisure Class*. New York: Viking

Vergara, C J (1995) *The New American Ghetto*. New Brunswick, NJ: Rutgers University Press

Vick, K (1997) '"Real TV" at heart of lawsuit over fatal crash', *The Arizona Republic* (12 December), p. A4

Virilio, P (1986) *Speed and Politics*. New York: Semiotext(e)

Virilio, P (1991) *The Aesthetics of Disappearance*. New York: Semiotext(e)

Visano, L (1996) 'What do "they" know? delinquency as mediated texts', in G O'Bireck (ed.), *Not a Kid Anymore*. Scarborough, Ontario: Thompson

Vold, G, Bernard, T and Snipes, J (1998) *Theoretical Criminology*. Oxford: Oxford University Press

Wacquant (2002) From Slavery to Mass Incarceration: Rethinking the 'Race Question', *New Left Review* 13 (Jan/Feb): 41–60

Wakefield, A (2003) *Selling Security: The Private Policing of Public Space*. Cullompton: Willan

Walker, D (1999) 'Hands up! "COPS" hits valley for 400th show', *The Arizona Republic* (30 April), pp. D11, D12

Walklate, S (1997) 'Risk and criminal victimization', *British Journal of Criminology* 37(1): 35–45

Walters, R (2003) *Deviant Knowledge*. Cullompton: Willan

Ward, A (2006) 'Defend yourself', *Ft. Worth Star-Telegram* (16 July), p. 3G

Warren, J (2006) 'Introduction: performance ethnography: a *TPQ* symposium', *Text and Performance Quarterly* 26(4): 317–19

Watts, E K (1997) 'An exploration of spectacular consumption: gangsta rap as cultural commodity', *Communication Studies* 48: 42–58

Webber, C (2007) 'Background, foreground, foresight: the third dimension of cultural criminology?', *Crime, Media, Culture* 3(2): 139–57

Weber, M (1978) *Economy and Society*. Berkeley, CA: University of California Press

Websdale, N and Alvarez, A (1998) 'Forensic journalism as patriarchal ideology', in F Bailey and D Hale (eds), *Popular Culture, Crime, and Justice*. Belmont, CA: Wadsworth

Weisburd, D and Piquero, A (2008) 'How well do criminologists explain crime: statistical modelling in published studies', *Crime and Justice*, 37, 453

Wender, J (2001) 'The eye of the painter and the eye of the police: what criminology and law enforcement can learn from Manet', paper presented at the 53rd Conference of the American Society of Criminology, November, Atlanta, GA

Whitehead, J and Lab, S (2006) *Juvenile Justice*. New York: LexisNexis

Whyte, D (2007) 'The crimes of neo-liberal rule in occupied Iraq', *British Journal of Criminology* 47: 177–95

Whyte, W H (1956) *The Organization Man*. New York: Simon and Schuster

Wilkinson, I (2005) *Suffering: A Sociological Introduction*. Cambridge: Polity

Williamson, J (1978) *Decoding Advertisements*. London: Marian Boyars.

Williams, J (1998) 'Comic books: a tool of subversion?', in S Anderson and G Howard (eds), *Interrogating Popular Culture*. Guilderland, NY: Harrow and Heston

Williams, S (2001) *Emotion and Social Theory*. London: Sage

Willis, P (1977) *Learning to Labour*. New York: Columbia University Press

Willis, P (2000) *The Ethnographic Imagination*. Cambridge: Polity Press

Wilson, B and Atkinson, M (2005) 'Rave and Straightedge, the virtual and the real: exploring online and offline experiences in Canadian youth subcultures', *Youth and Society* 36(3): 276–311

Wilson, J Q and Kelling, G (2003 [1982]) 'Broken windows: the Police and neighborhood safety', reprinted in E McLaughlin et al. (eds), *Criminological Perspectives*. London: Sage

Winlow, S and Hall, S (2006) *Violent Night*. Oxford: Berg

Woodson, P (2003) '"COPS" still rocks', *Ft. Worth Star-Telegram* (22 February), pp. 1F, 11F

Wouters, C (2002) 'On Jack Katz: *How Emotions Work*', *Theoretical Criminology* 6(3) 369–73

Wright, E (2004) *Generation Kill*. New York: Berkley Caliber

Wright, R and Decker, S (1994) *Burglars on the Job*. Boston: Northeastern University Press

Wyatt, E (2005) 'Even for an expert, blurred TV images became a false reality', *The New York Times* (8 January), p. B7

Wynn, J, (2001) *Inside Riker's*. New York: St. Martin's Griffith

Yanich, D (2001) 'Location, location, location: urban and suburban crime on local TV', *Journal of Urban Affairs* 23(3–4): 221–41

Yar, M (2005) 'The global "epidemic" of movie "piracy": crime-wave or social construction?', *Media, Culture & Society* 27(5): 677–96

Yar, M (Forthcoming) 'Neither *Scylla* nor *Charybdis*: transcending the criminological dualism between rationality and the emotions', *Theoretical Criminology*

Young, A (2004) *Judging the Image*. London: Routledge

Young, A (2007) 'Images in the aftermath of trauma: responding to September 11th', *Crime, Media, Culture* 3(1): 30–48

Young, A (2008) 'Culture, critical criminology, and the Imagination of crime', in T Anthony and C Cuneen (eds), *The Critical Criminology Companion*. Cullompton: Federation Press

Young, A (2009) 'The scene of the crime: is there such a thing as just looking?', in Hayward, K and Presdee, M (eds) *Framing Crime: Cultural Criminology and the Image*. London: Routledge

Young, J (1971) *The Drugtakers*. London: Paladin

Young, J (1973) 'The amplification of drug use', in S Cohen and J Young (eds), *The Manufacture of News*. Beverley Hills, CA: Sage

Young, J (1998) 'Breaking windows: situating the new criminology', in P Walton and J Young (eds), *The New Criminology Revisited*. London: Palgrave Macmillan

Young, J (1999) *The Exclusive Society*. London: Sage

Young, J (2002) 'Critical criminology in the twenty-first century: critique, irony and the always unfinished', in R Hogg and K Carrington (eds), *Critical Criminology*. Cullompton: Willan Publishing

Young, J (2003) 'Merton with energy, Katz with structure', *Theoretical Criminology* 7(3): 389–414

Young, J (2004a) 'Voodoo criminology and the numbers game', in J Ferrell et al. (eds), *Cultural Criminology Unleashed*. London: GlassHouse

Young, J (2004b) 'Crime and the dialectics of inclusion/exclusion', *British Journal of Criminology* 44: 550–61

Young, J (2007) *The Vertigo of Late Modernity*. London: Sage

Zaitch, D and de Leeuw, T (2008) 'Virtual combats: othering, fun and violence among Argentinean and Dutch football supporters on the internet', in K Hayward, and M Presdee (eds), *Framing Crime*. London: GlassHouse

Zimring, F (2007) *The Great American Crime Decline*. New York: Oxford University Press

Index

rational choice theory (RCT), 65, 66–9,
    81, 113–114, 204
Real virtuality, 145
reality
    reconstituting, 138, 145
    and virtuality, 145–9
reality television, 131, 132, 135, 143
Recycled Life, 121
recycling, 116–17
Redmon, D., 187
reflexivity, 130–1
Regoli, R., 102
Research Assessment Exercise (RAE), 163
research methods *see* methods/methodology
research subjects, 163–5, 171
resistance, 1–2, 74, 79, 104, 124
    commodification of, 19–21, 150–2
    crime, culture and, 16–19
    in late modernity, 60, 111–12, 117
    and mediated spirals of meaning, 150–4
    and politics of cultural criminology, 20–3,
        192, 196–7
    romanticization of, 21–2
    through video games, 148–9
retail sector, 110–11, 113–14
Retort Collective, 75–6
Retromacking, 137
Riker's Island, 57–8
risk, 72–4, 118
Robbins, K., 145
Rodriguez, R., 183
romanticization of resistance, 21–2
Rowbotham, S., 46
Rules of Sociological Method, The, 33

Sabin, A., 187
Said, E., 77
Samaddar, S., 211
San Precario, 111–12
Sanders, C., 136
Schleiner, A.-M., 148, 149
Schmalleger, F., 103
Schuilenburg, M., 141, 146, 148
scientific criminology, 162
    critique of, 168–74, 205
Scranton, D., 144
security, 58
    private, 79, 97, 203
Seductions of Crime, 49, 69, 70, 180
self-fulfilling social dynamics, 51–2
Sellin, T., 3
sensual metamorphoses, 70
sexuality, 207
shoplifting, 110–11
Siegel, D., 3
Simon, T., 187
situational aspects of emotion, 70
situational crime prevention, 65, 67
Situationists, 5–6, 75, 152–3, 199

Smith, W.E., 88, 185, 188
Smiths, The, 206–7
Snyder, G., 184
social anthropology, 4
social bulimia, 62
social change, 89
    see also resistance
social class, 15–16, 35–6, 52, 201–4
    underclass, 62–3, 73–4, 119
social control, 117, 118, 140–1
Sociological Imagination, The, 45
sociology of deviance, 29, 205
The Sociology of Youth Culture, 45
Soft City, 80
sousveillance, 112–113
Spare Parts, 84
speed culture, 129
spirals, 133–7, 206
    see also cultural flow
Starace, A., 159
Starbucks, 103
state, criminology of, 75–80
Steal This Book, 115
story
    criminology of everyday life, 89–96
        analysis of, 96–121
    see also fiction
street codes, 137–9
strikers, 2, 202
Struckoff, D., 102
structural analysis, 19
Strummer, J., 150
Stubbs, J., 22
style, 100, 198–9
subcultural ethnographies, 162
subcultural narratives, 52–3
subcultural theory, 4, 5, 26, 32–6
    British, 42–7
subcultures, 34, 53
    Matza and Sykes on, 39–42
Subterranean values, 41–42
success, 34
SuicideGirls.com, 207–8
surveillance, 98–100, 107–8, 112–113, 197
    of research, 162–5
survey research, 162–3, 166–7
Sutherland, E., 166
Sykes, G., 34, 39–42
Symbolic interactionism, 88
symbolism of urban environment, 104–6

Target, 97–8
Taste of Honey, A, 55
tattoos, 99–100
Taylor, F., 162
Taylor, I., 45
Techniques of neutralization, 39–40
television, 119–20, 131, 132, 135, 143
Temporary autonomous zone, 204